LOBSTER THER
MOOSE PICK-UP LINES
CARTOONS FROM MAINE

Edited by Mike Lynch

Cartoons by
DAVID JACOBSON
JOHN KLOSSNER
MIKE LYNCH
JEFF PERT
BILL WOODMAN

Down East Books
CAMDEN, MAINE

Down East Books

Published by Down East Books
An imprint of The Rowman & Littlefield Publishing Group, Inc.
4501 Forbes Blvd., Ste. 200
Lanham, MD 20706
www.rowman.com

Distributed by NATIONAL BOOK NETWORK

Copyright © 2018 by Mike Lynch
Individual cartoons © by artist

ISBN 978-1-60893-965-7 (paperback)
ISBN 978-1-60893-966-4 (e-book)

∞™ The paper used in this publication meets the minimum requirements of American National Standard for Information Sciences—Permanence of Paper for Printed Library Materials, ANSI/NISO Z39.48-1992.

Printed in the United States of America

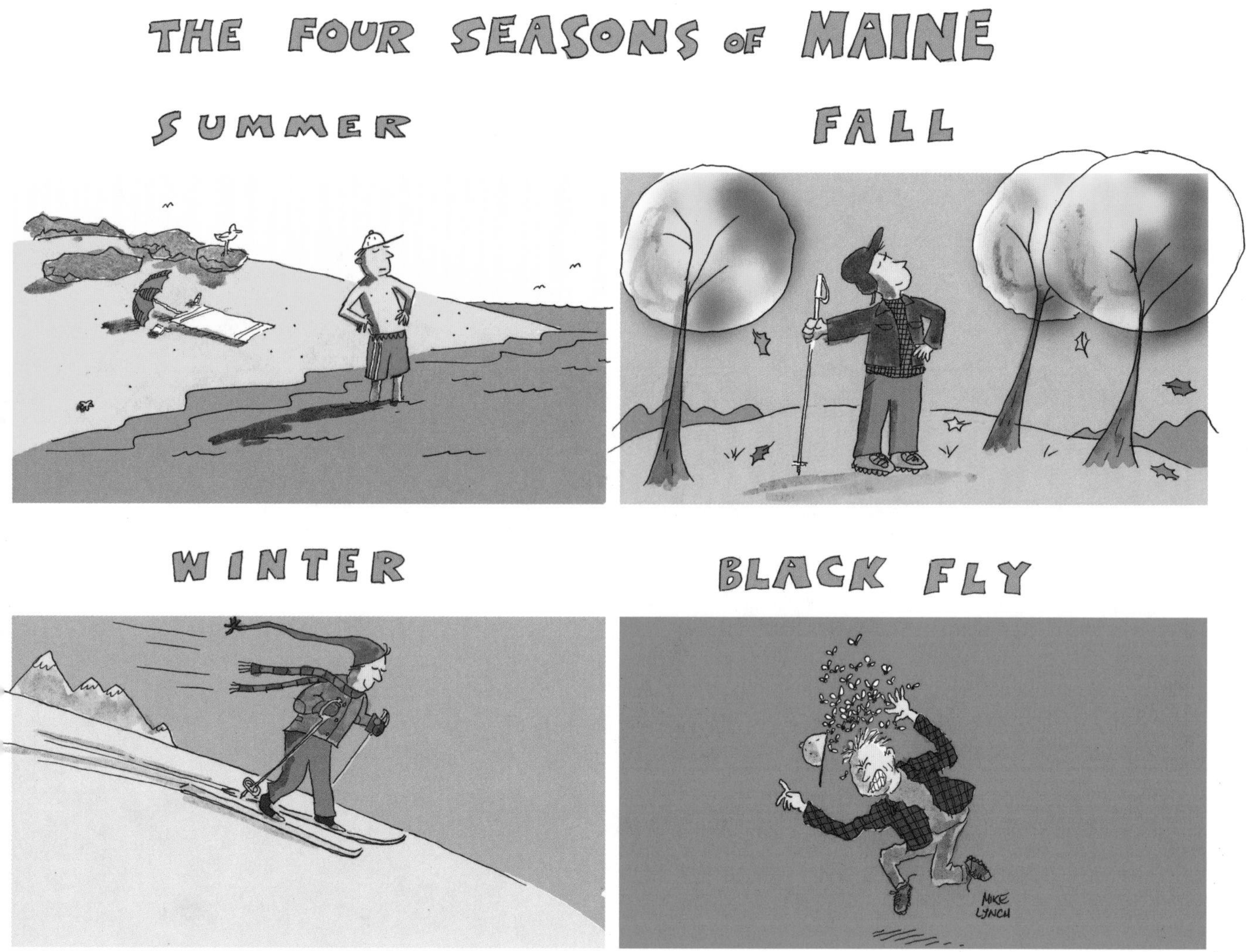
THE FOUR SEASONS OF MAINE
SUMMER
FALL
WINTER
BLACK FLY
MIKE LYNCH

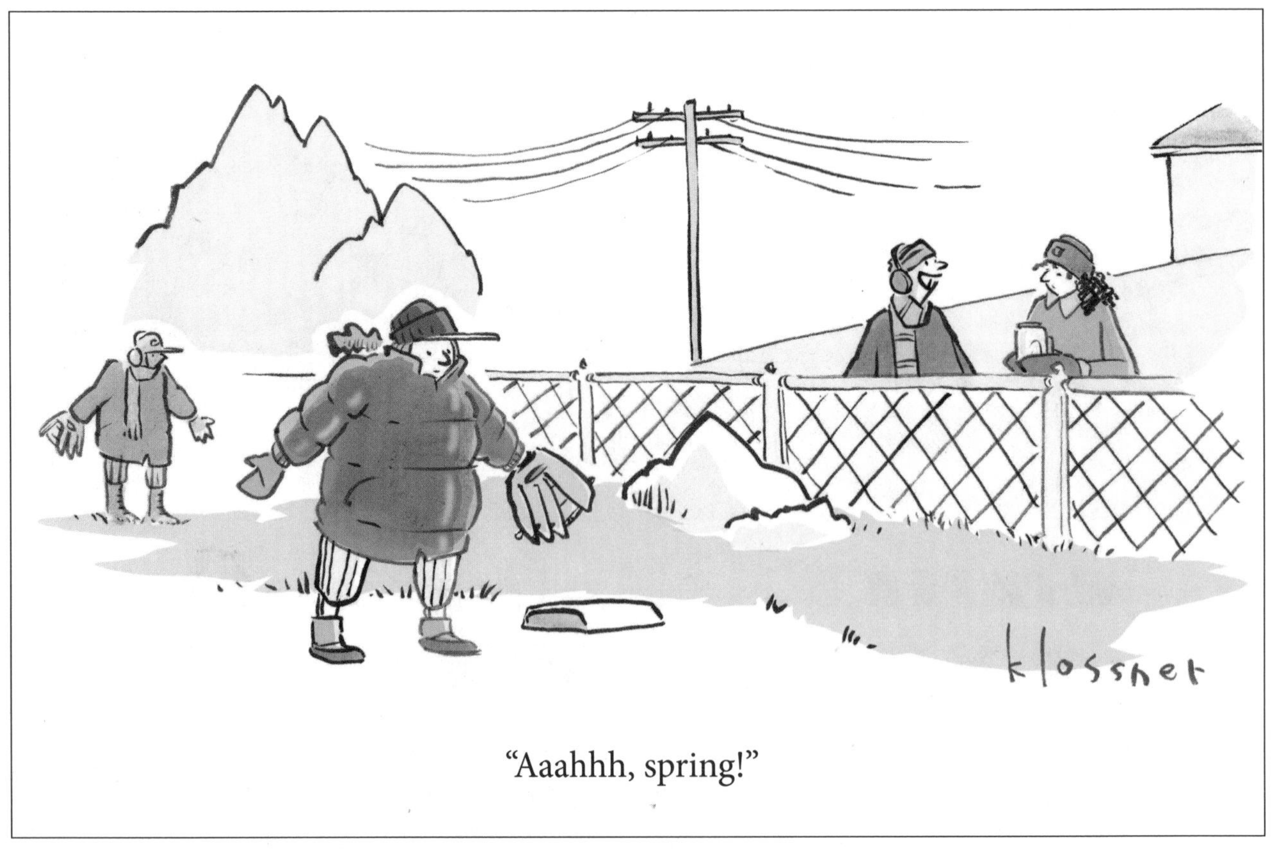
klossner

"Aaahhh, spring!"

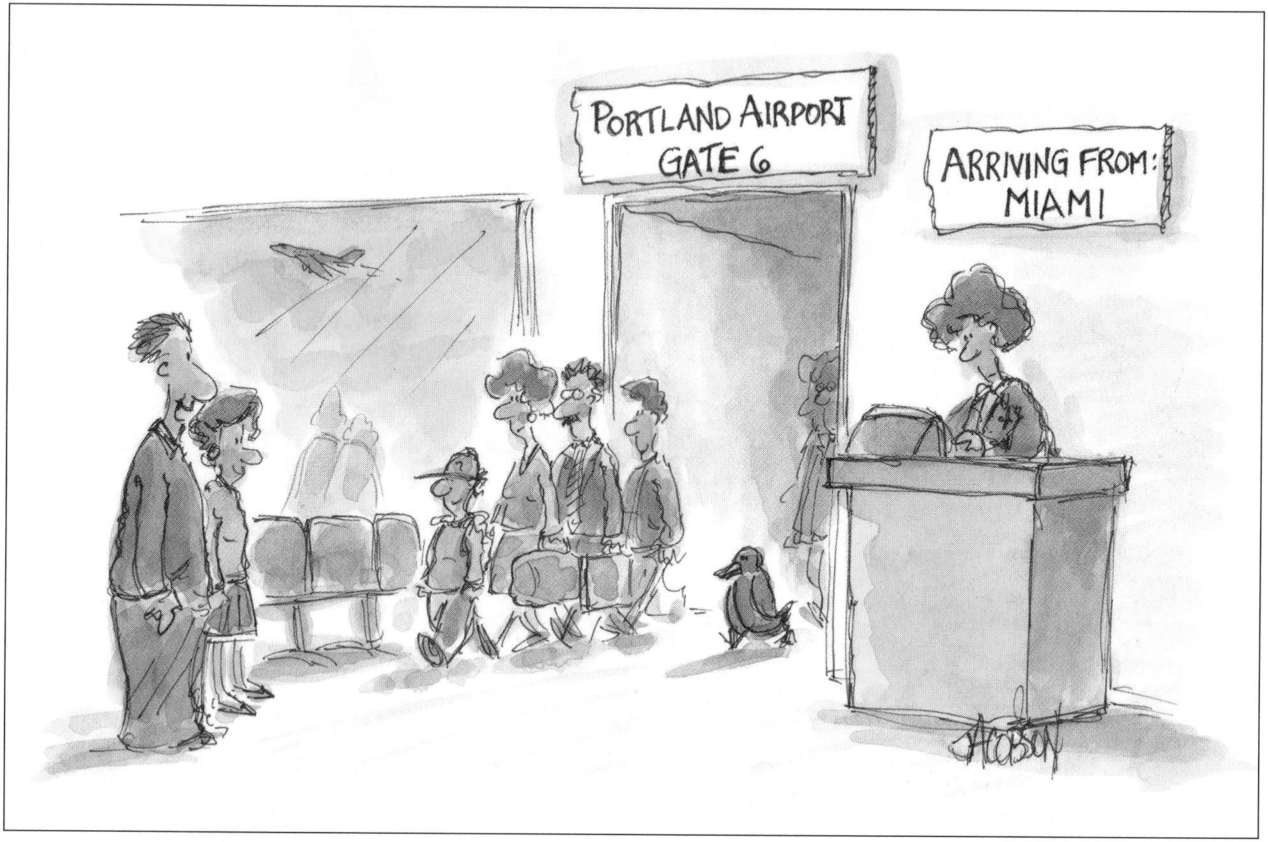
PORTLAND AIRPORT
GATE 6
ARRIVING FROM:
MIAMI
JACOBSON

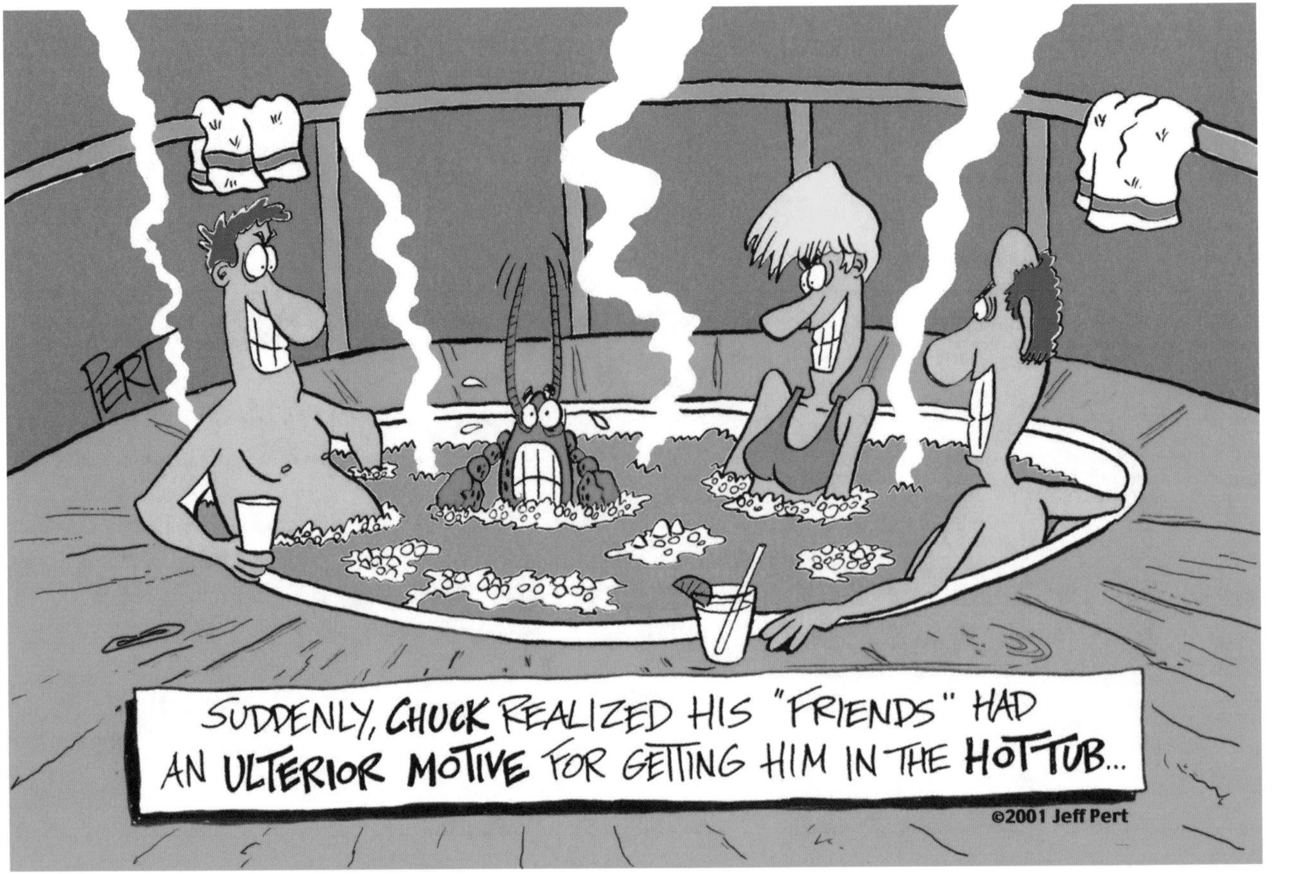
PERT
SUDDENLY, CHUCK REALIZED HIS "FRIENDS" HAD AN ULTERIOR MOTIVE FOR GETTING HIM IN THE HOT TUB...
©2001 Jeff Pert

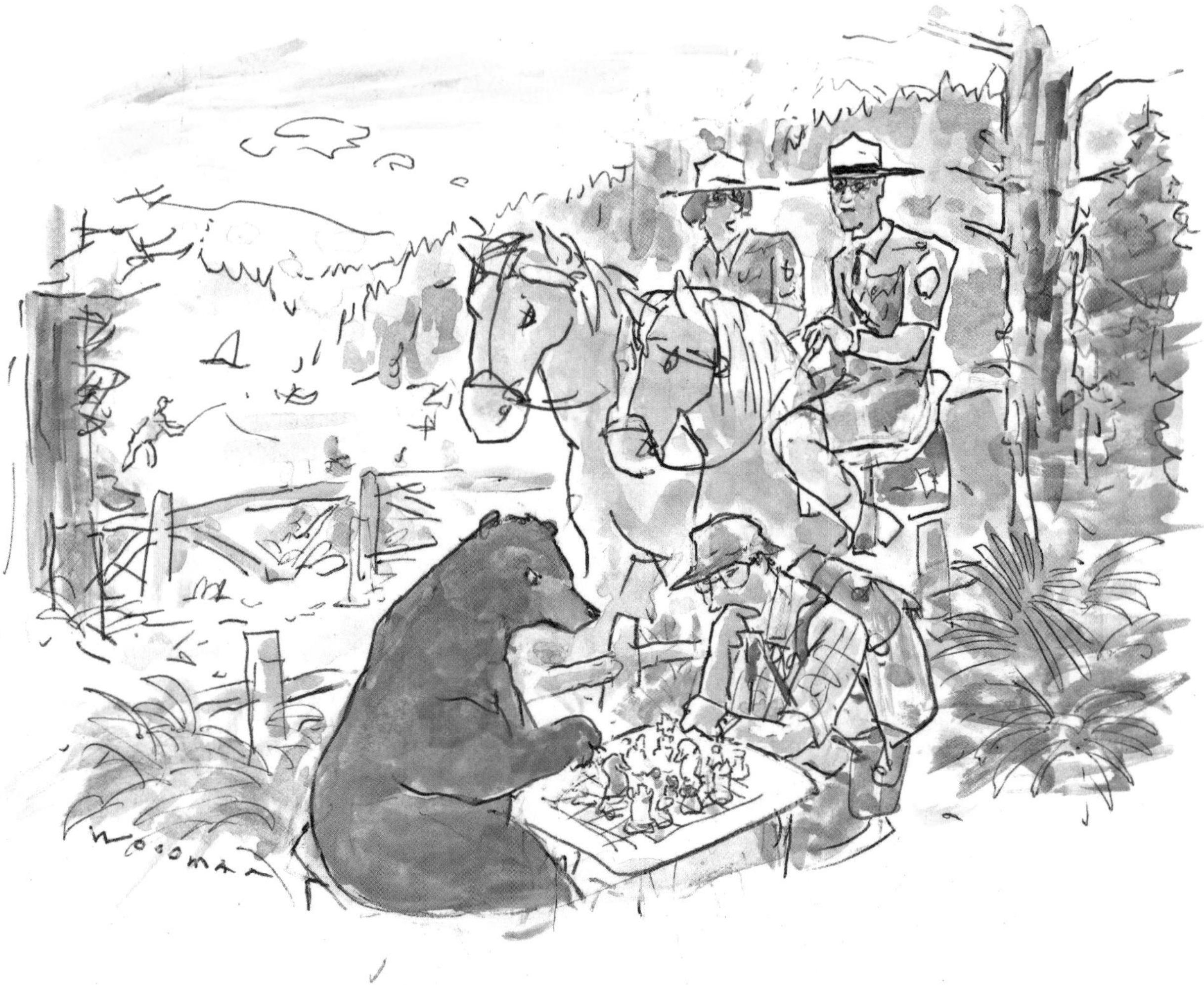

“When I first came to the park, all they could do was beg.”

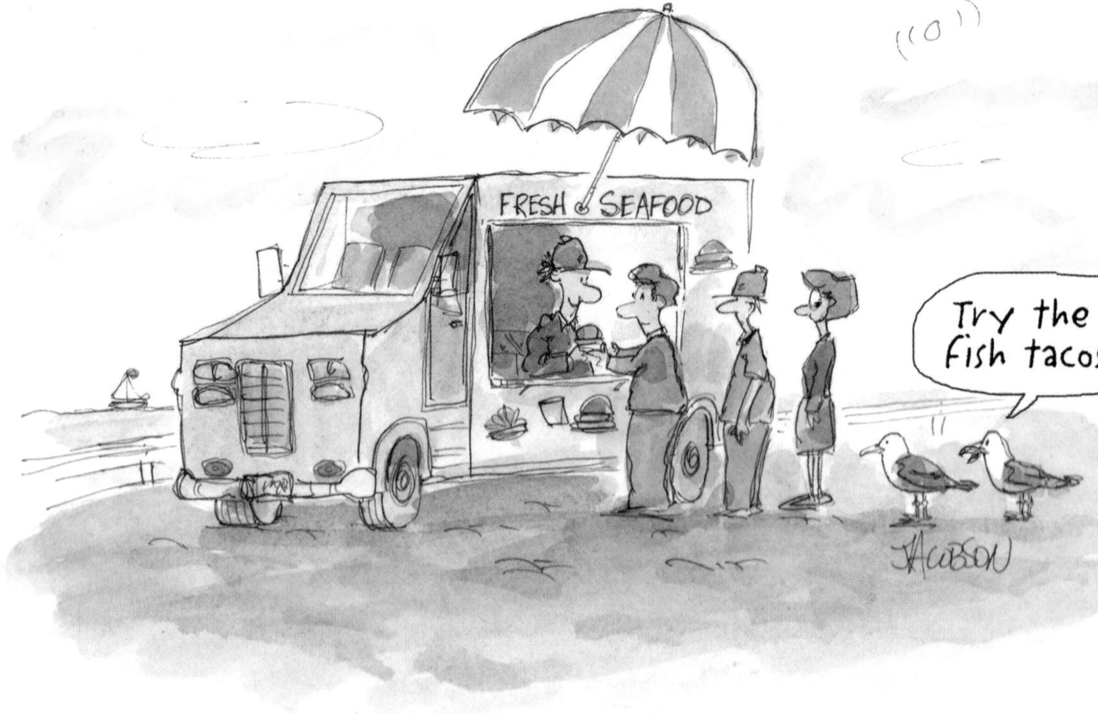
FRESH SEAFOOD
Try the fish tacos.
JACOBSON

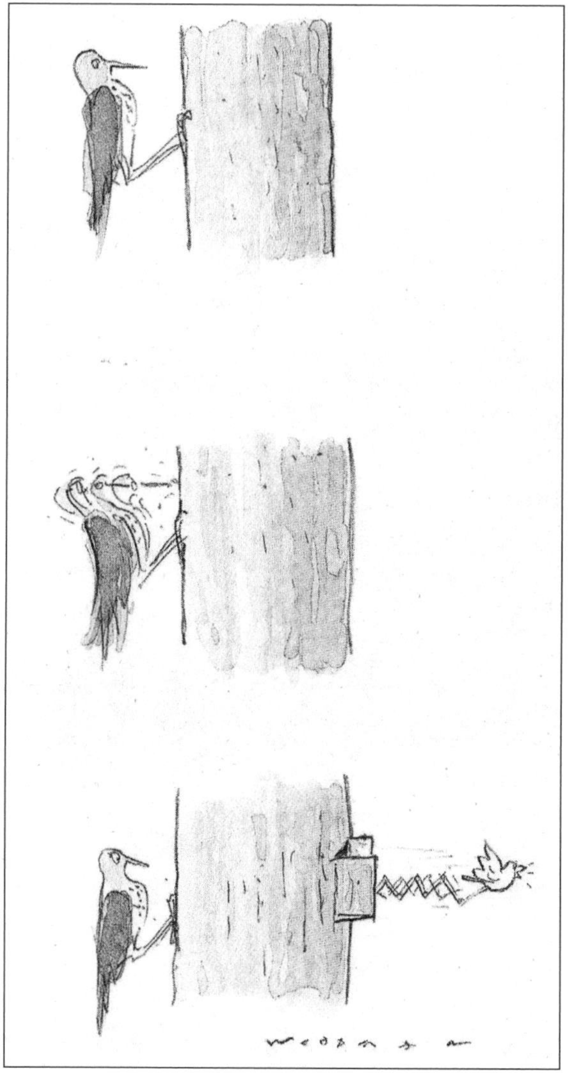

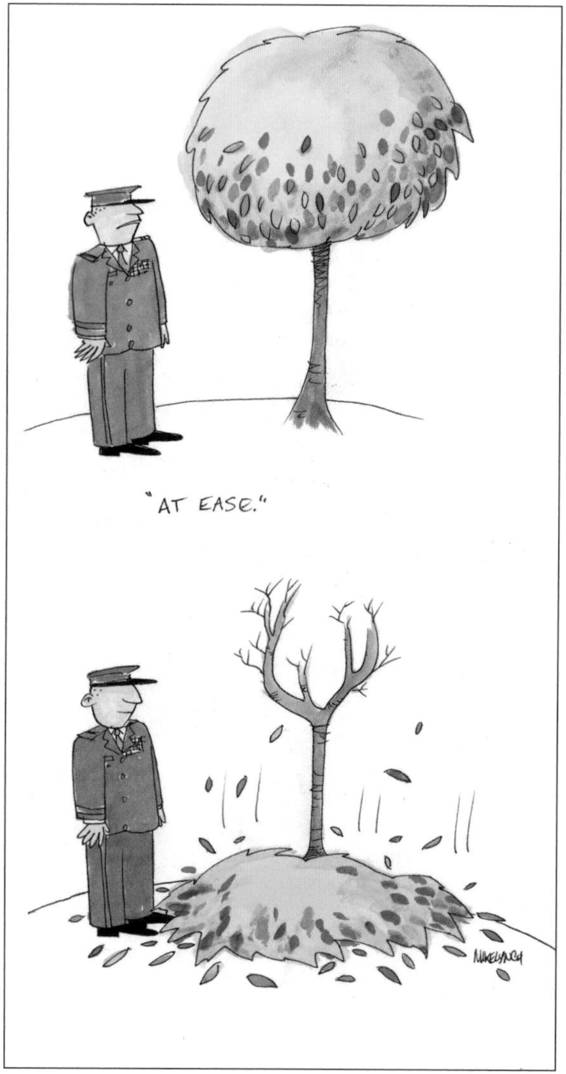
"AT EASE."
MIKELYNCH

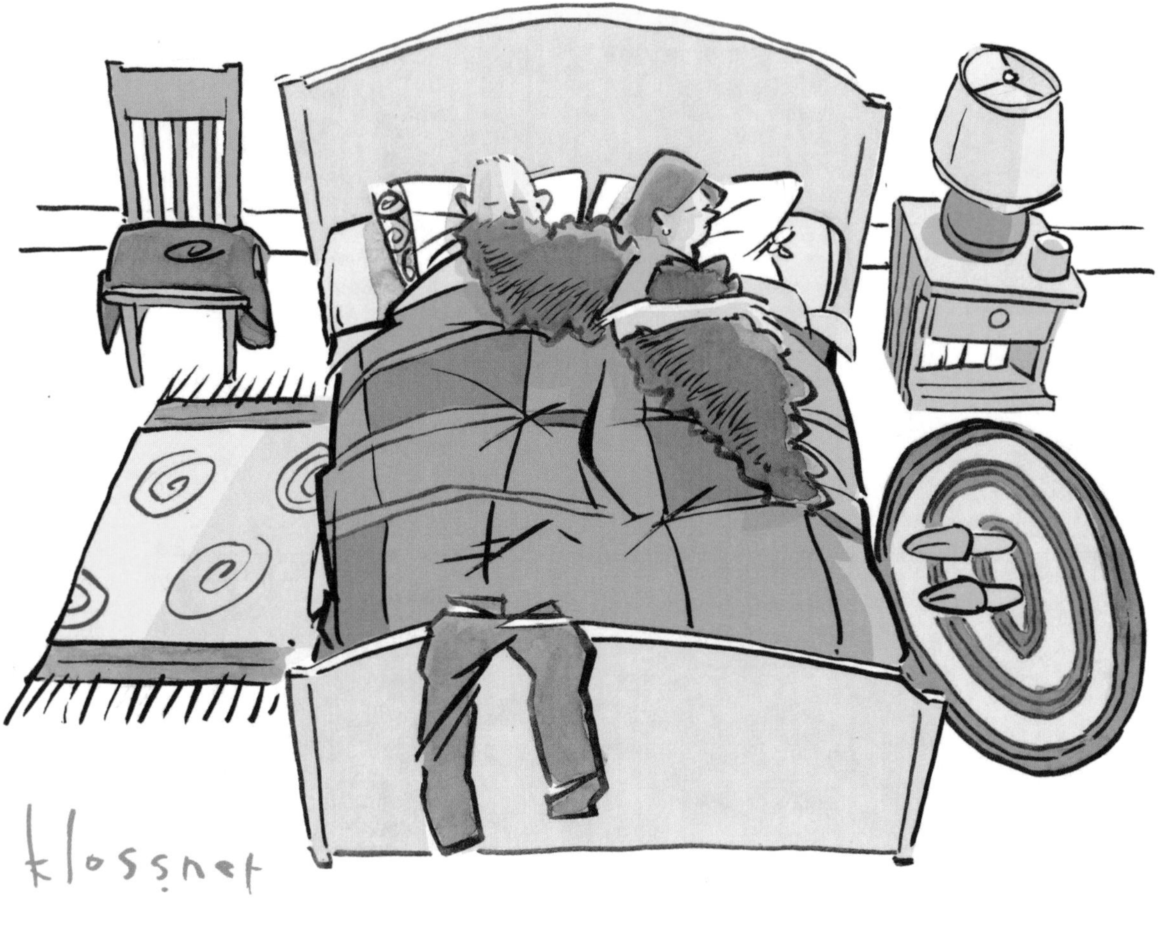
klossner

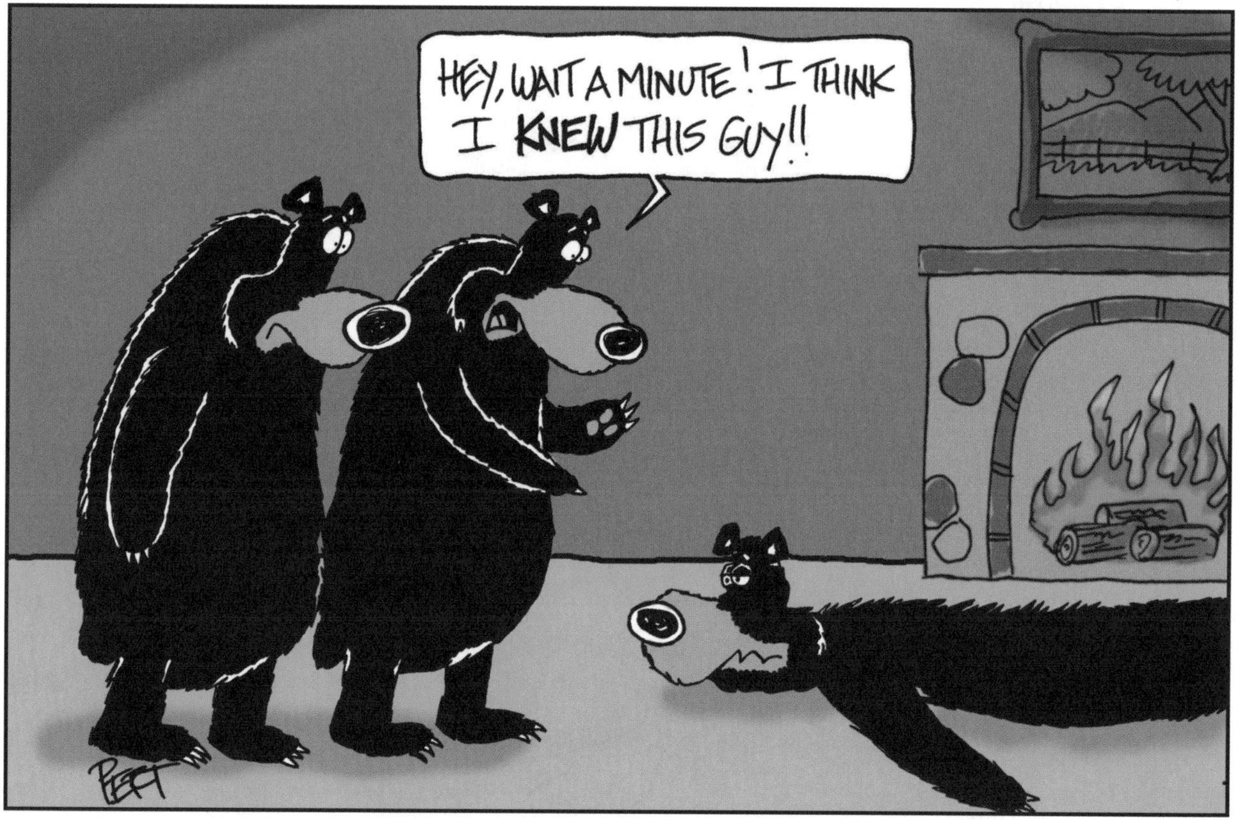
HEY, WAIT A MINUTE! I THINK I KNEW THIS GUY!!

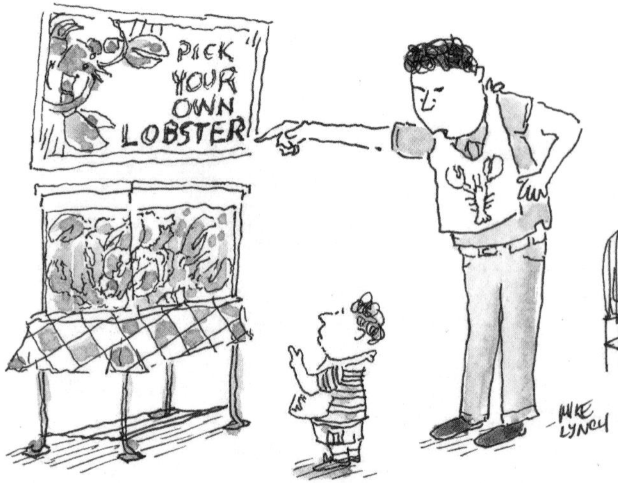
PICK
YOUR
OWN
LOBSTER
MIKE LYNCH

“Stop giving them names.
Just pick one out to eat!”

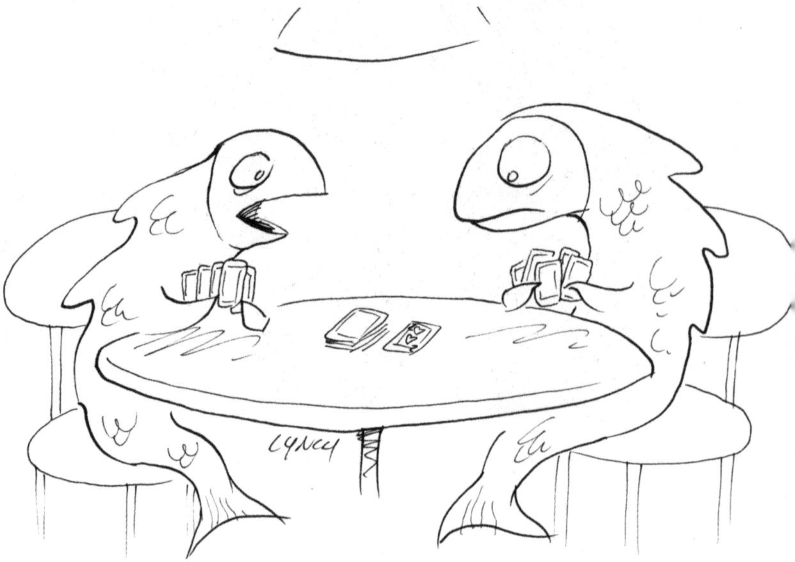
LYNCH

“Go human!”

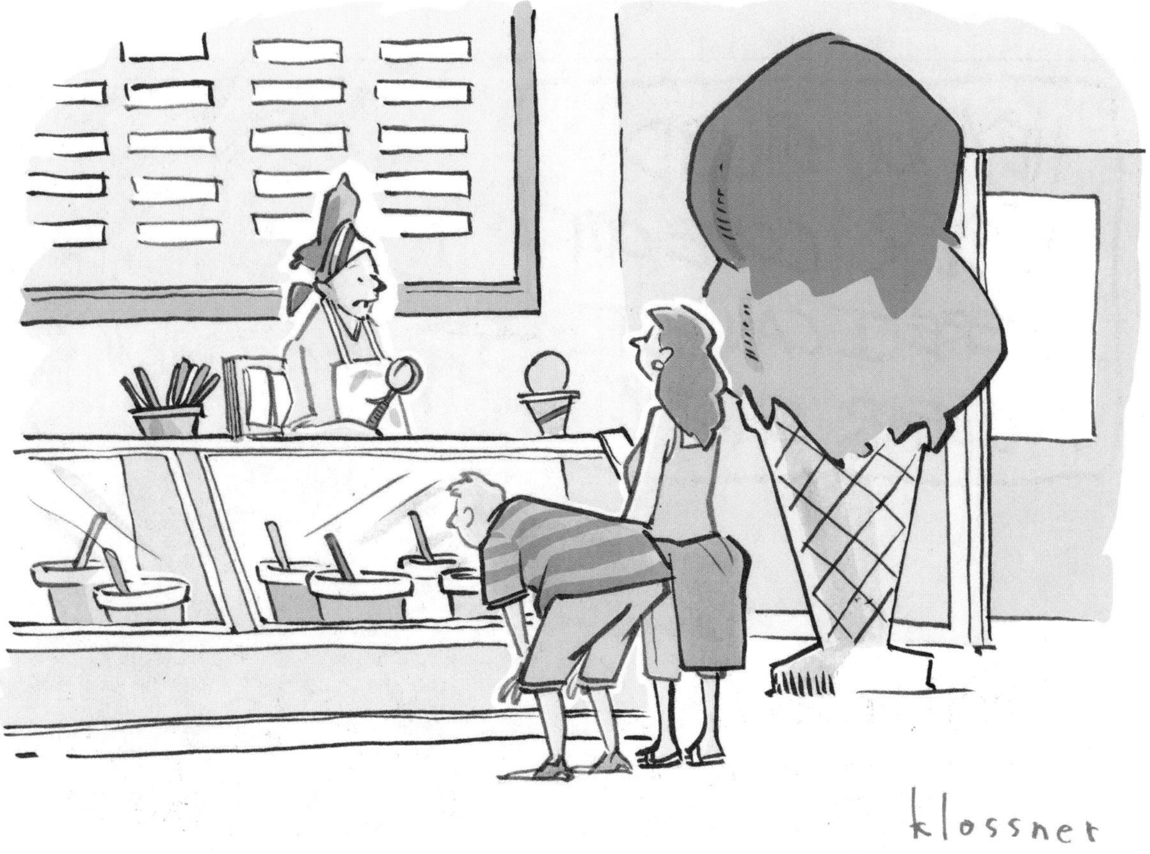
klossner

"We have 89 flavors and 17 accidents."

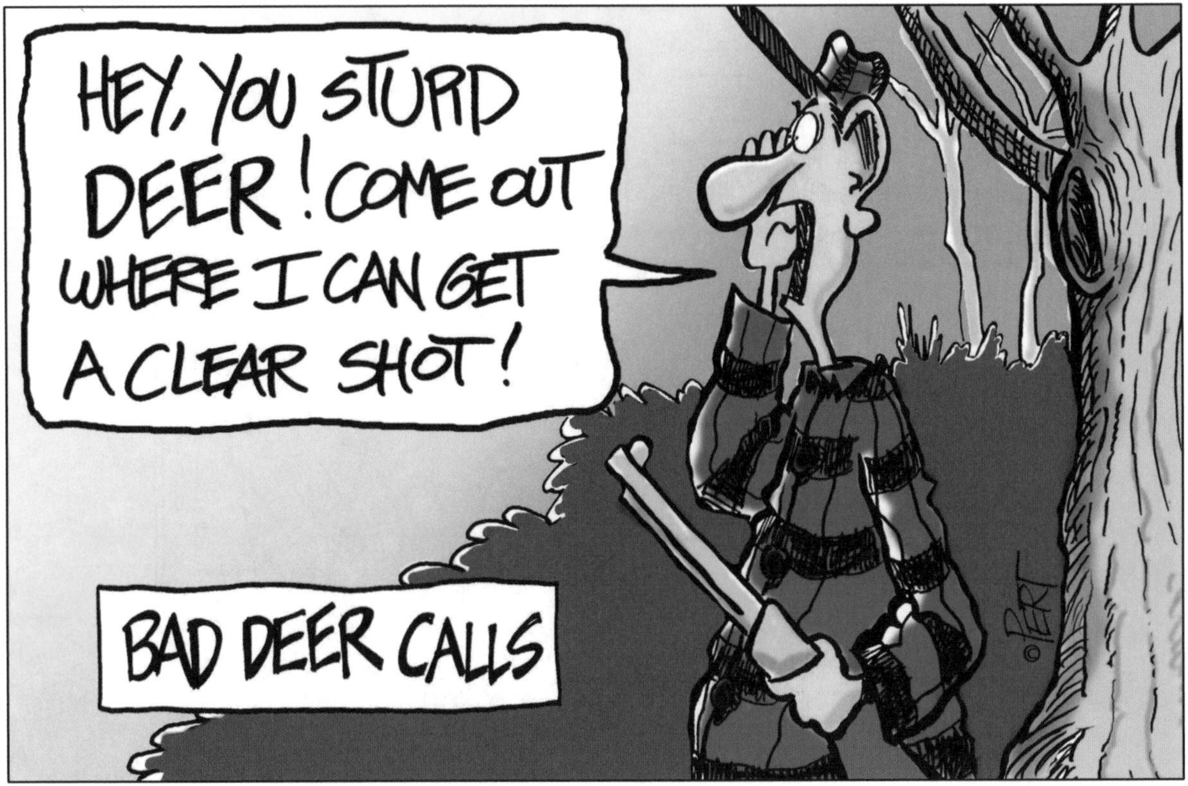
HEY, YOU STUPID DEER! COME OUT WHERE I CAN GET A CLEAR SHOT!
BAD DEER CALLS
©PERT

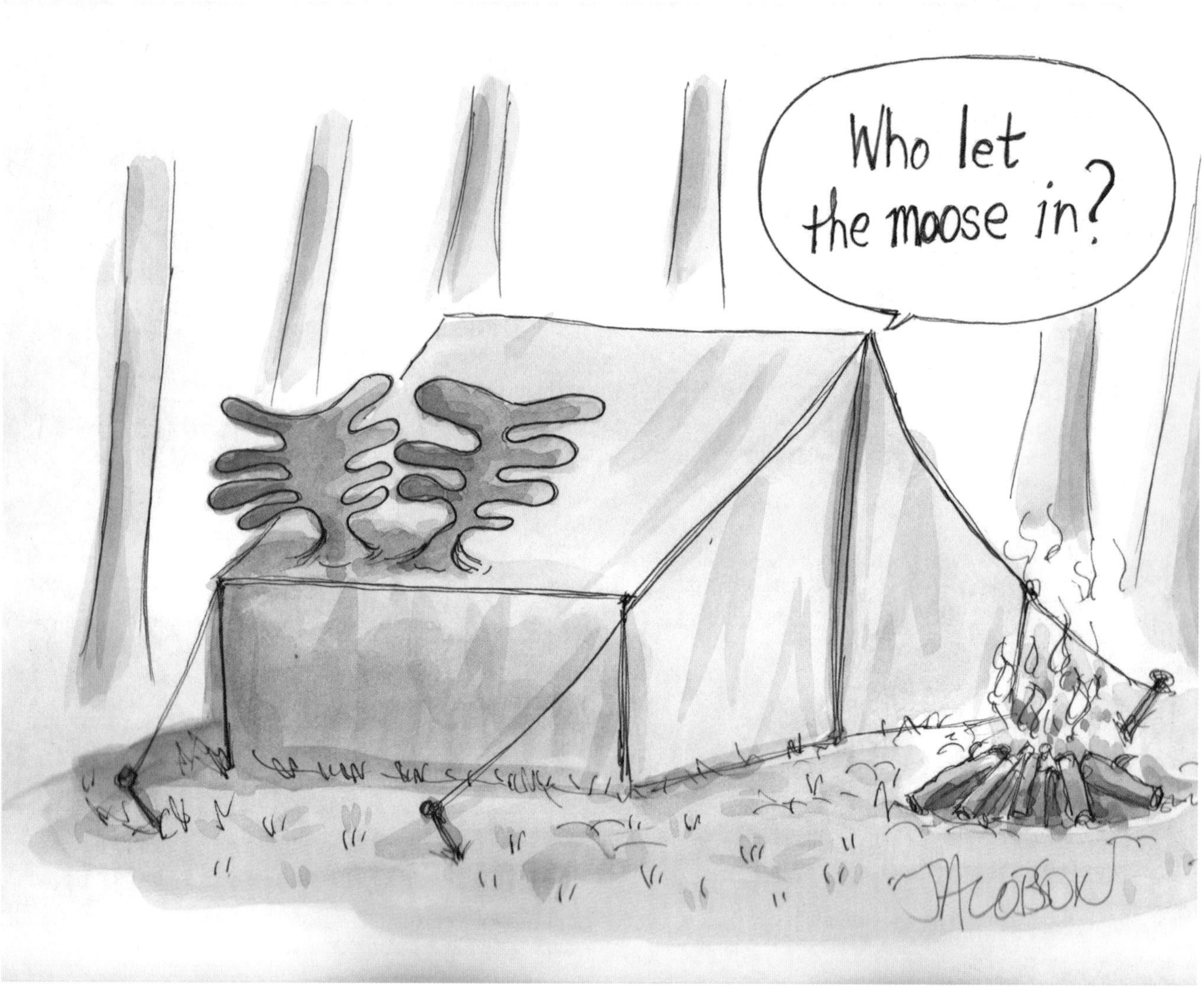
Who let the moose in?
JACOBSON

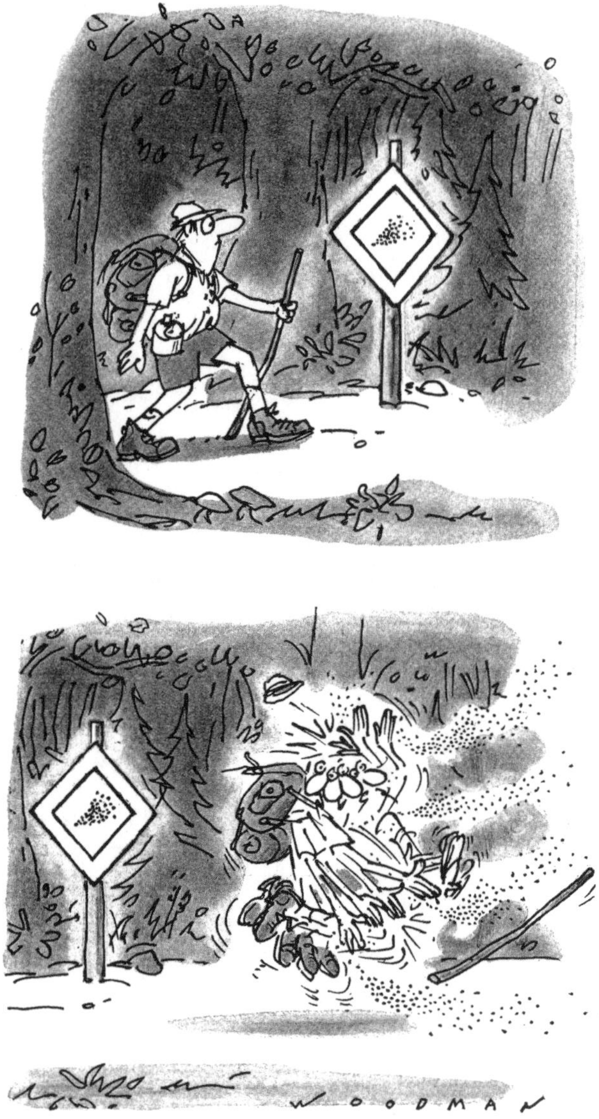
WOODMAN

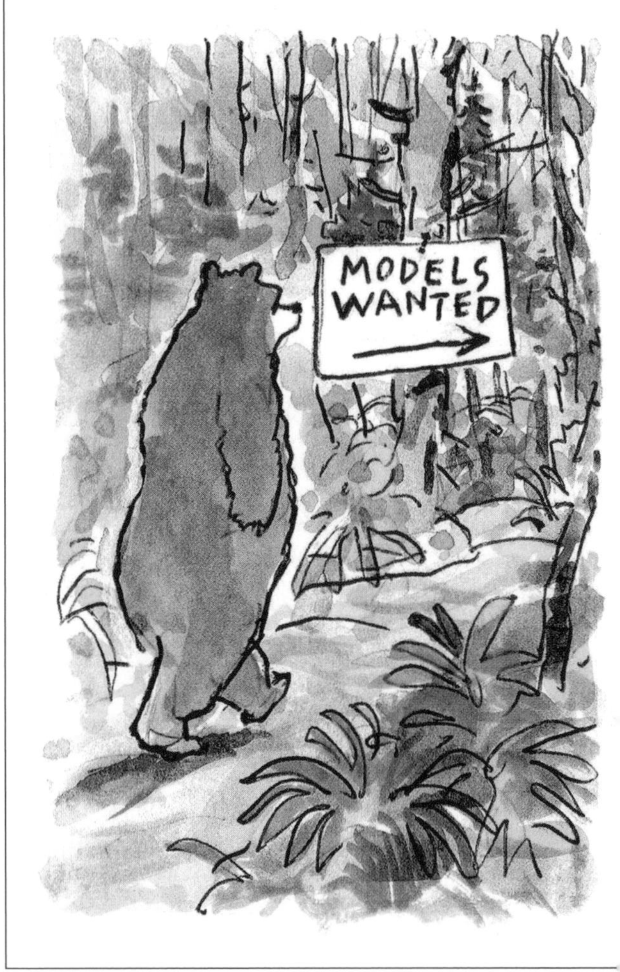
MODELS
WANTED

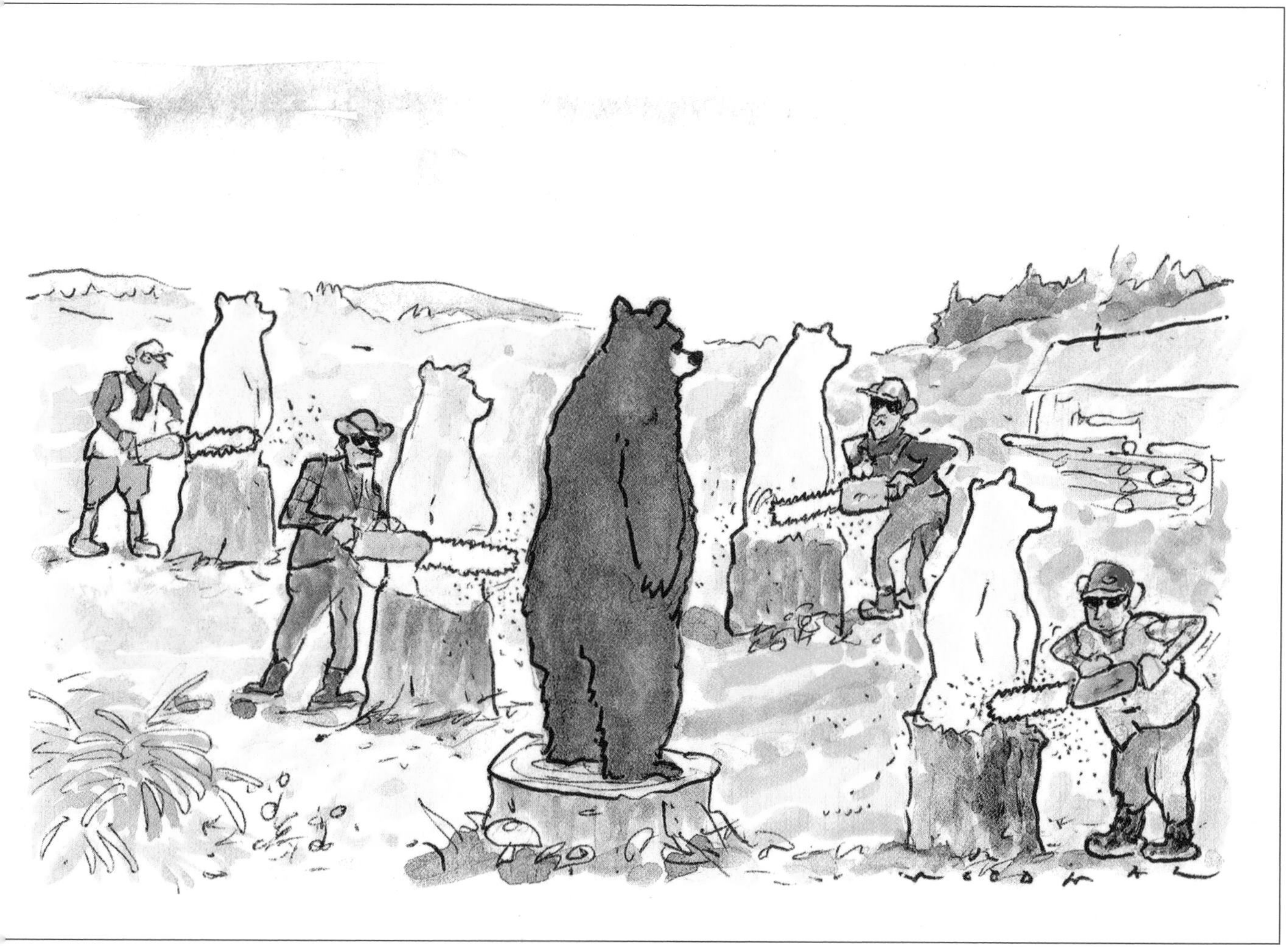

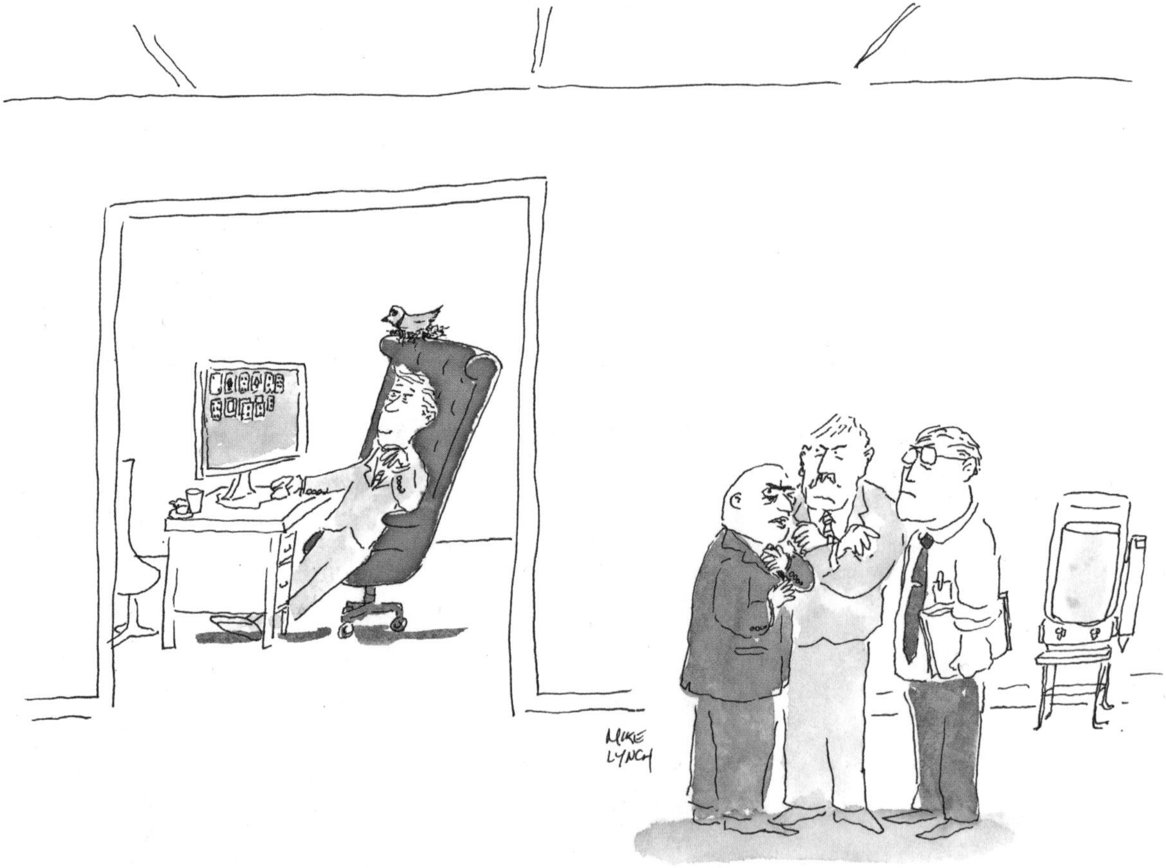
MIKE
LYNCH

"Hopkins deserves to be fired, but we can't touch him since that piping plover began roosting in his office."

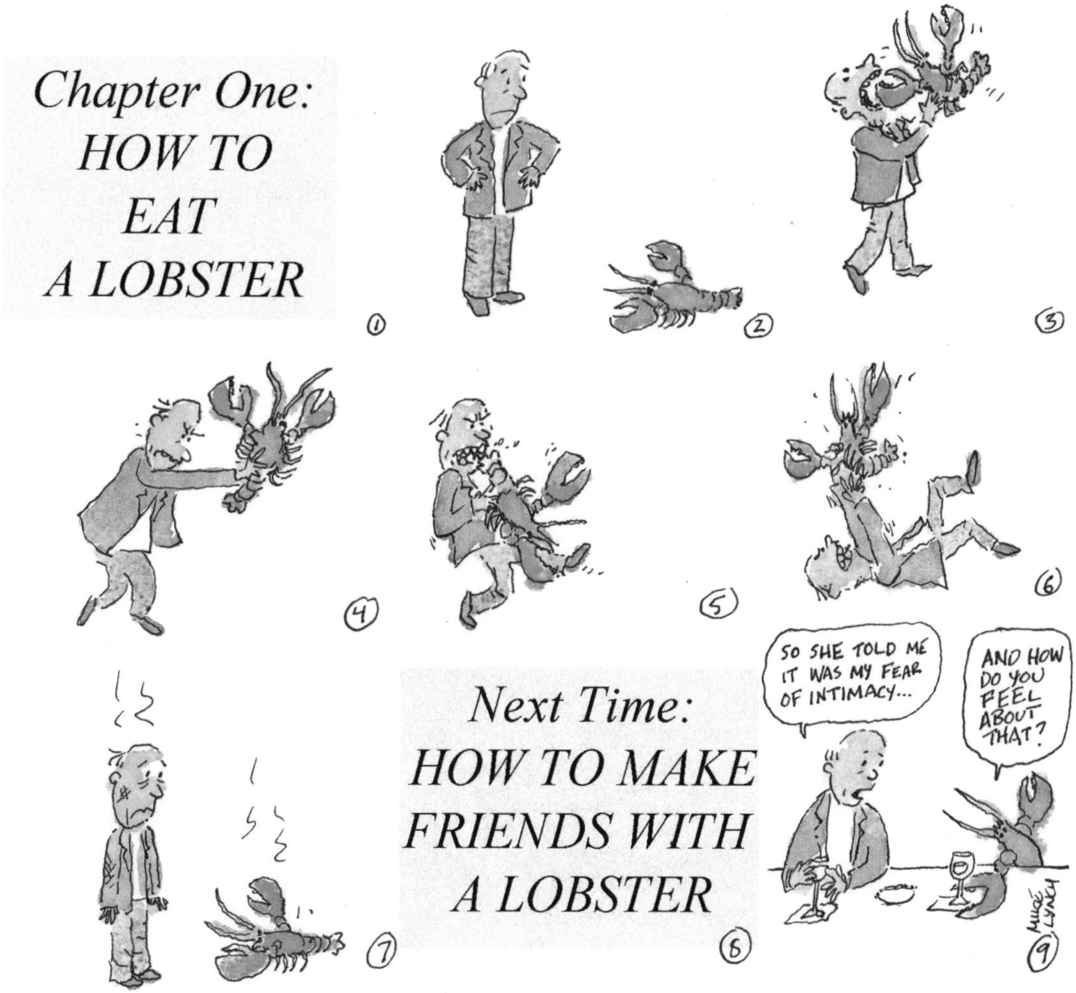
Chapter One:
HOW TO EAT A LOBSTER
Next Time:
HOW TO MAKE FRIENDS WITH A LOBSTER
SO SHE TOLD ME IT WAS MY FEAR OF INTIMACY...
AND HOW DO YOU FEEL ABOUT THAT?
MIKE LYNCH

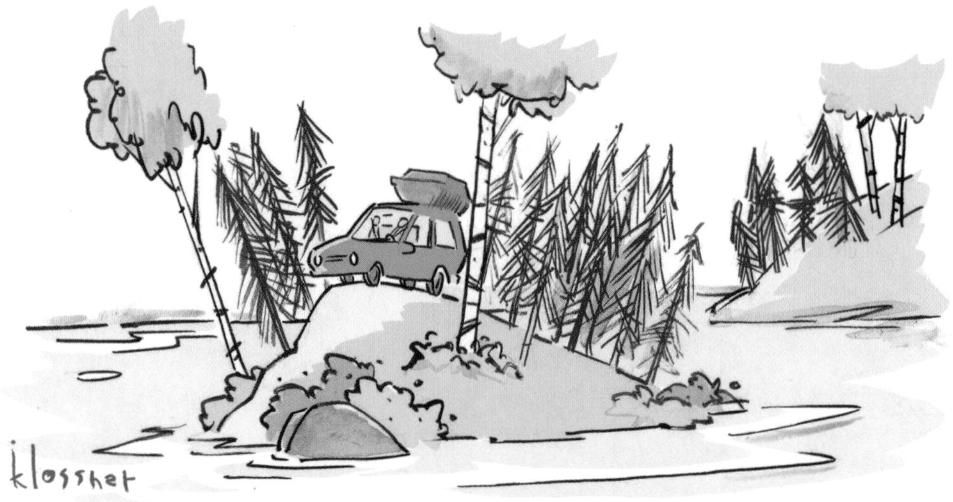
klossner

"You shouldn't have yelled at the GPS."

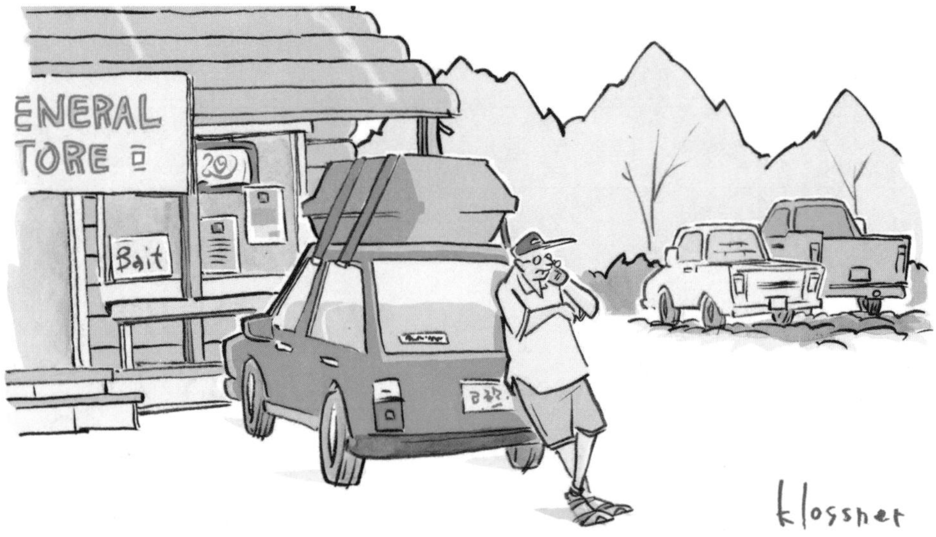
ENERAL
TORE
Bait
klossner

"It's God's country, if your god drives a truck."

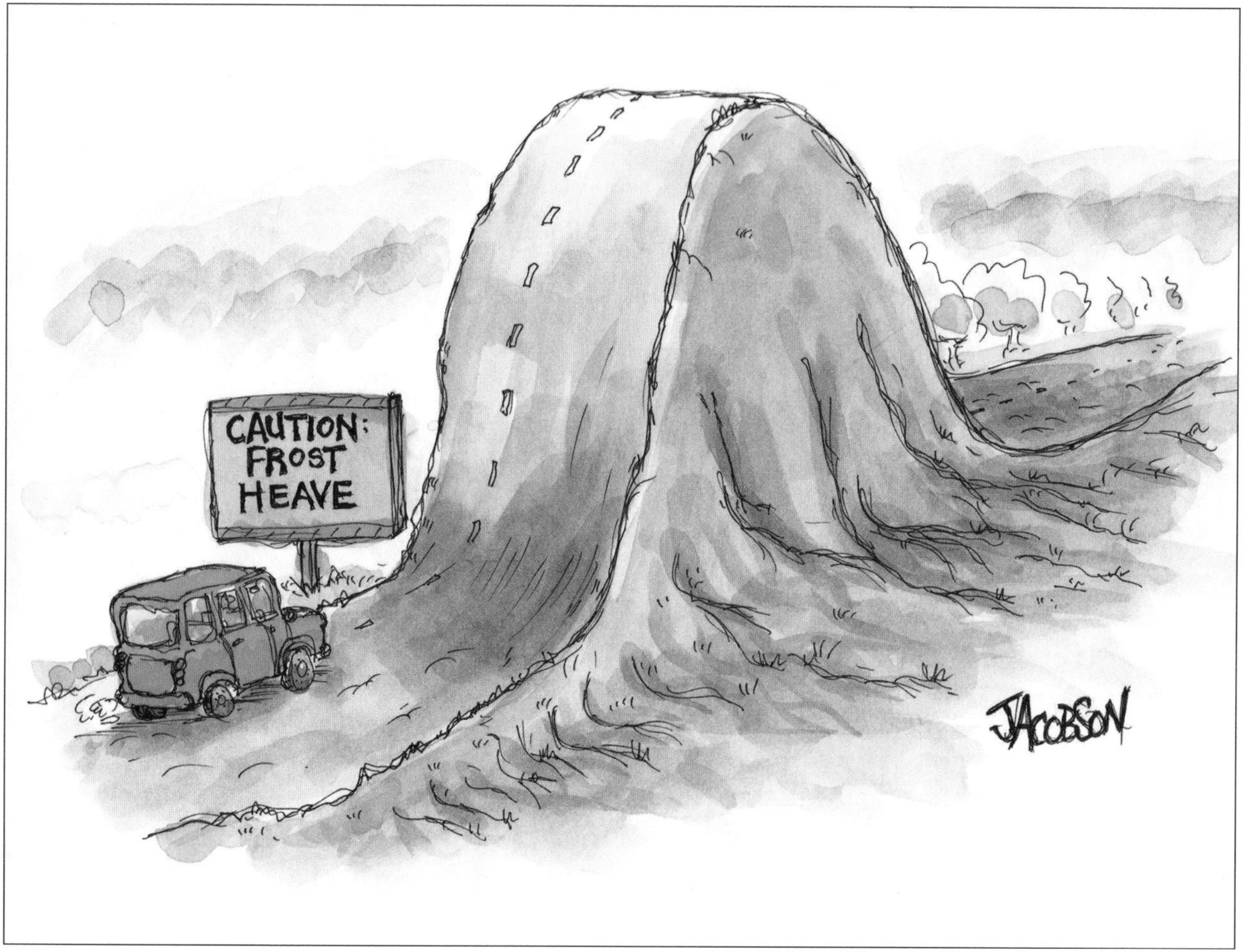
CAUTION:
FROST
HEAVE
JACOBSON

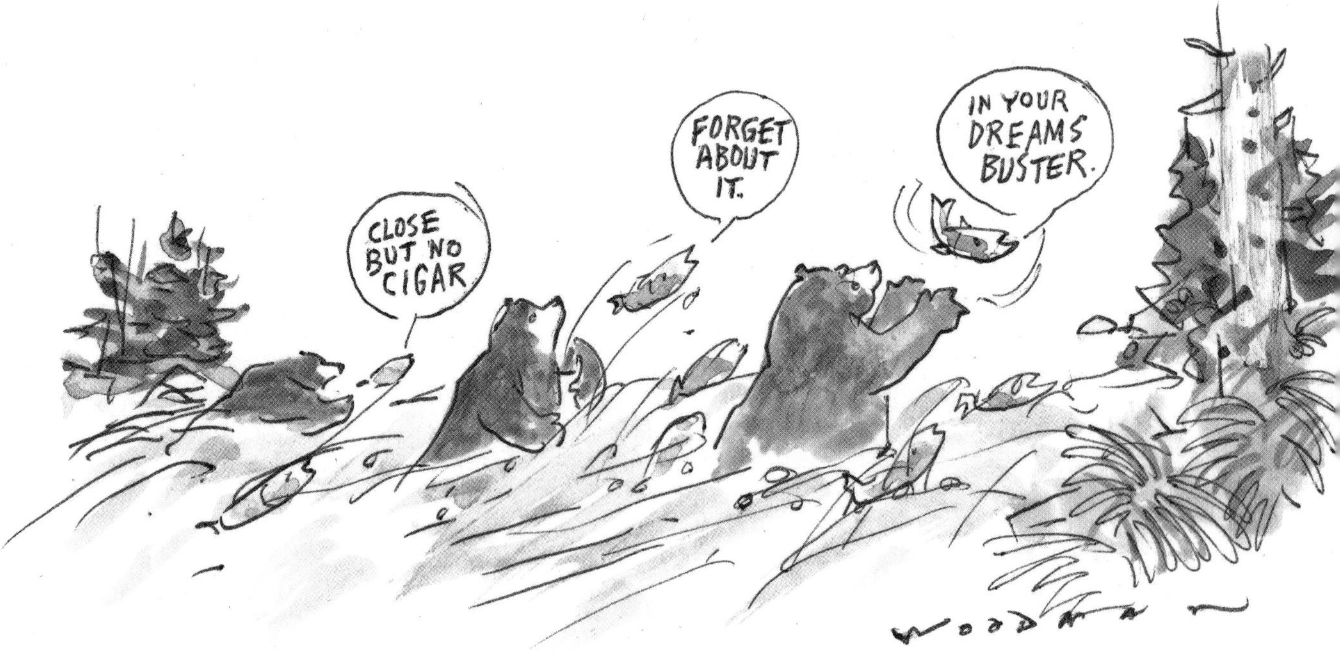
CLOSE BUT NO CIGAR
FORGET ABOUT IT.
IN YOUR DREAMS BUSTER.
WOODMAN

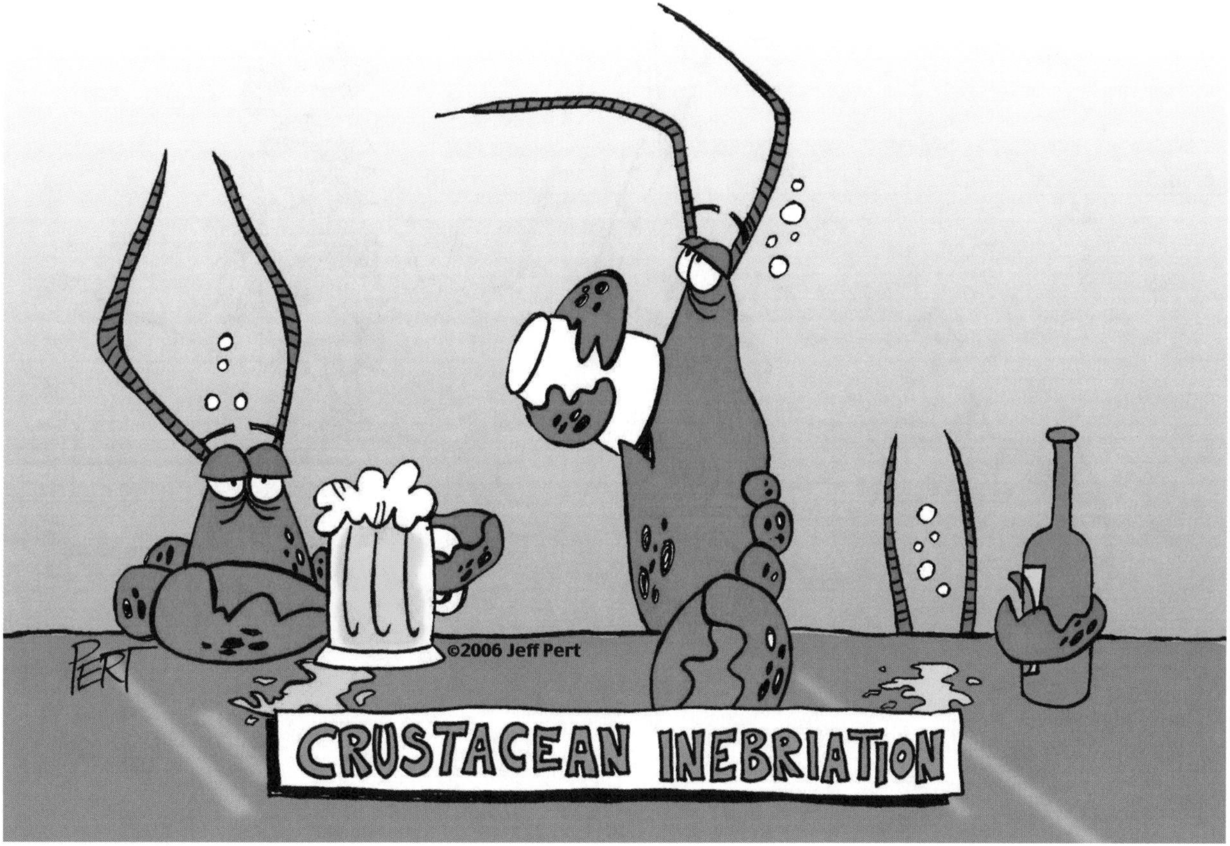
PERT
©2006 Jeff Pert
CRUSTACEAN INEBRIATION

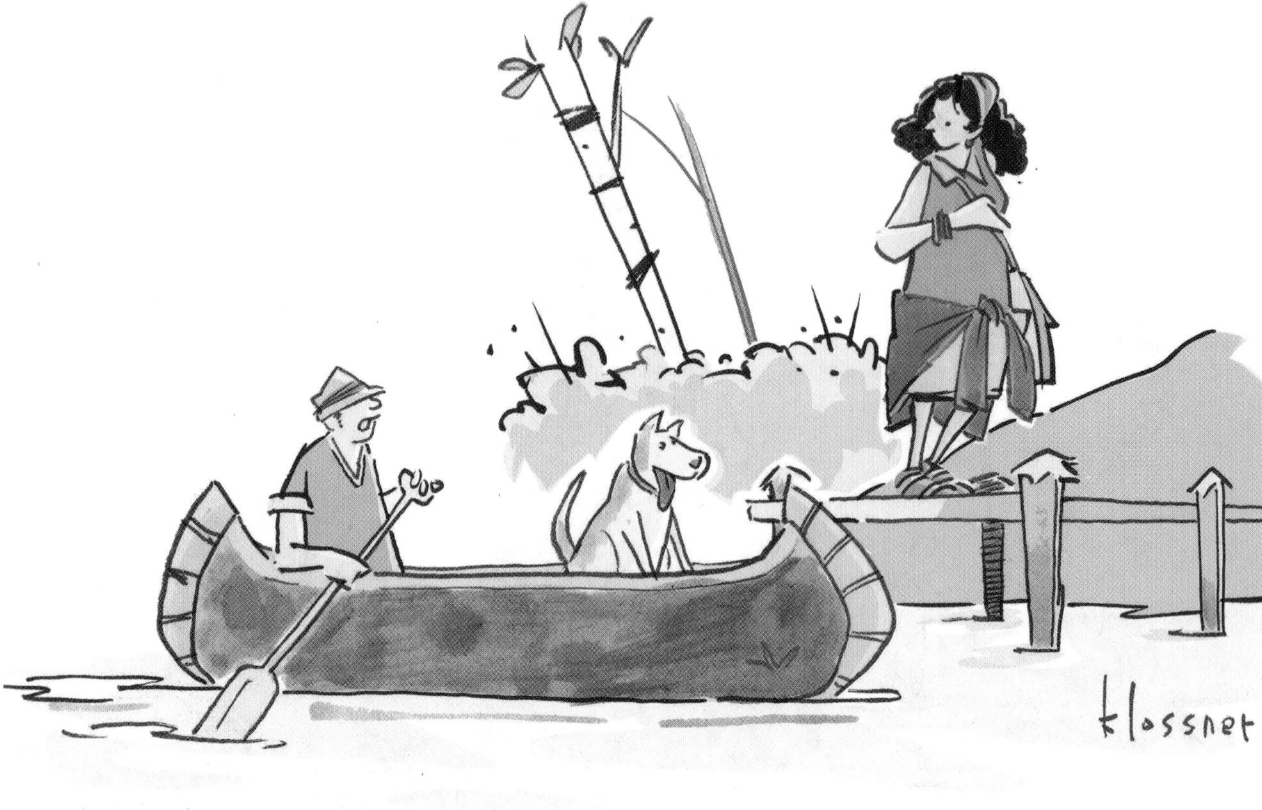
klossner

"I *am* the Uber."

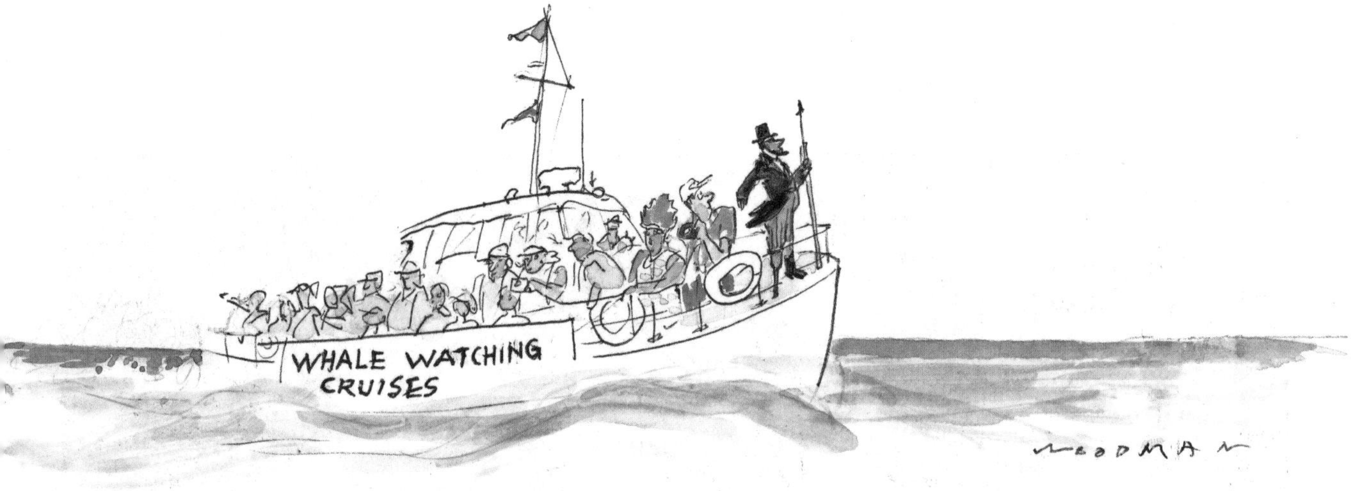
WHALE WATCHING
CRUISES
WOODMAN

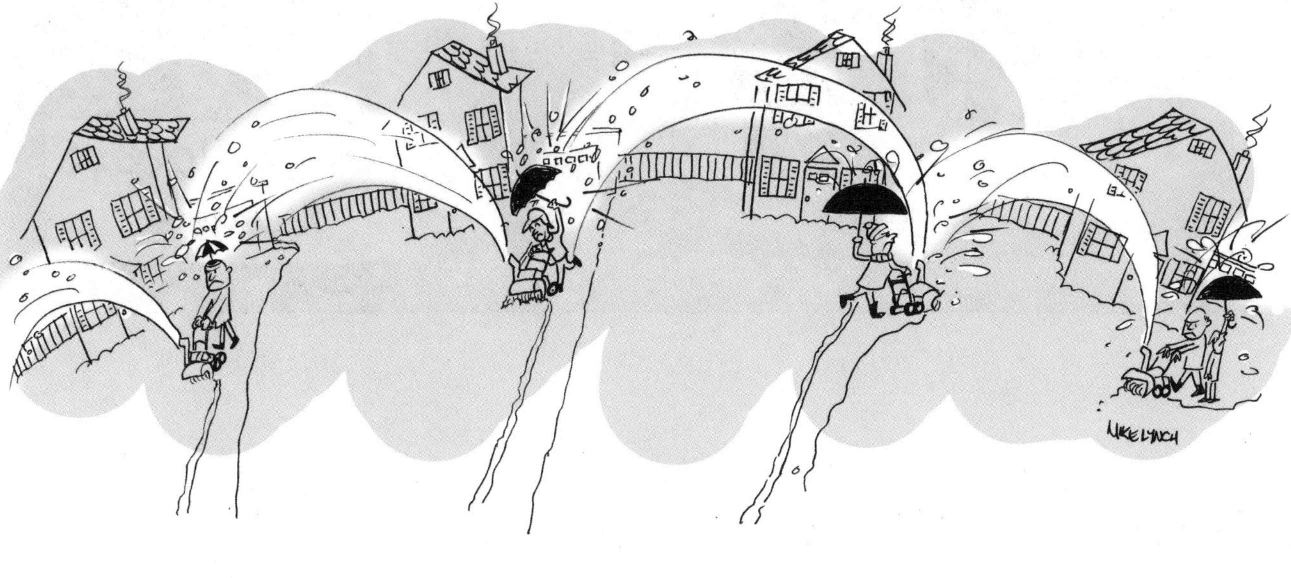
MIKE LYNCH

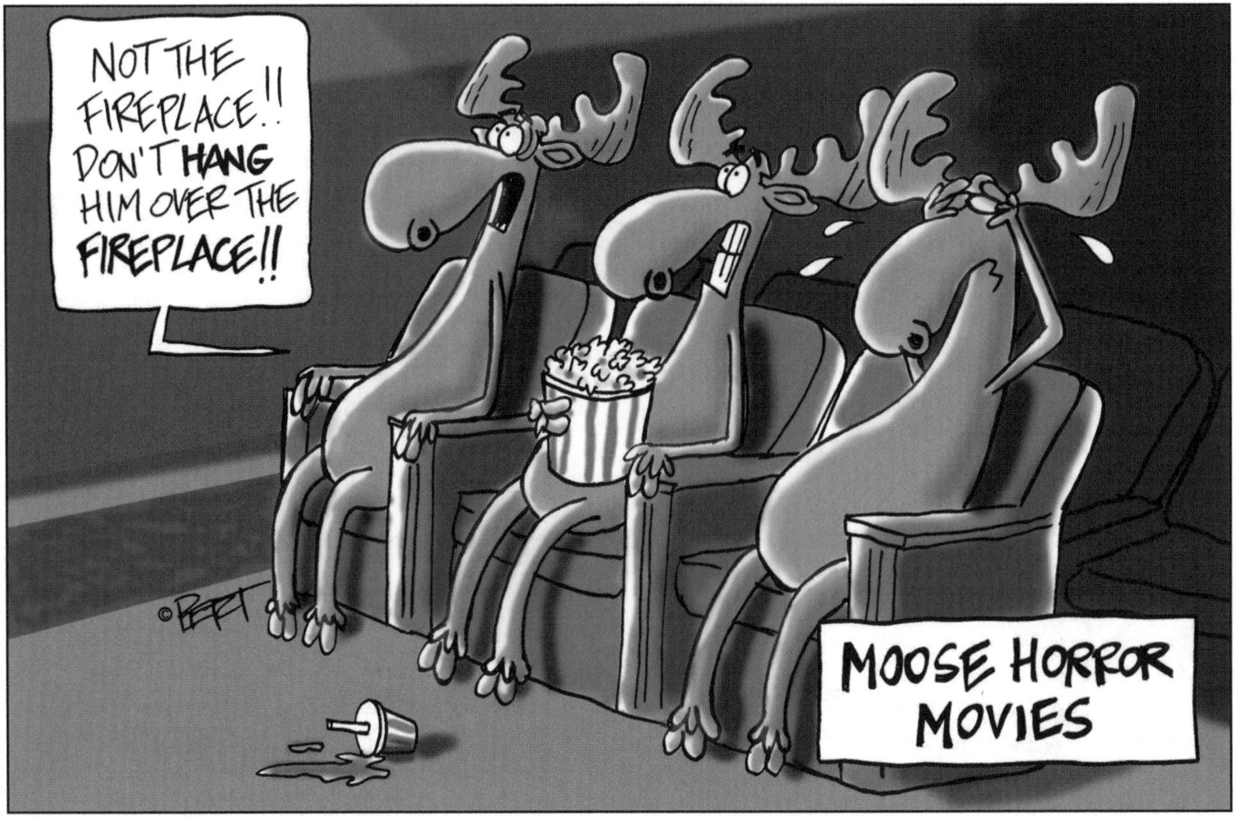
NOT THE FIREPLACE!! DON'T HANG HIM OVER THE FIREPLACE!!
MOOSE HORROR MOVIES

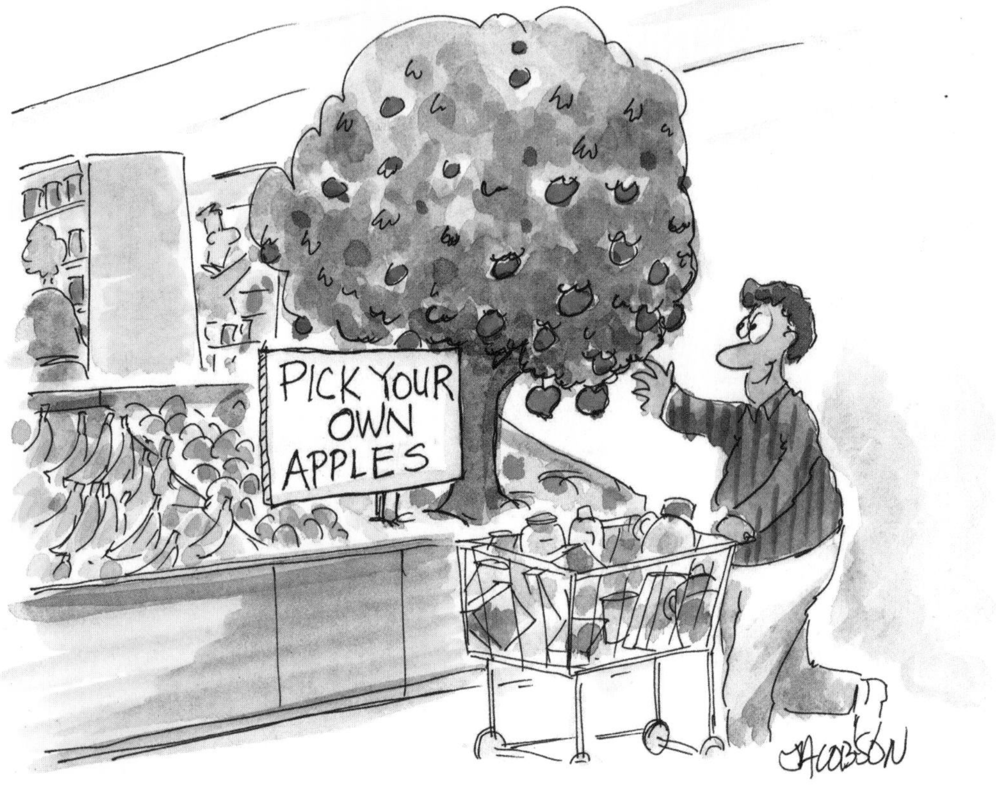
PICK YOUR OWN APPLES
JACOBSON

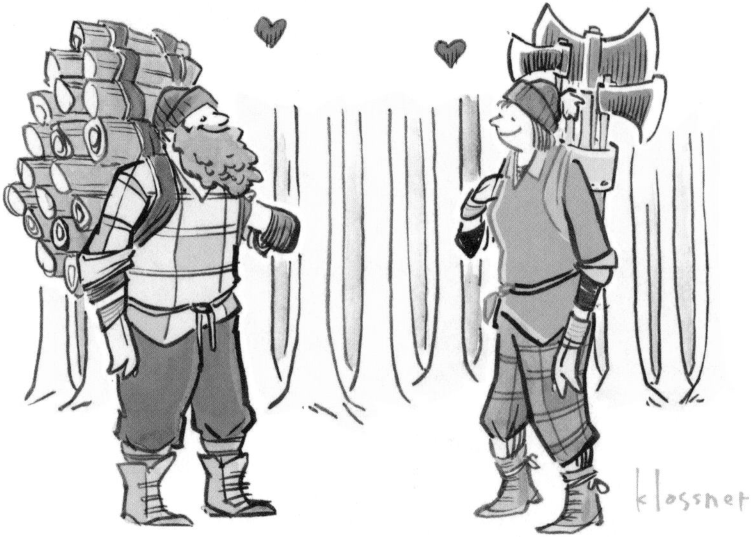
klossner

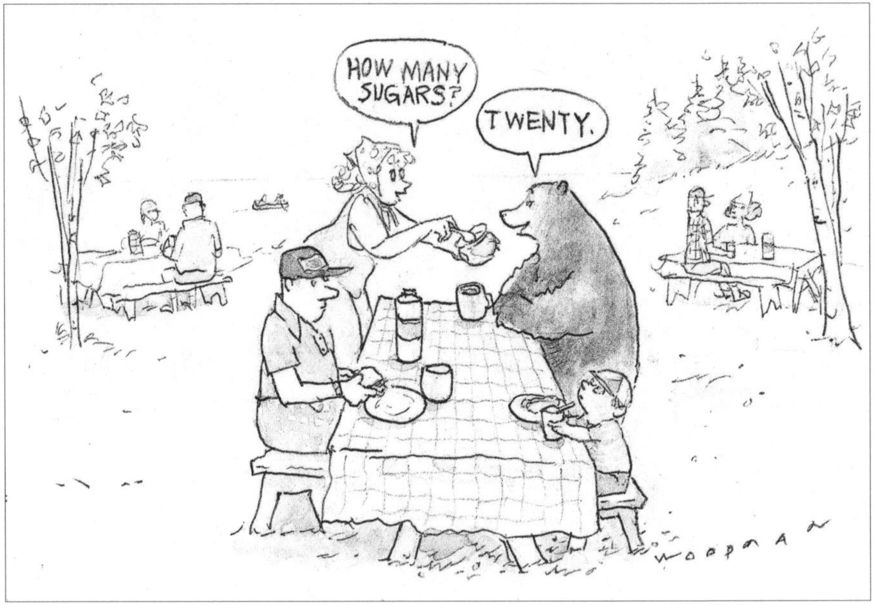
HOW MANY SUGARS?
TWENTY.
WOODMAN

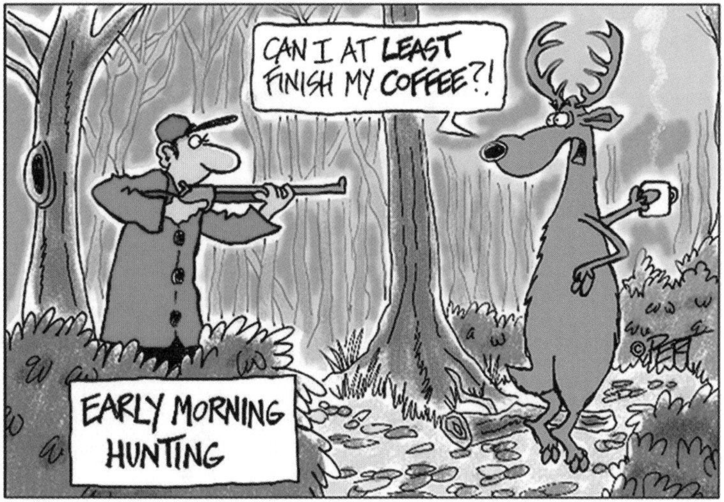
CAN I AT LEAST FINISH MY COFFEE?!
EARLY MORNING HUNTING
©PETT

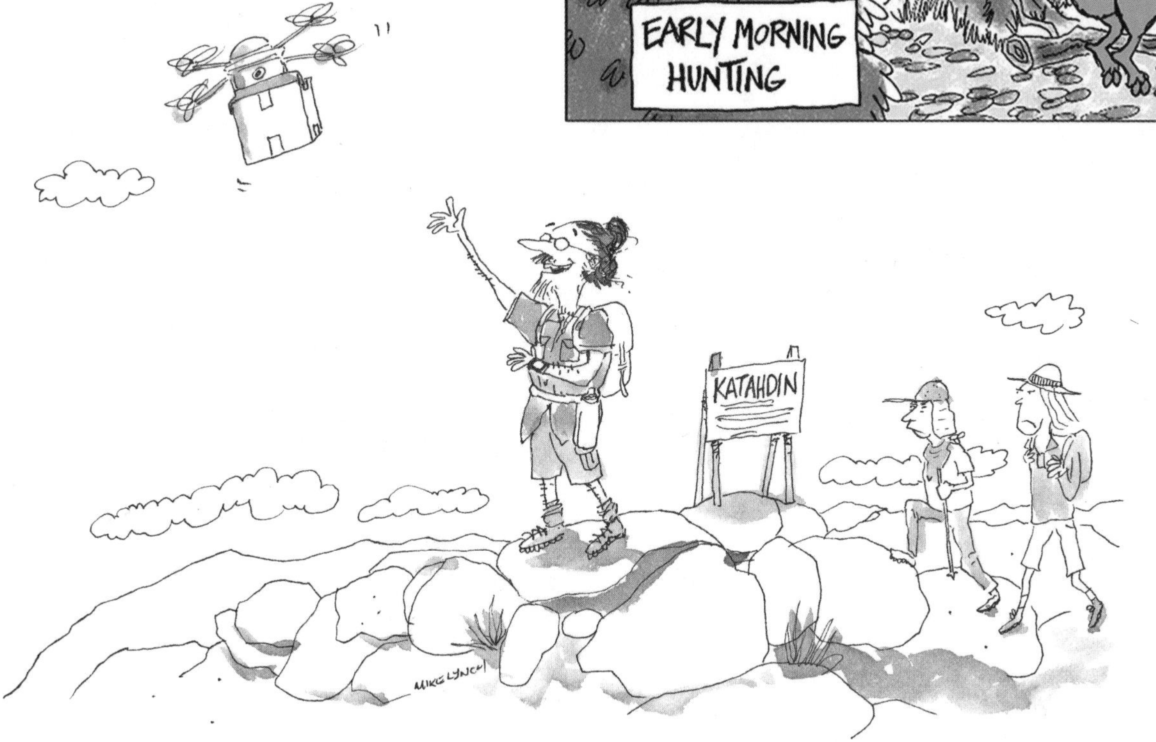
KATAHDIN
MIKE LYNCH

“First to get an Amazon drone delivery on Mount Katahdin.”

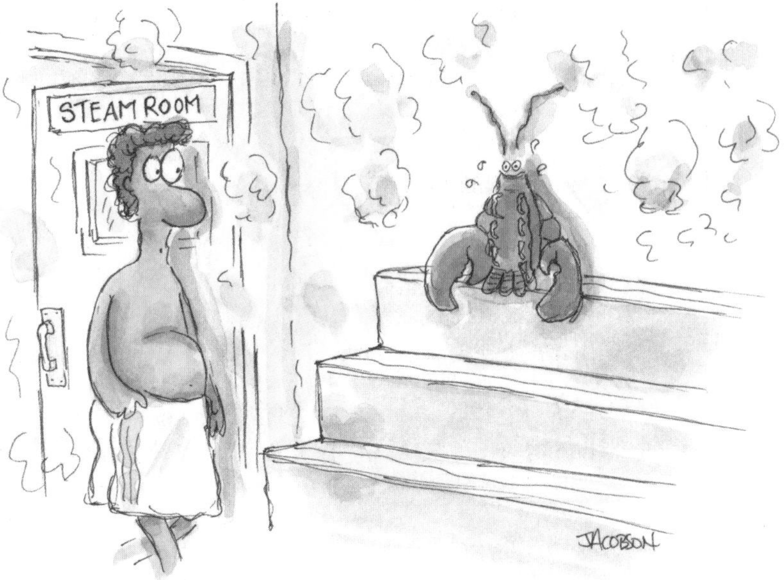
STEAM ROOM
JACOBSON

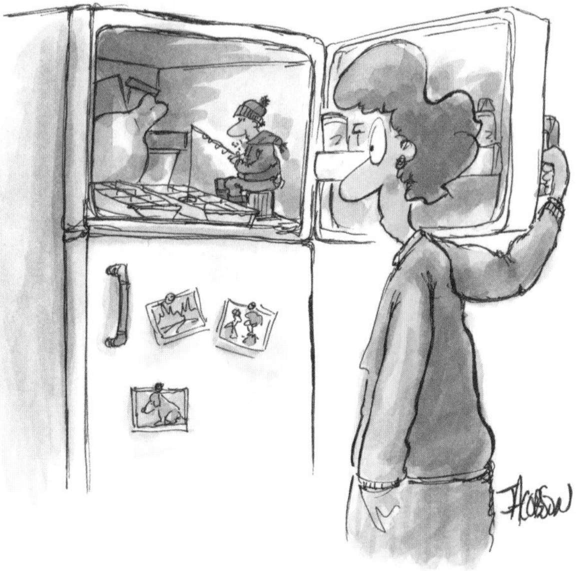
JACOBSON

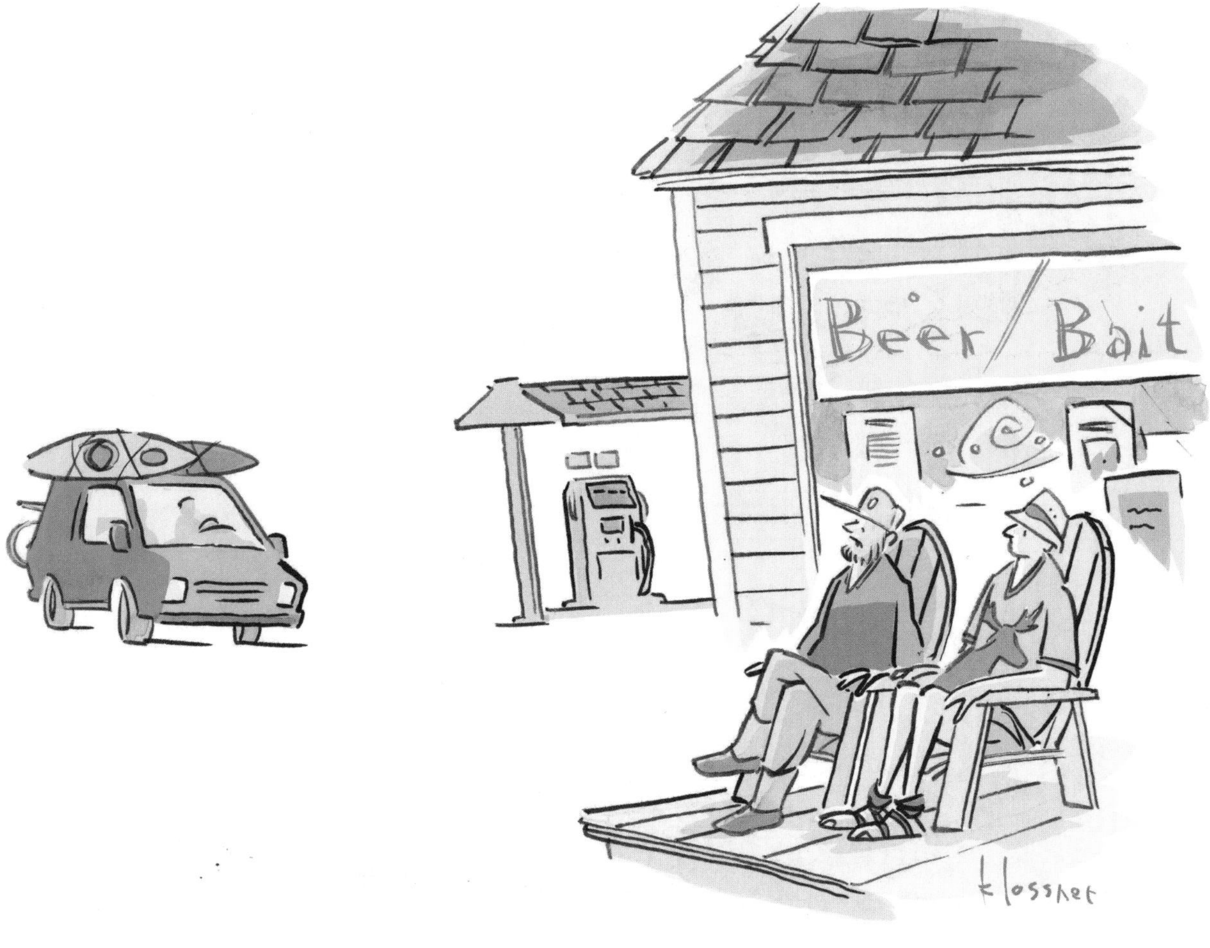
Beer/Bait
klossner

"Here comes the economy."

BOAT LAUNCHING 101

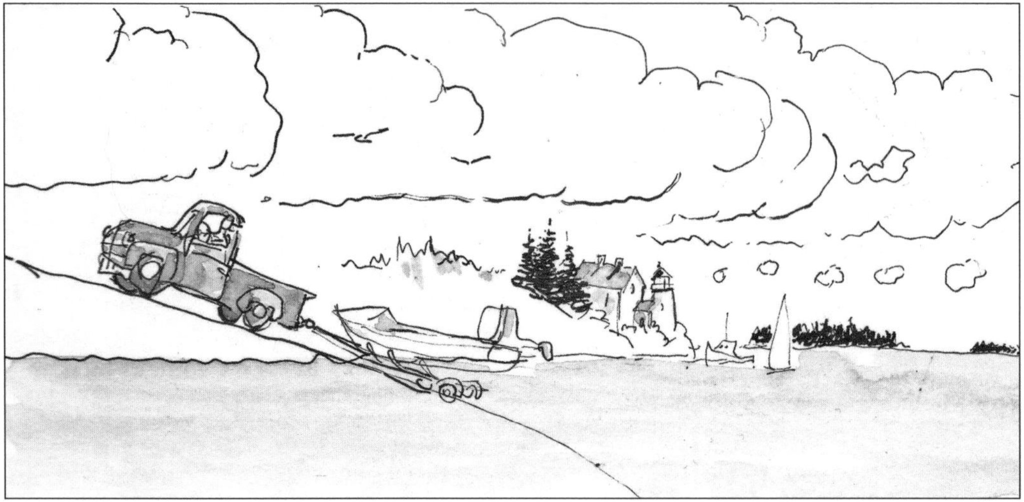

Right

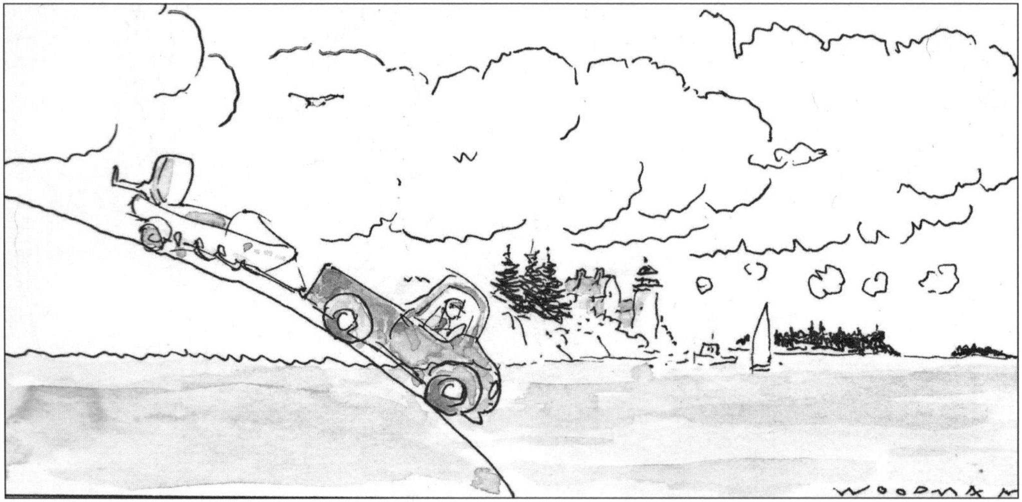

Wrong

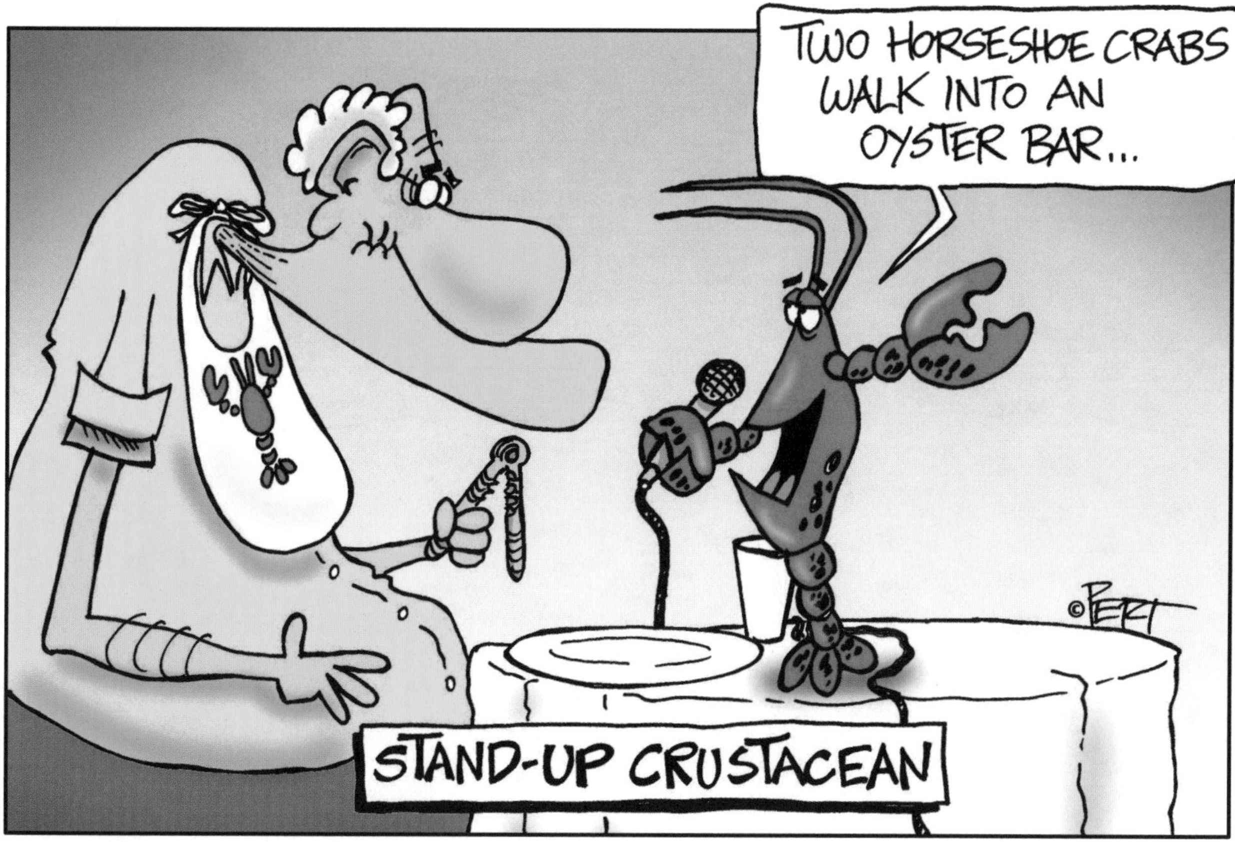
TWO HORSESHOE CRABS WALK INTO AN OYSTER BAR...
©PERT
STAND-UP CRUSTACEAN

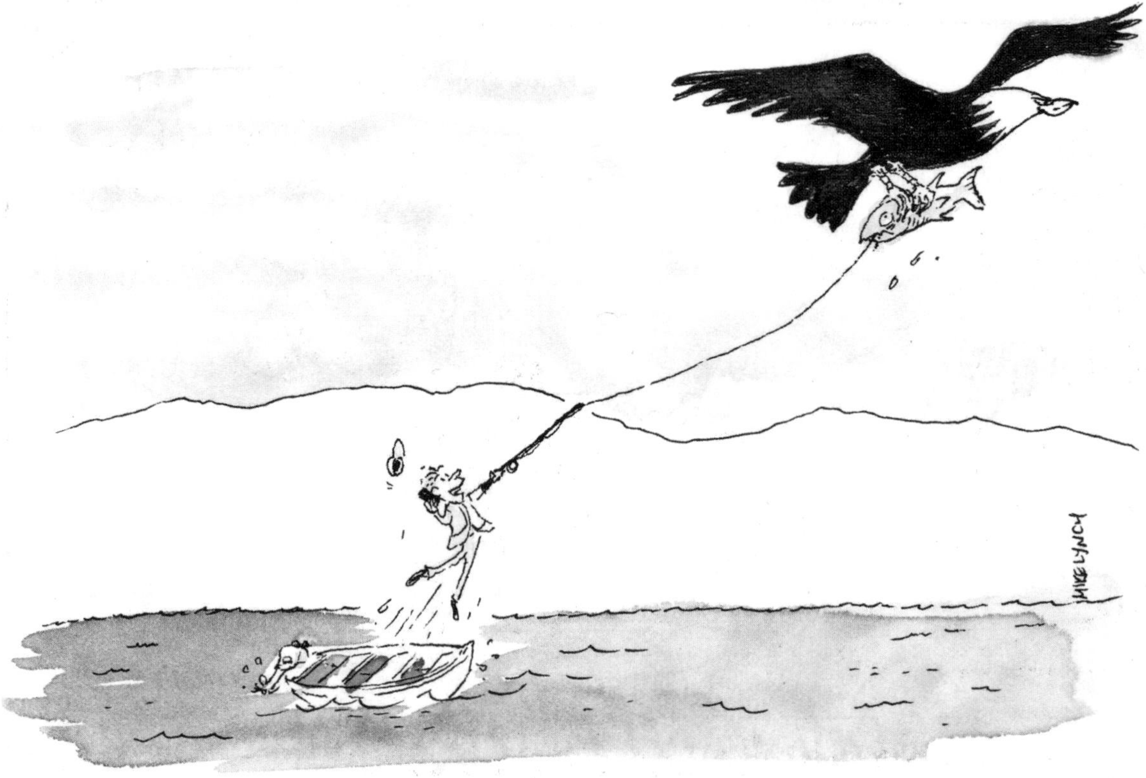
MIKE LYNCH

"Hi Hon. You wouldn't believe the time I'm having!"

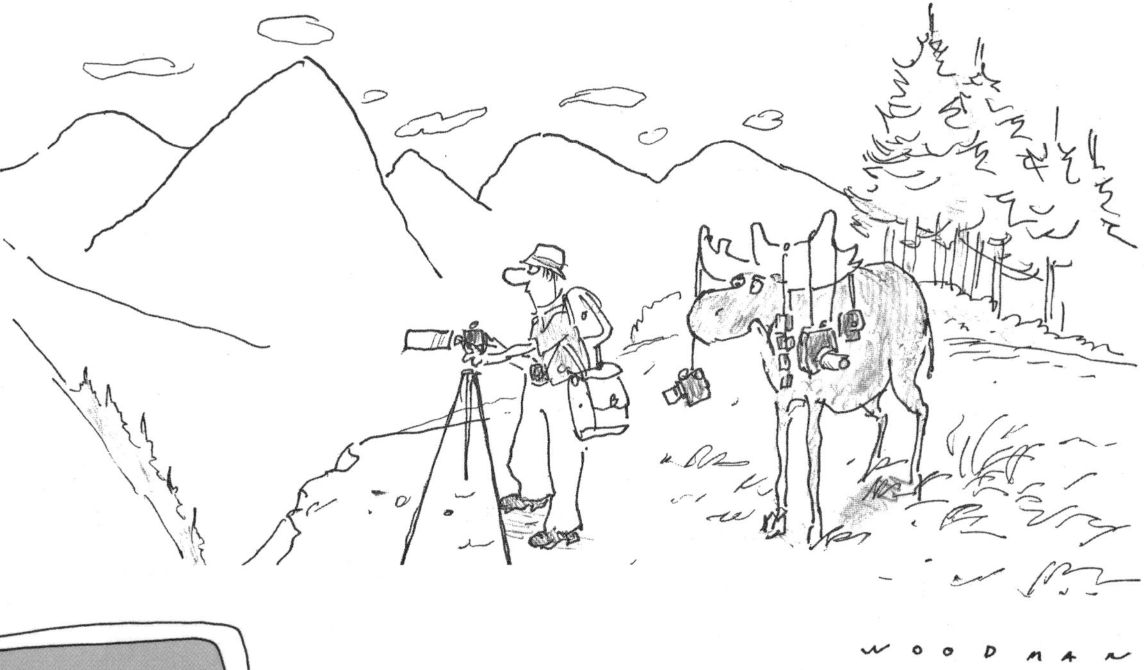
WOODMAN

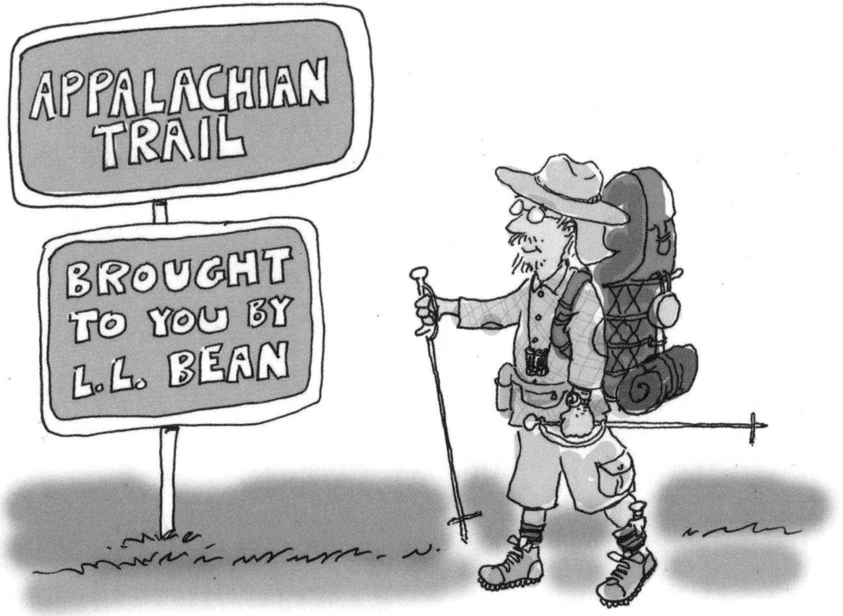
APPALACHIAN TRAIL
BROUGHT TO YOU BY L.L. BEAN

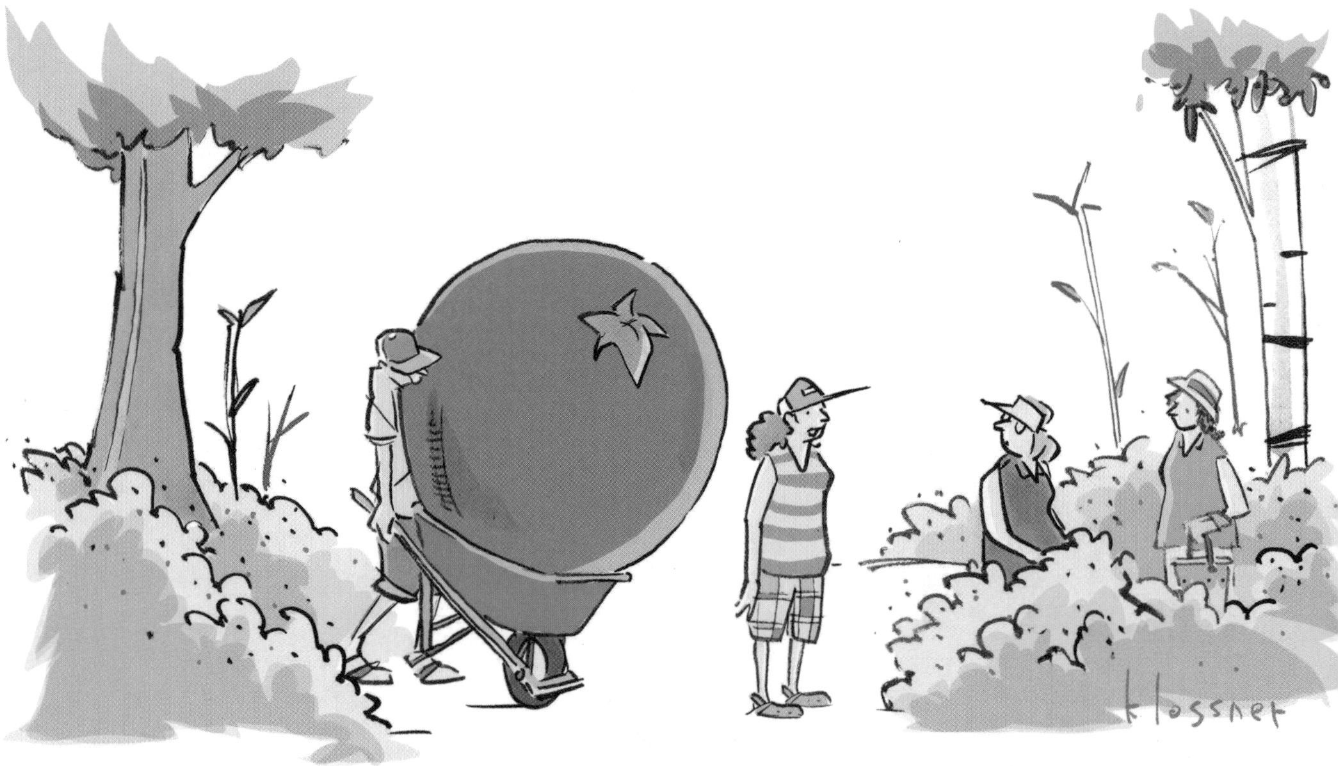
klossner

"If you locate the right bush,
the picking is so much quicker."

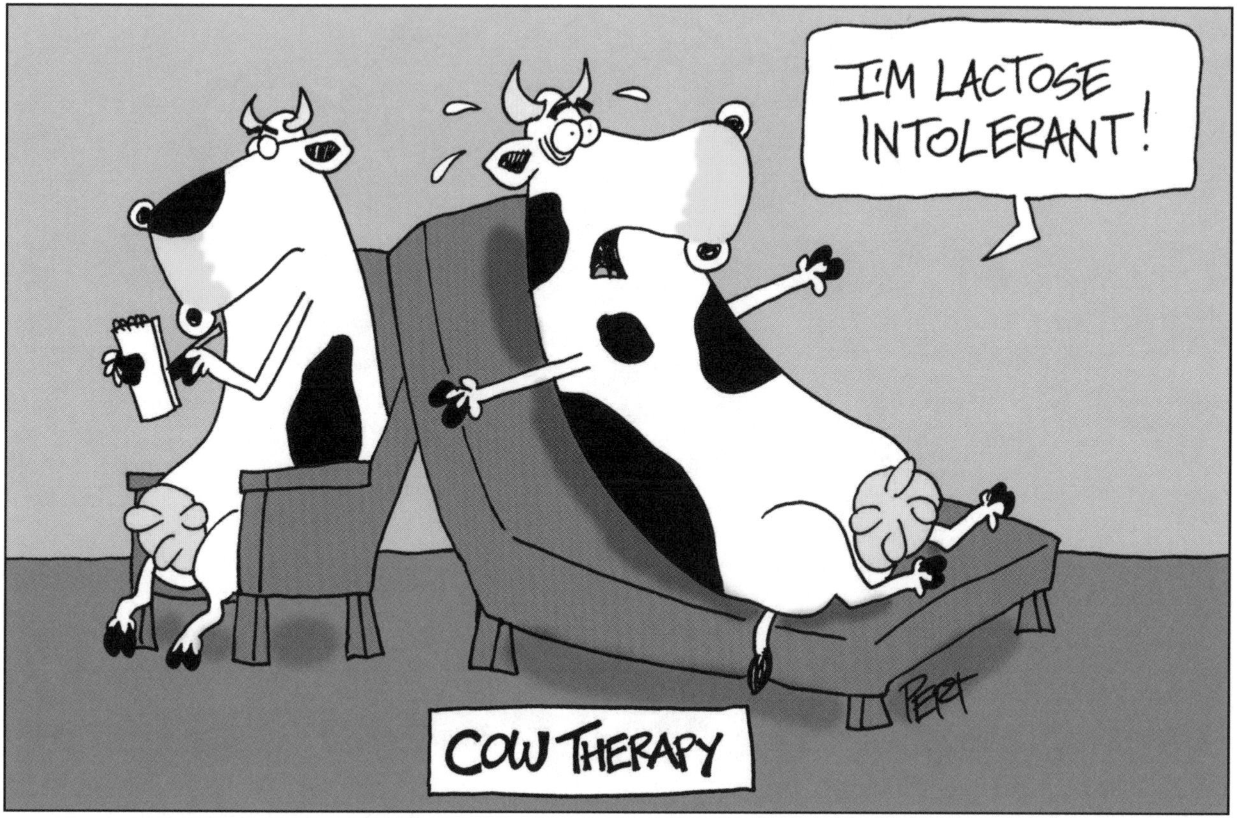
I'M LACTOSE INTOLERANT!
PERT
COW THERAPY

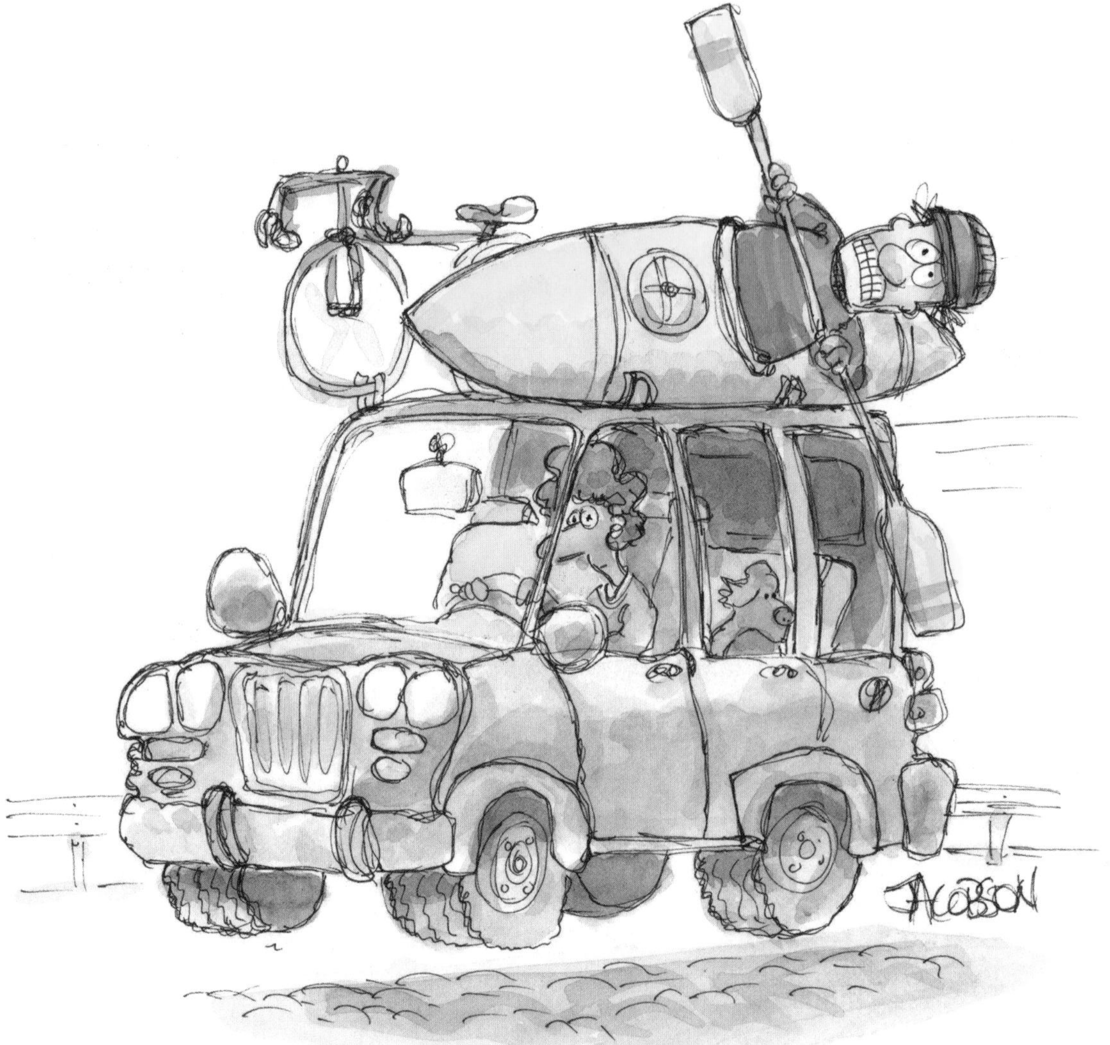
JACOBSON

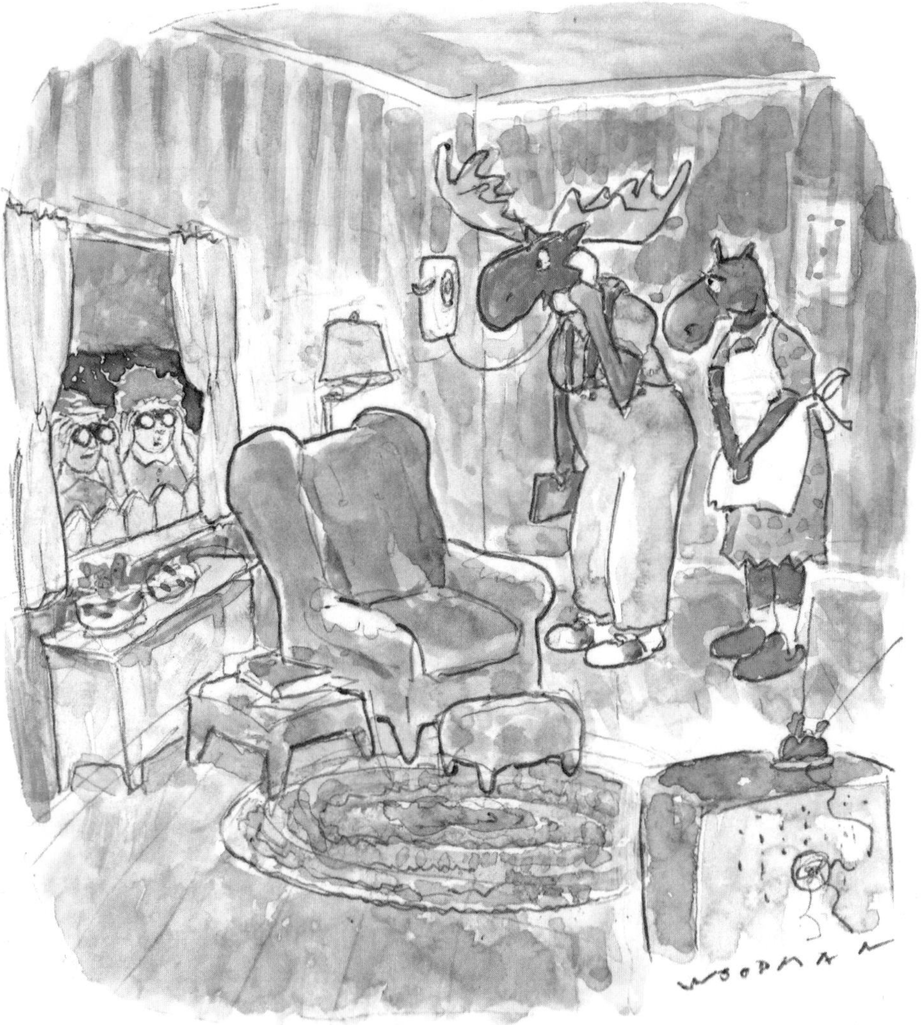
WOODMAN

"Hello, Sheriff, Bill and Dotty Moose here. We'd like to report two moose watchers in our backyard."

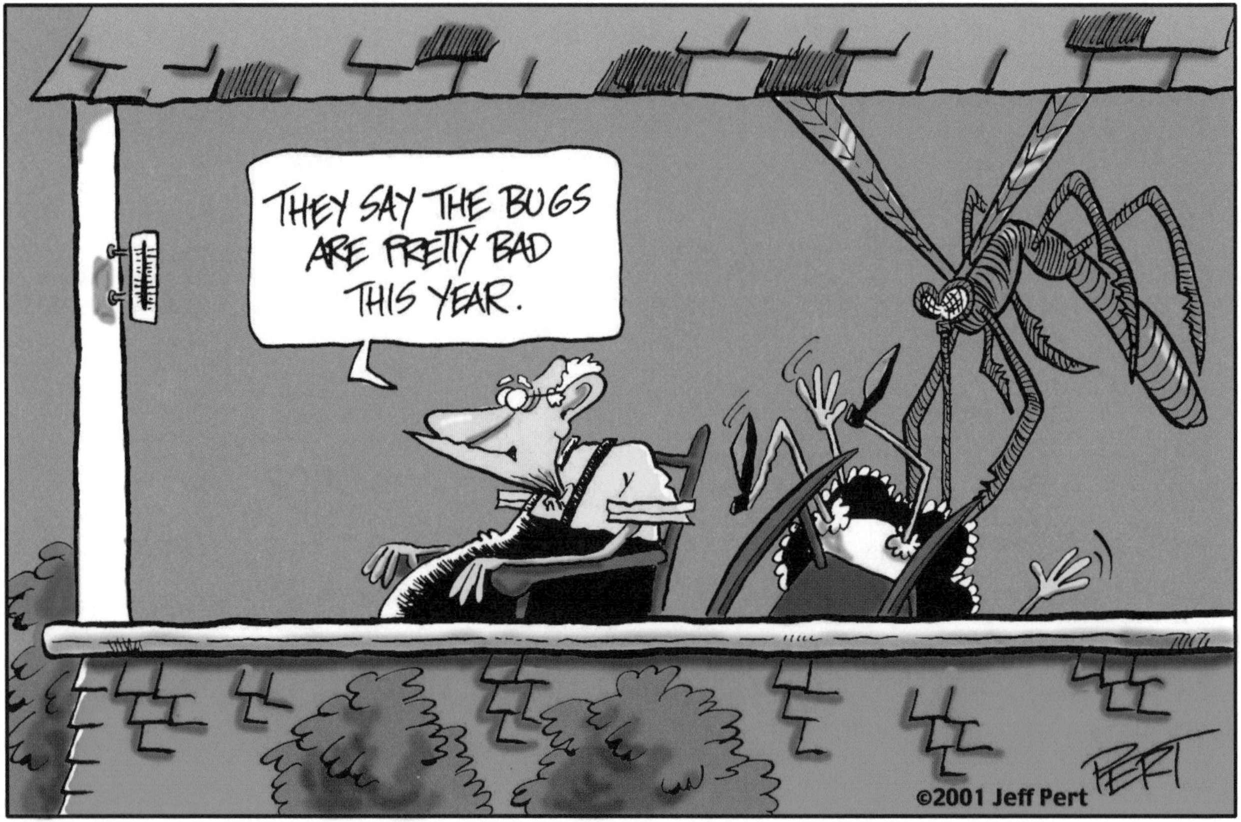
THEY SAY THE BUGS ARE PRETTY BAD THIS YEAR.
PERT
©2001 Jeff Pert

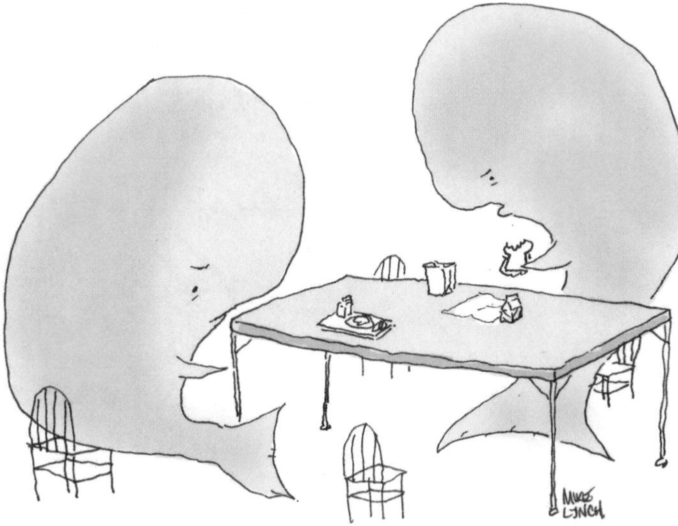
MIKE LYNCH

"Darn it! Mom made me a krill sandwich for lunch again."

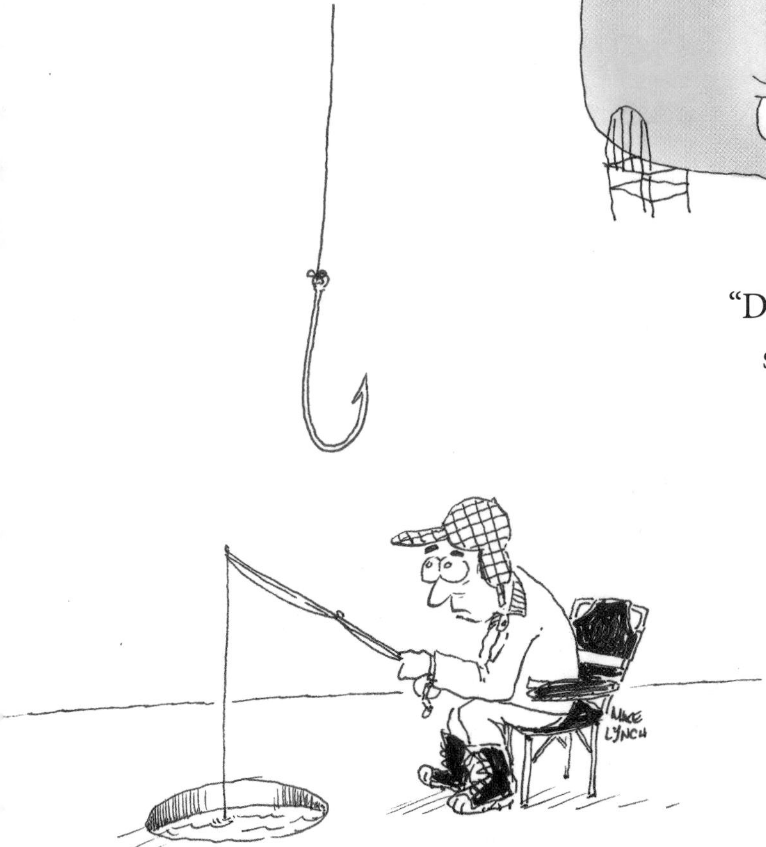
MIKE LYNCH

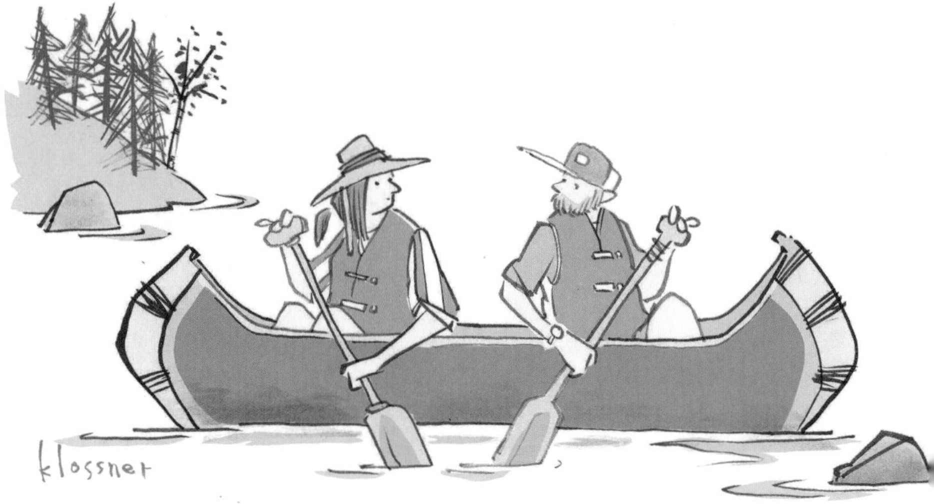
klossner

"When they first realized that the relationship would take some work."

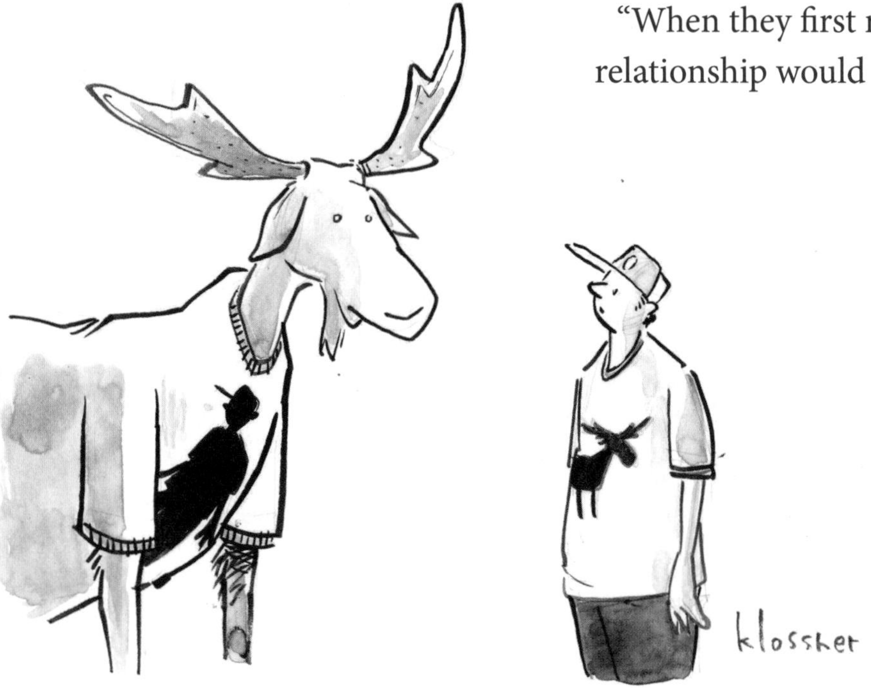
klossner

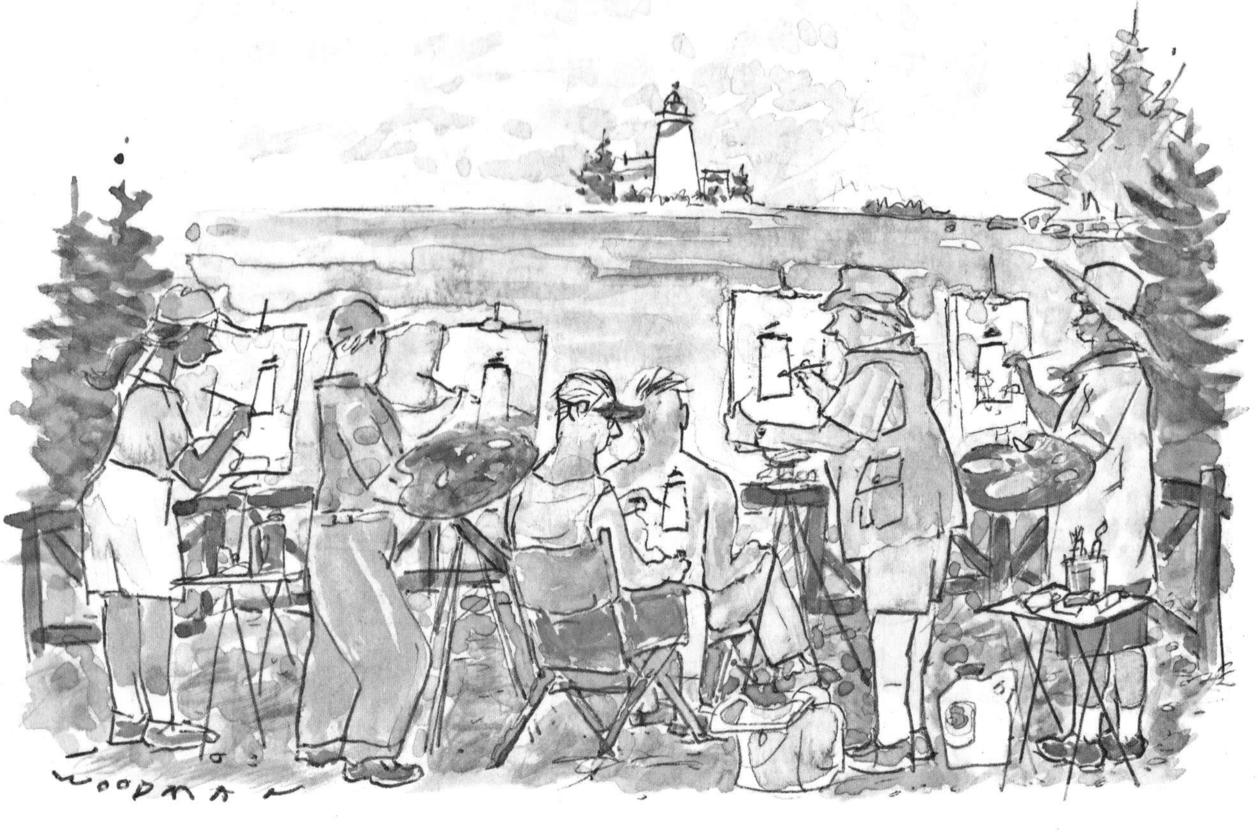
WOODMAN

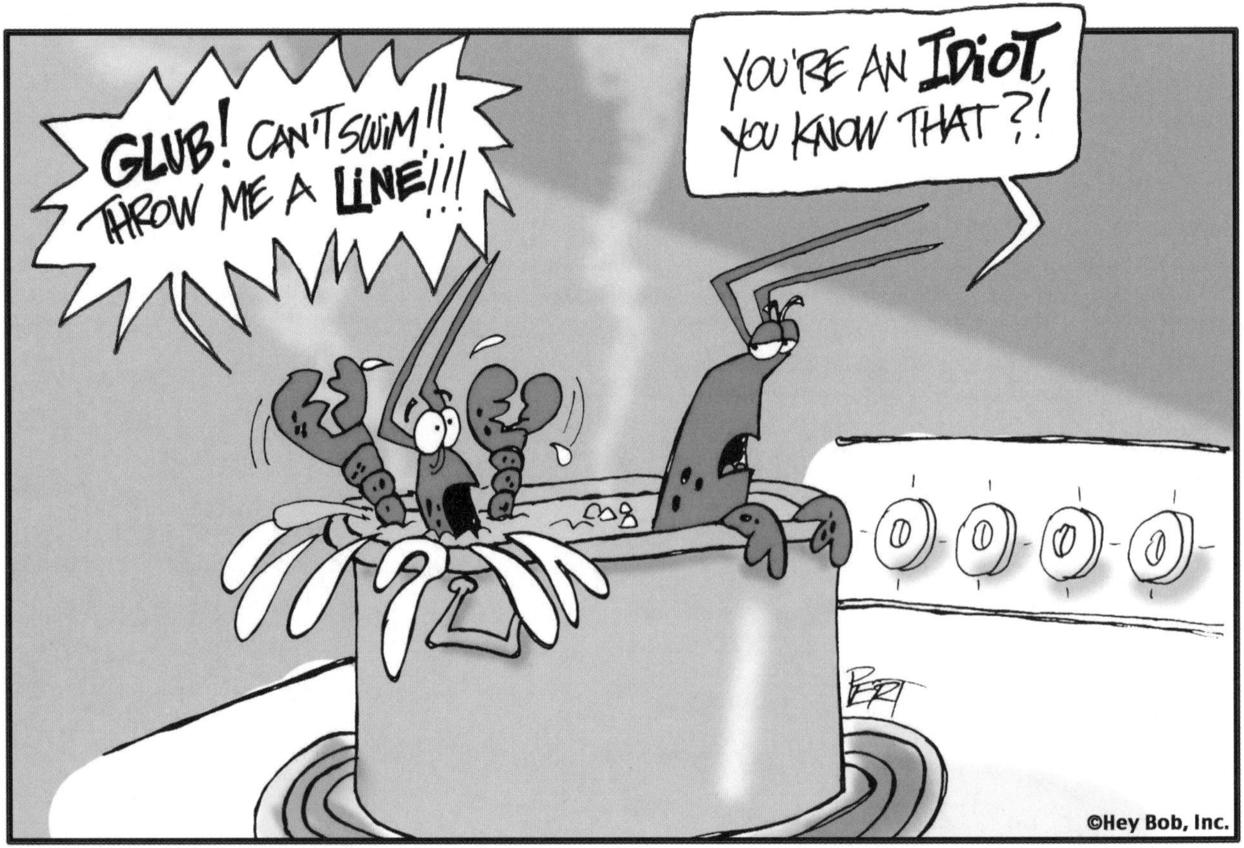
GLUB! CAN'T SWIM!! THROW ME A LINE!!!
YOU'RE AN IDIOT, YOU KNOW THAT?!
BERT
©Hey Bob, Inc.

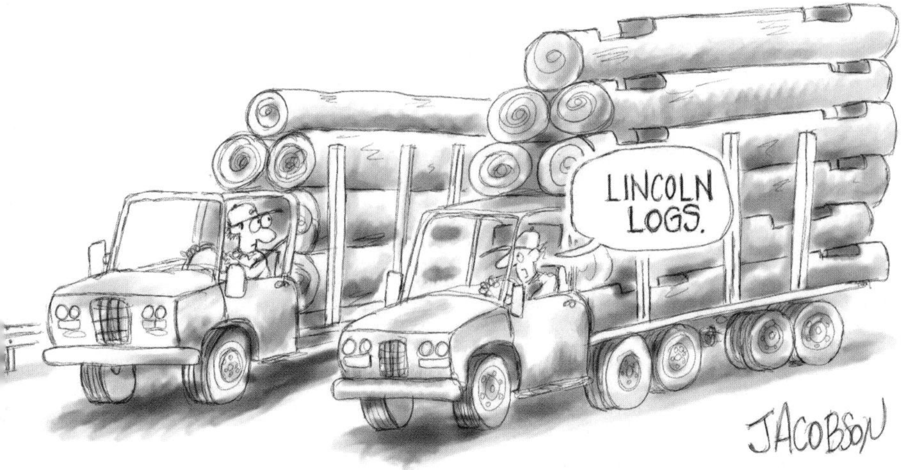
LINCOLN LOGS.
JACOBSON

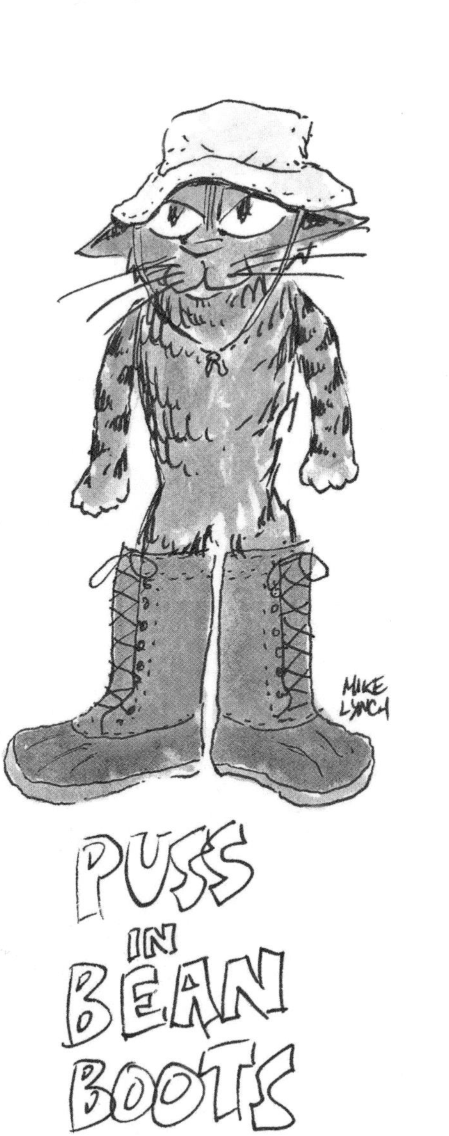
MIKE LYNCH
PUSS IN BEAN BOOTS

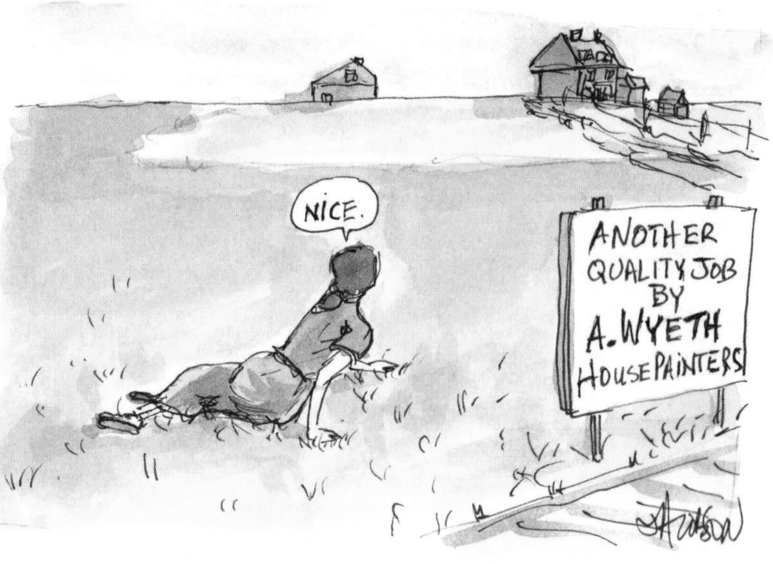
NICE.
ANOTHER QUALITY JOB BY A. WYETH HOUSEPAINTERS

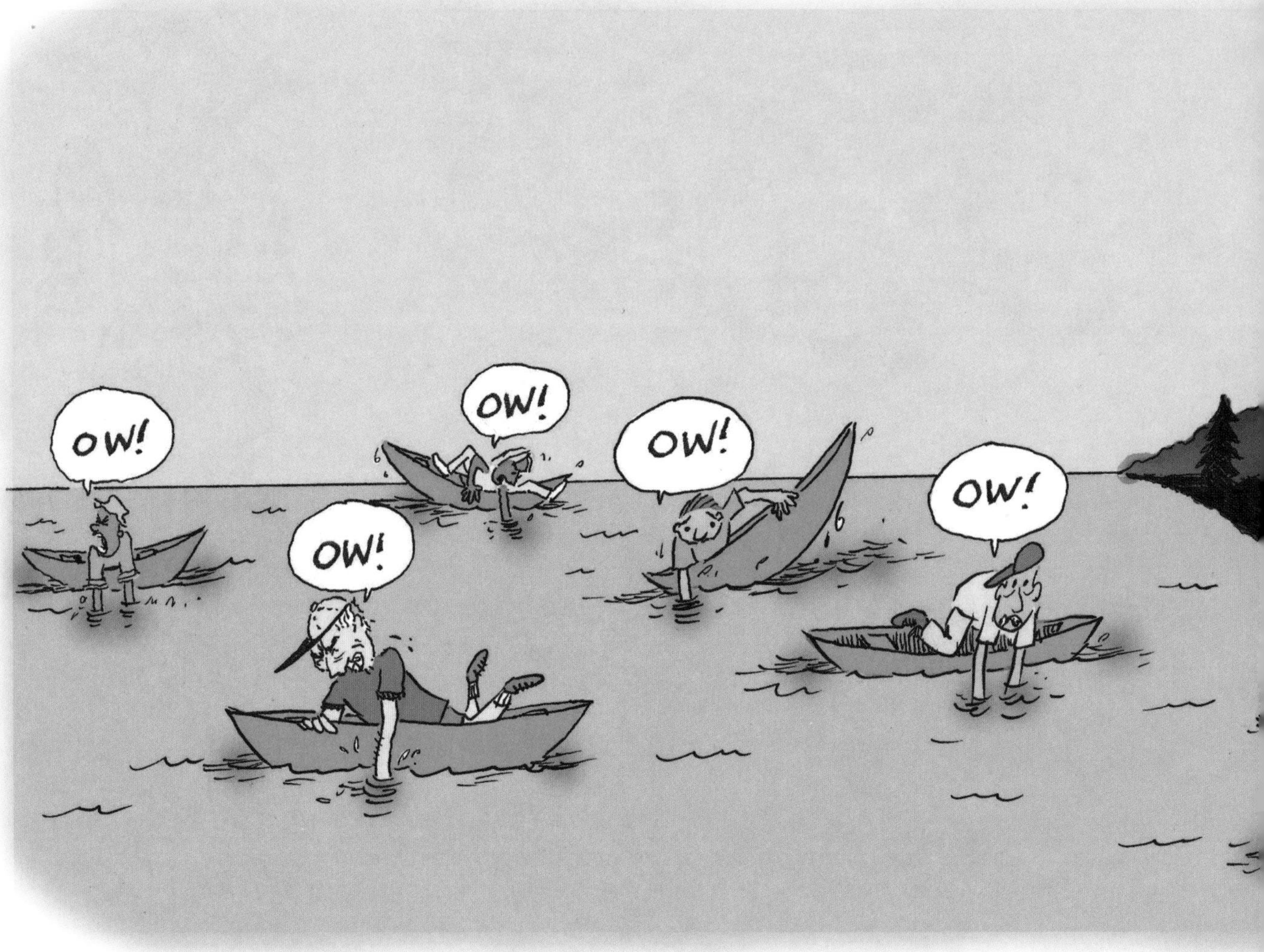

OW!
OW!
OW!
OW!
OW!

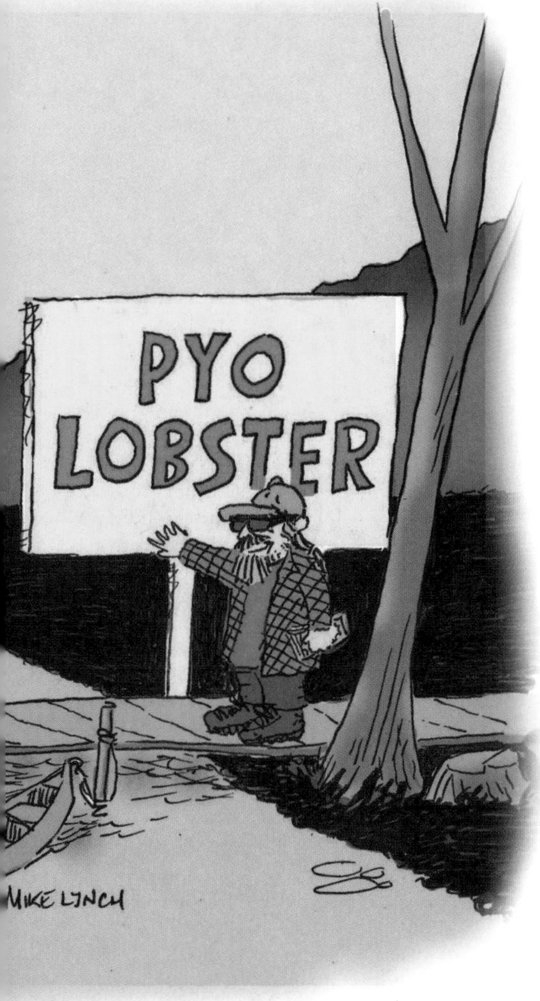
PYO
LOBSTER
MIKE LYNCH

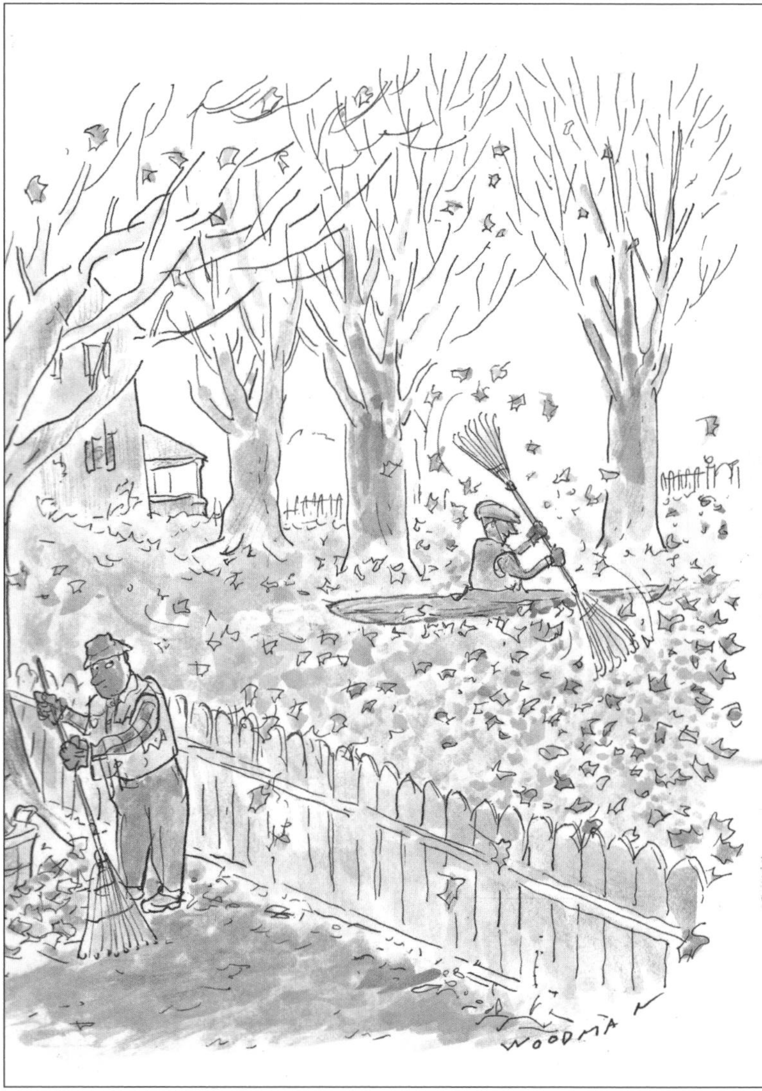
WOODMAN

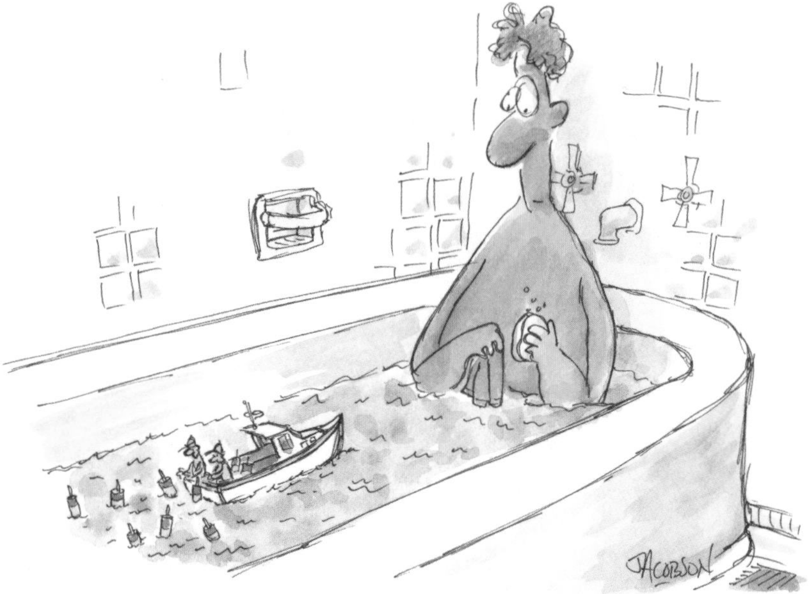

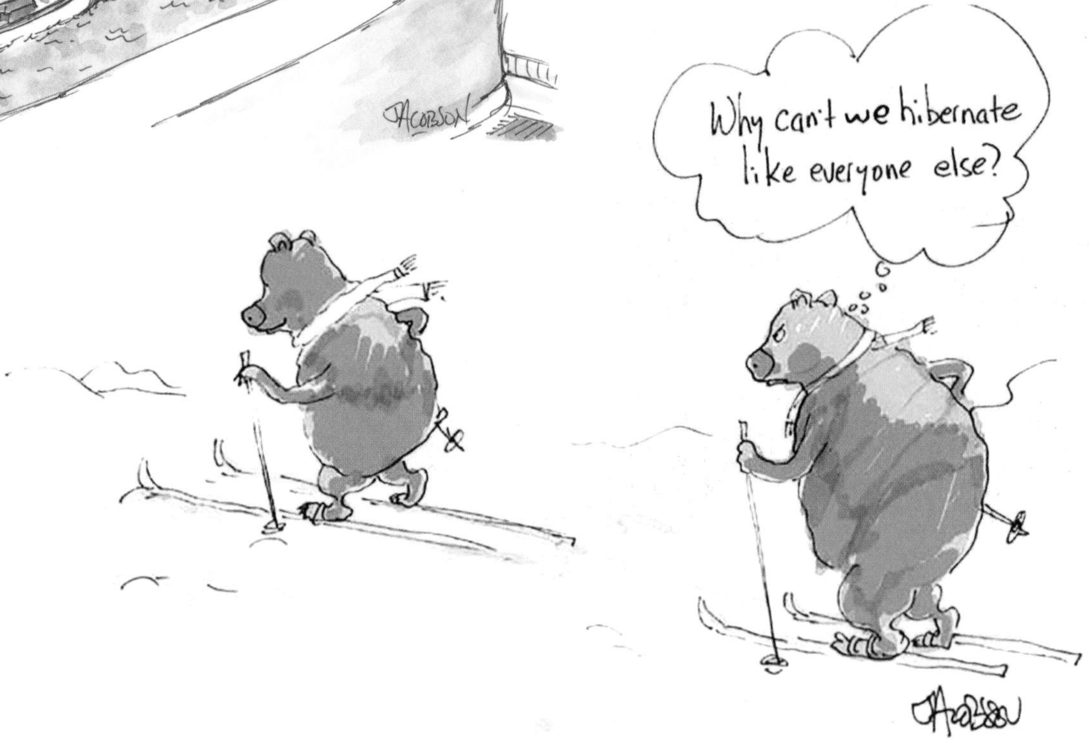

Why can't we hibernate like everyone else?

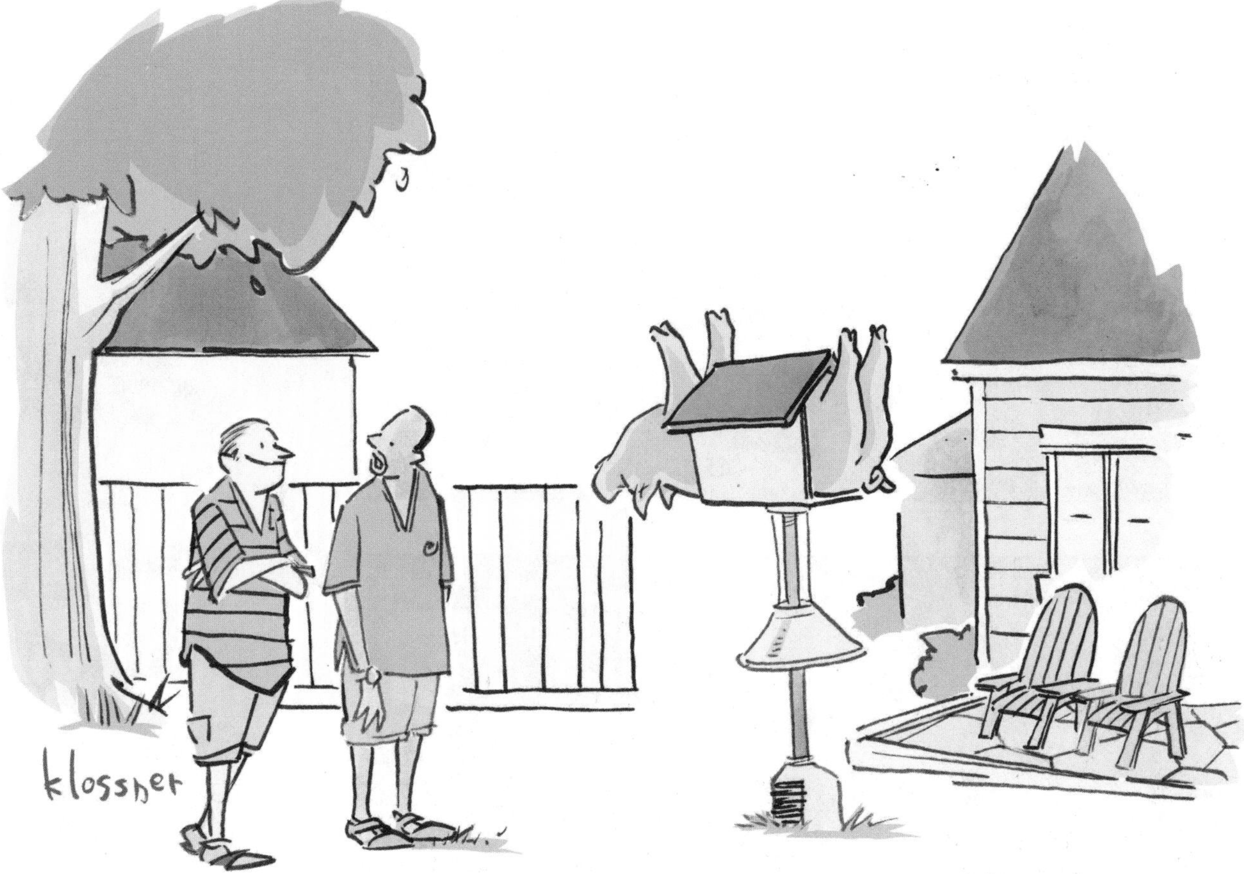
klossner

"What birds are you trying to attract?"

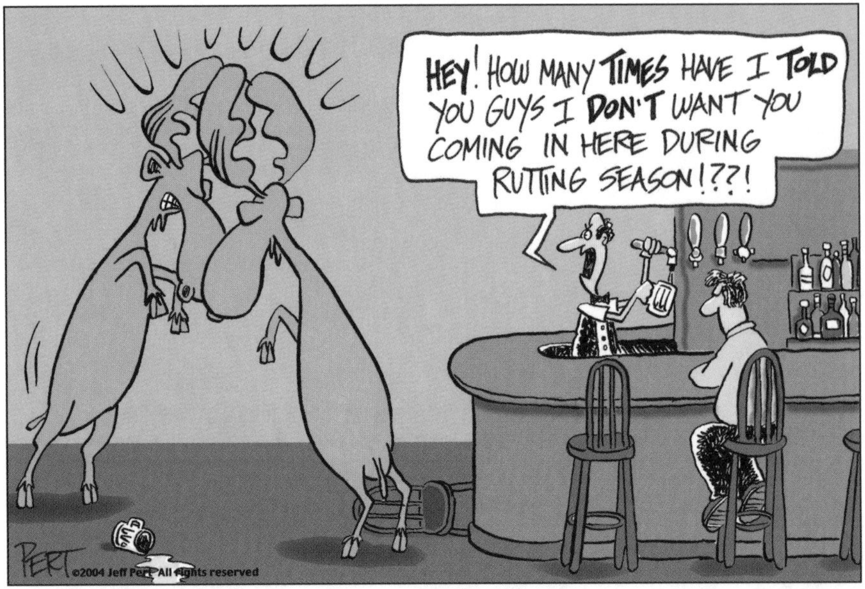
HEY! HOW MANY TIMES HAVE I TOLD YOU GUYS I DON'T WANT YOU COMING IN HERE DURING RUTTING SEASON!??!
PERT
©2004 Jeff Pert. All rights reserved

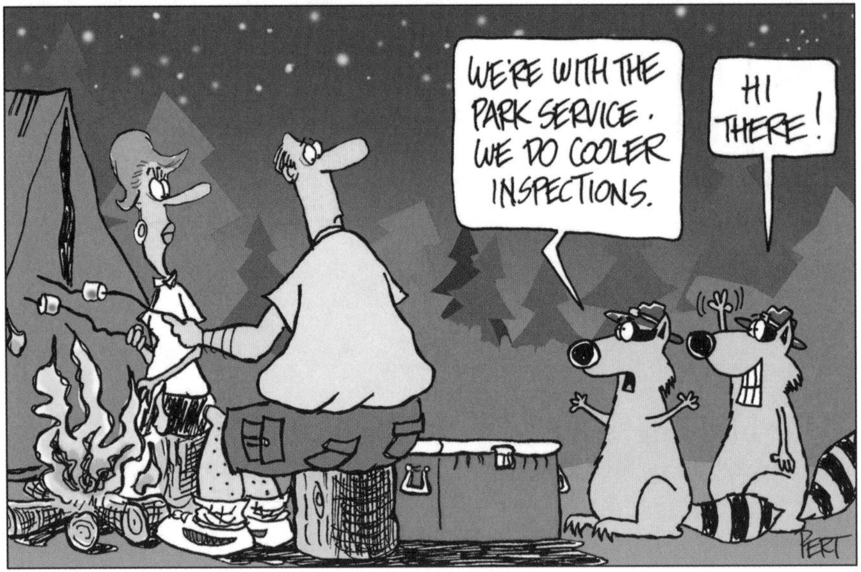
WE'RE WITH THE PARK SERVICE. WE DO COOLER INSPECTIONS.
HI THERE!
PERT

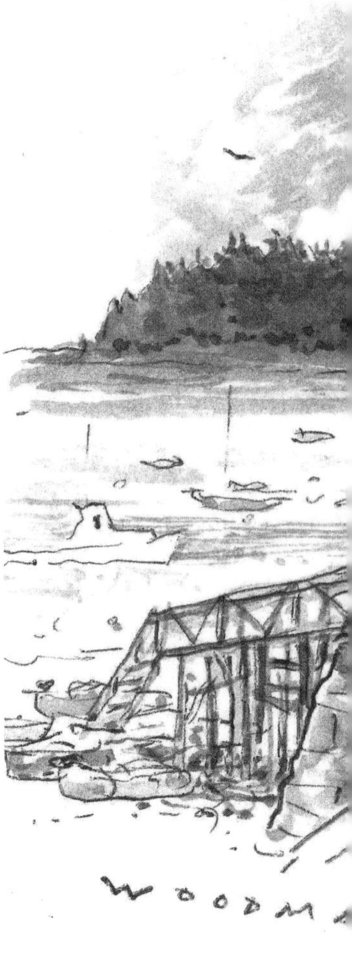

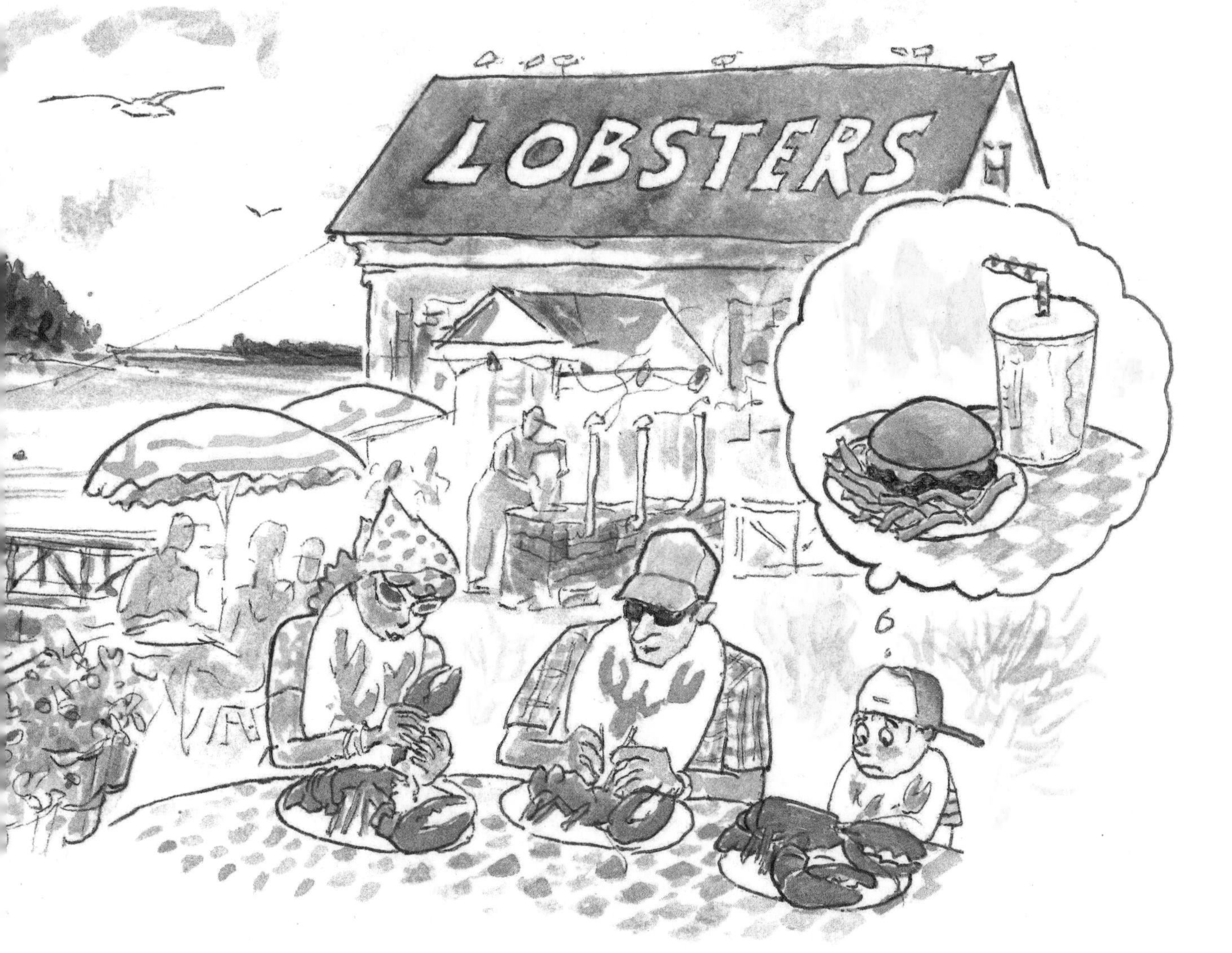
LOBSTERS

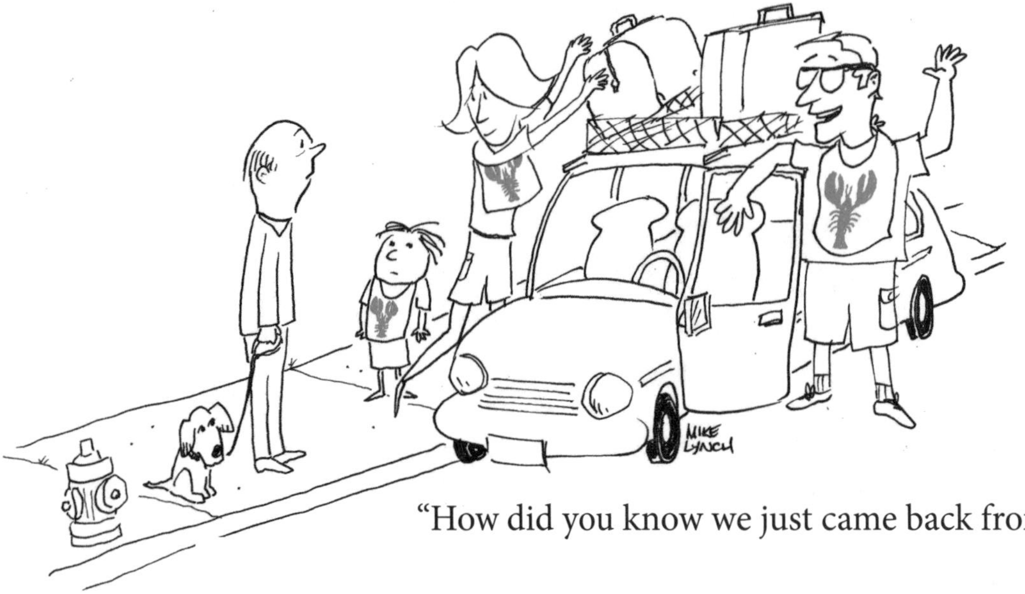
MIKE
LYNCH

"How did you know we just came back from Maine?"

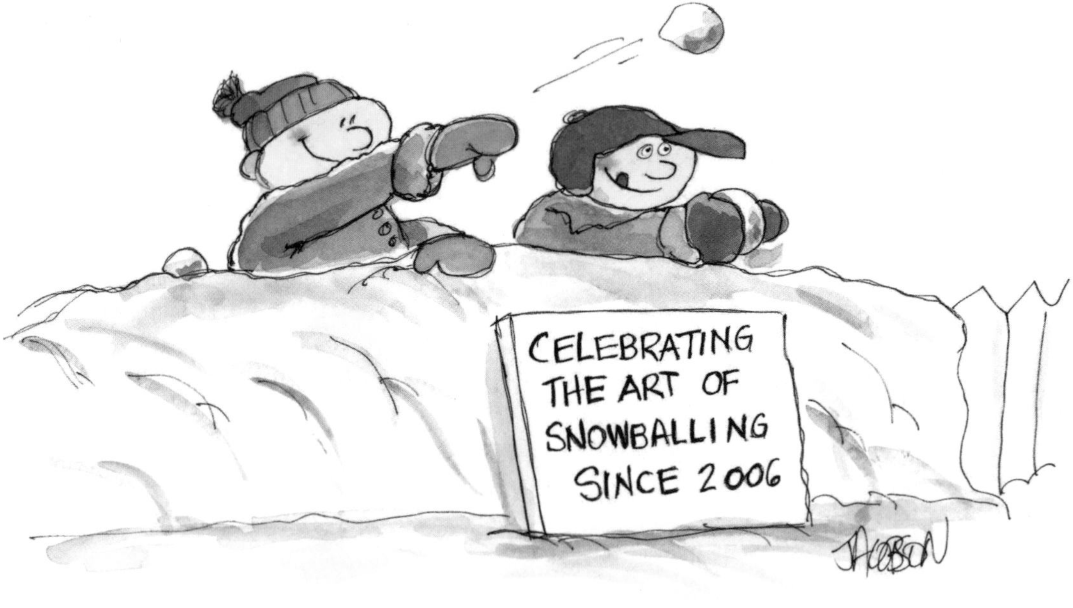
CELEBRATING
THE ART OF
SNOWBALLING
SINCE 2006
JACOBSON

"I'm not going to waste this gorgeous vacation day. Let's go to the outlet malls!"

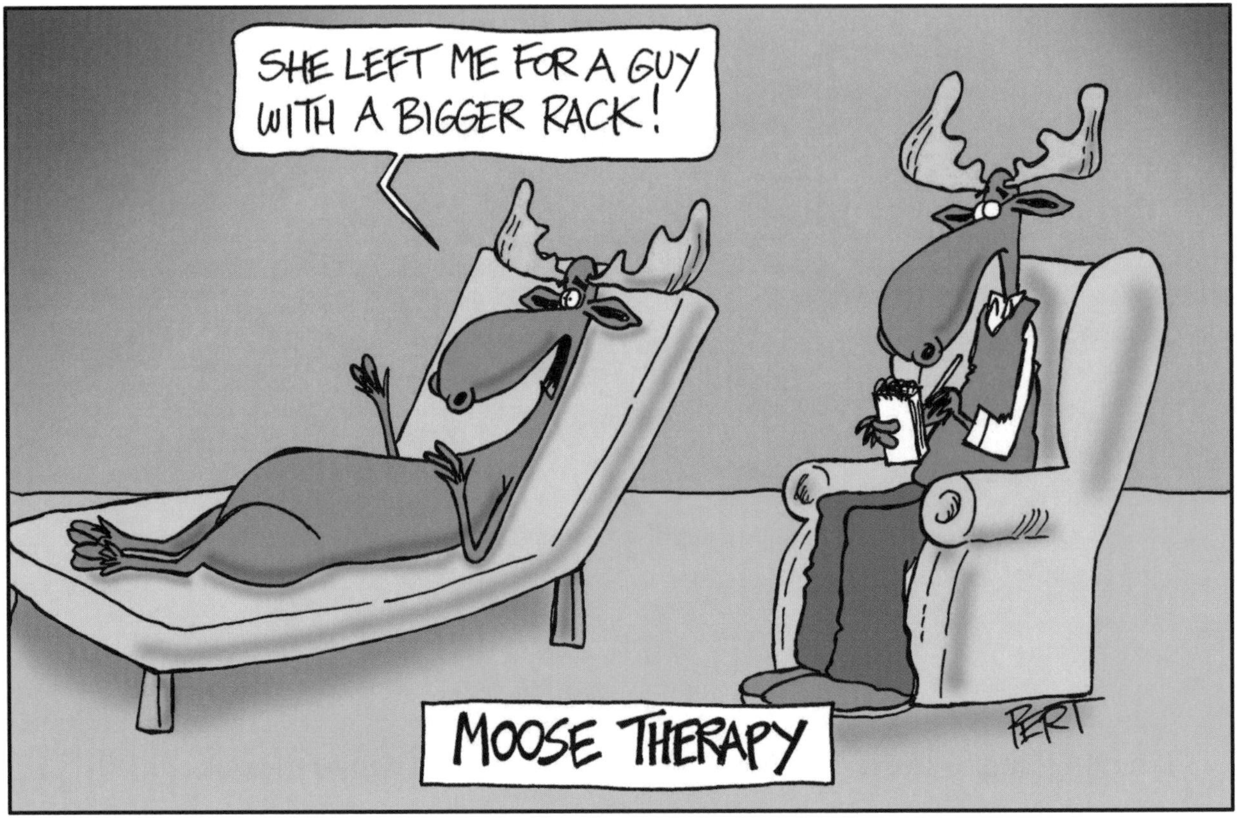
SHE LEFT ME FOR A GUY WITH A BIGGER RACK!
MOOSE THERAPY
BERT

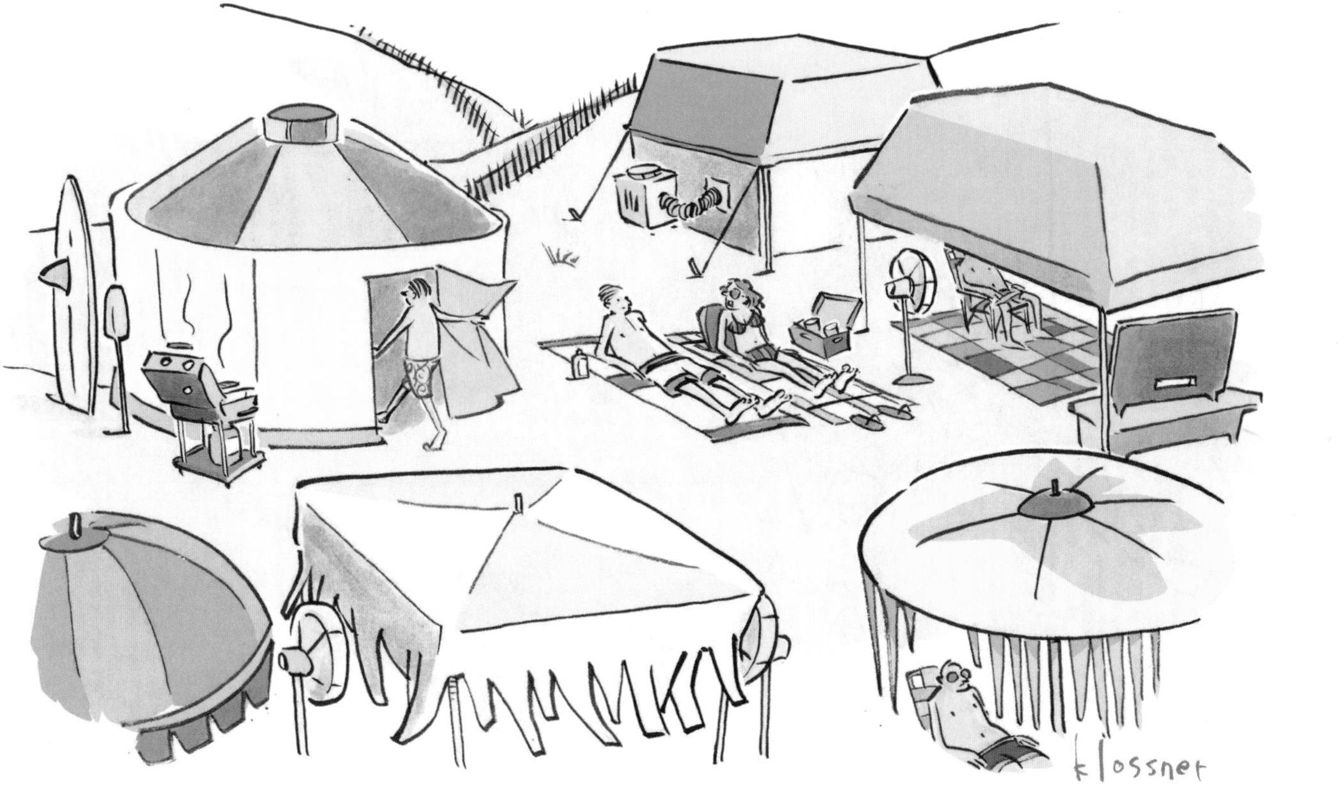
klossner

“Next year can we go to an amateur beach?”

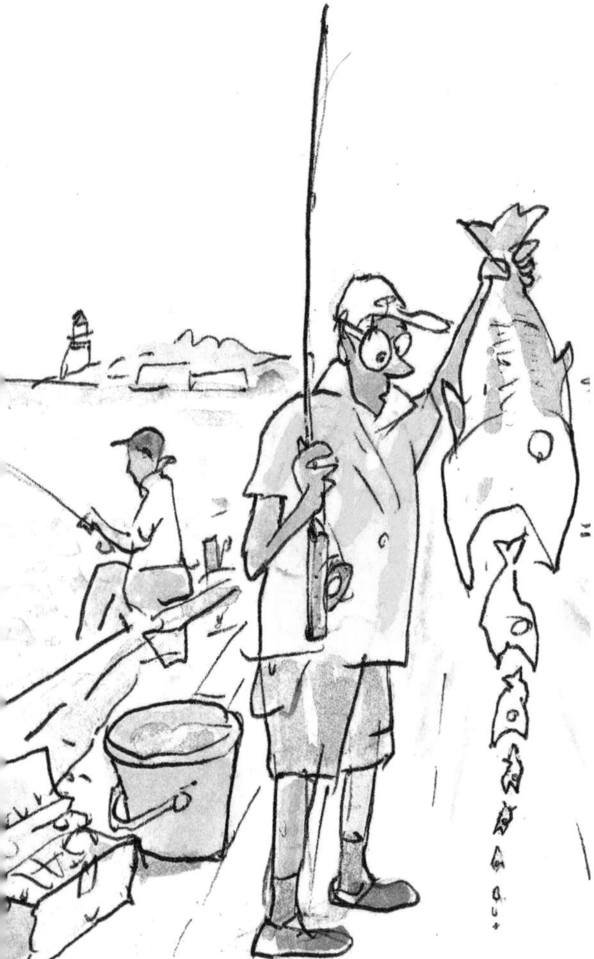

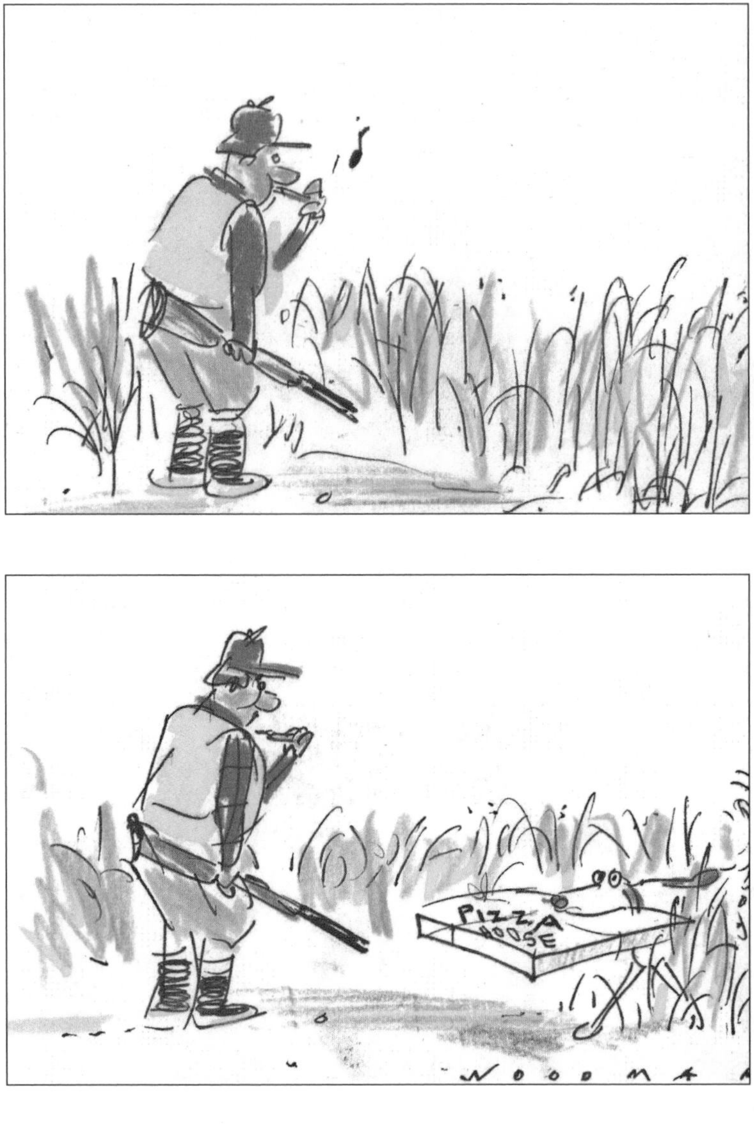
PIZZA
HOUSE

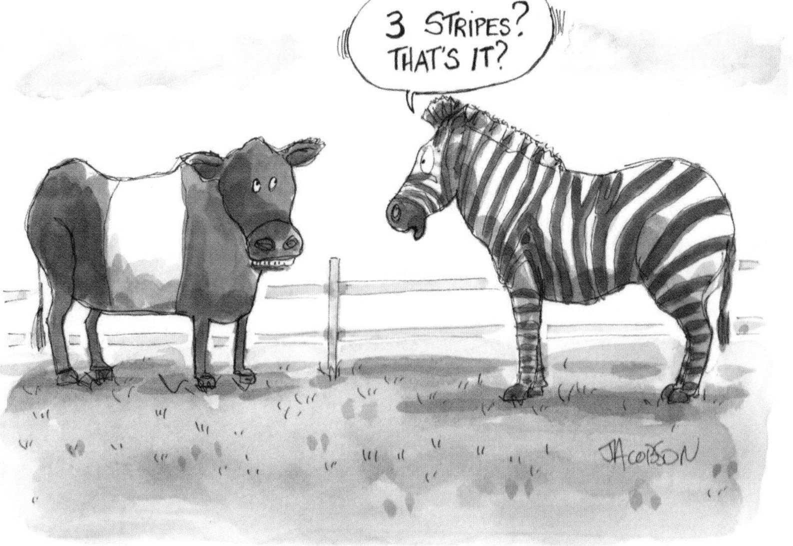
3 STRIPES? THAT'S IT?

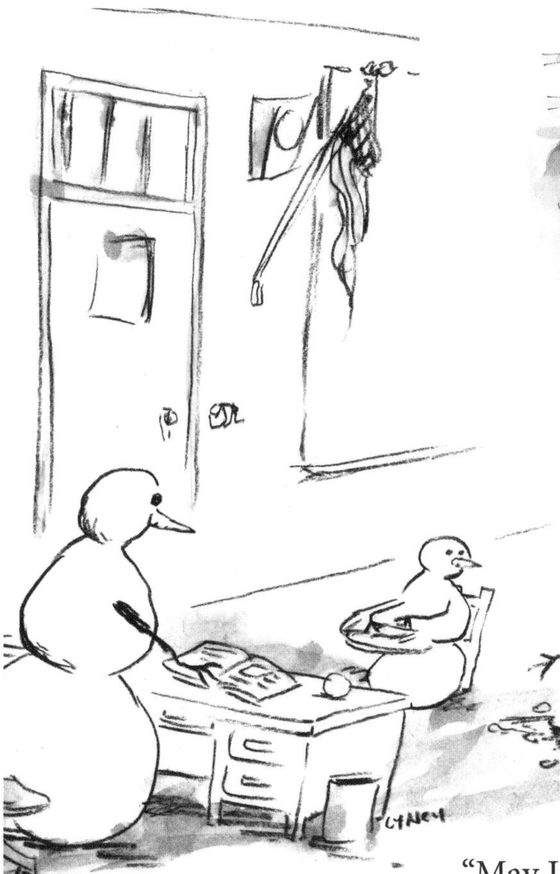

"May I be excused to go to the fridge?"

“The bugs are really bad this year.”

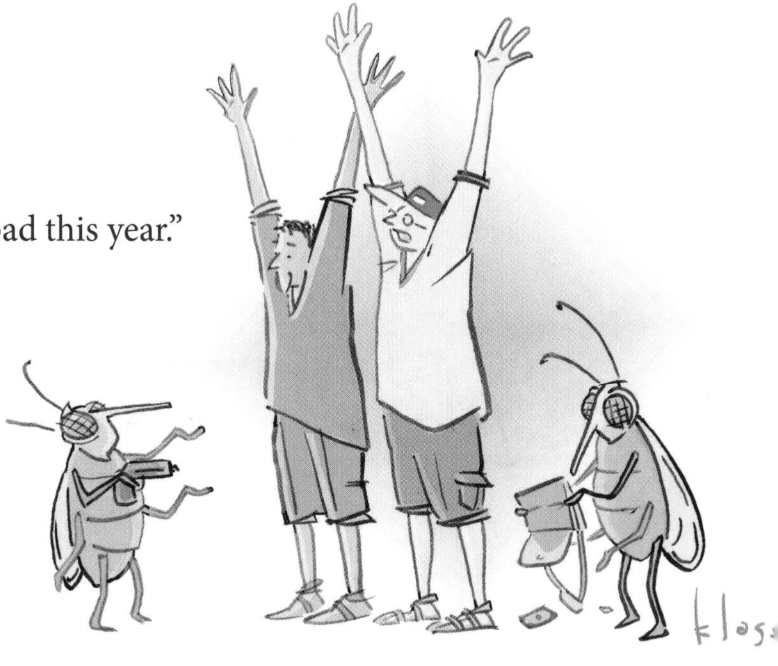

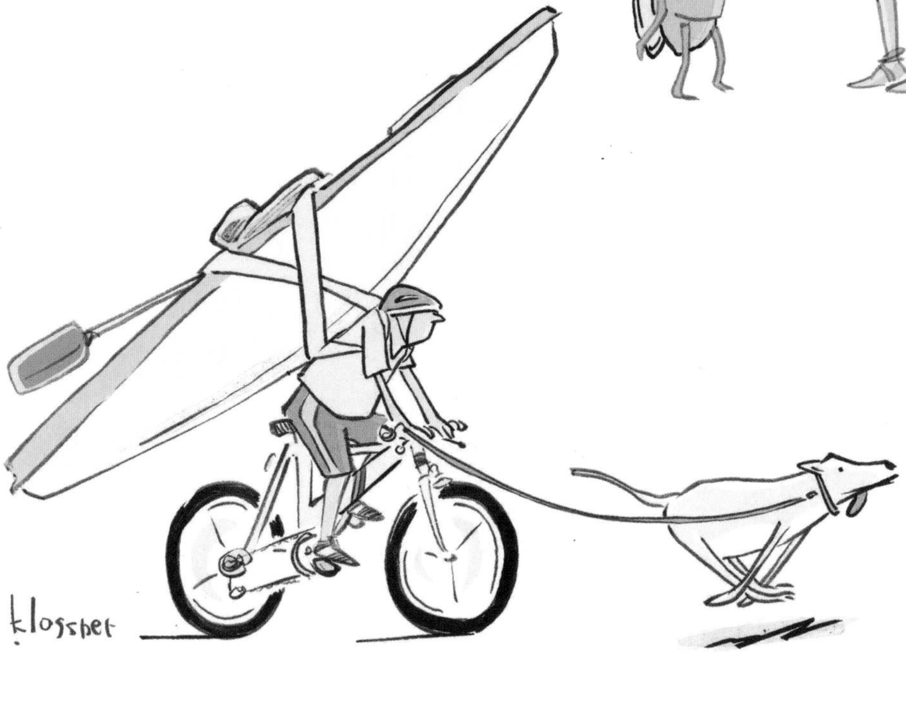

“Maine hybrid vehicle.”

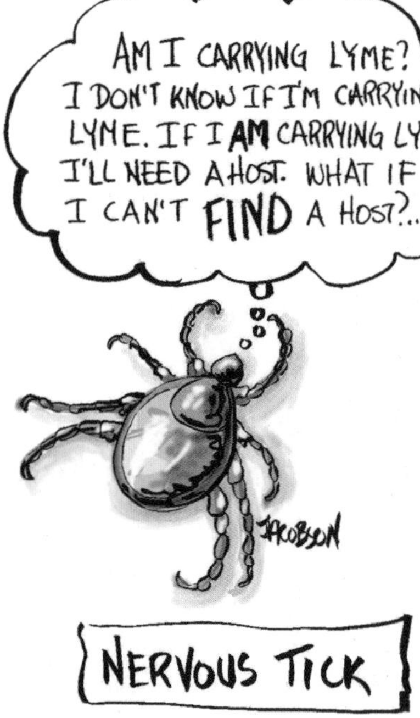
AM I CARRYING LYME? I DON'T KNOW IF I'M CARRYING LYME. IF I AM CARRYING LYME, I'LL NEED A HOST. WHAT IF I CAN'T FIND A HOST?...
NERVOUS TICK

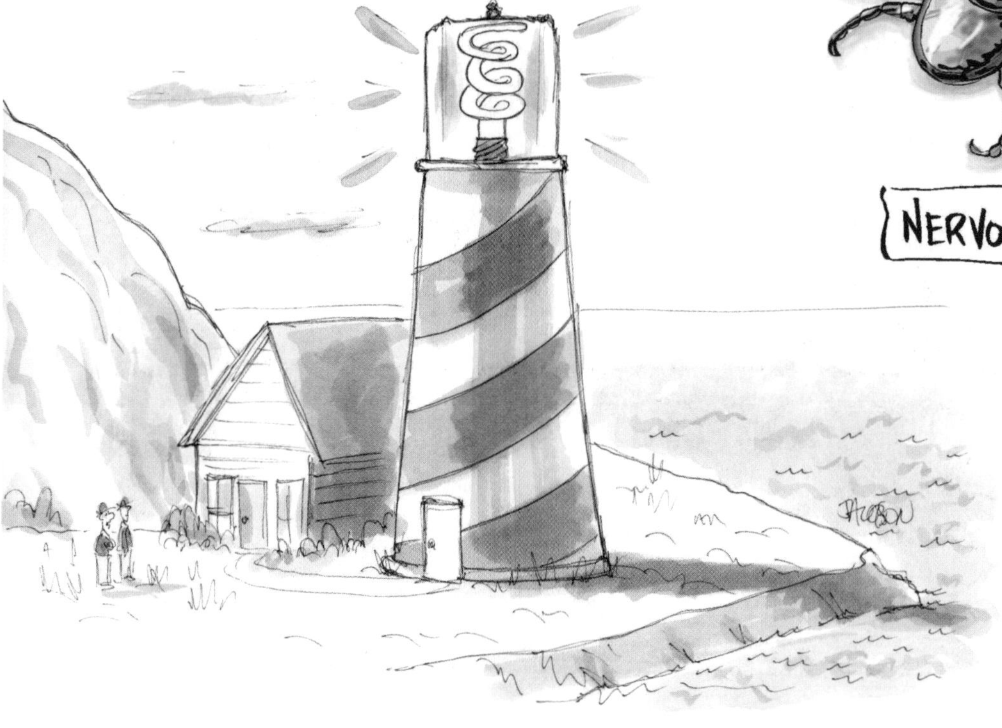

“It’s 40% more energy efficient.”

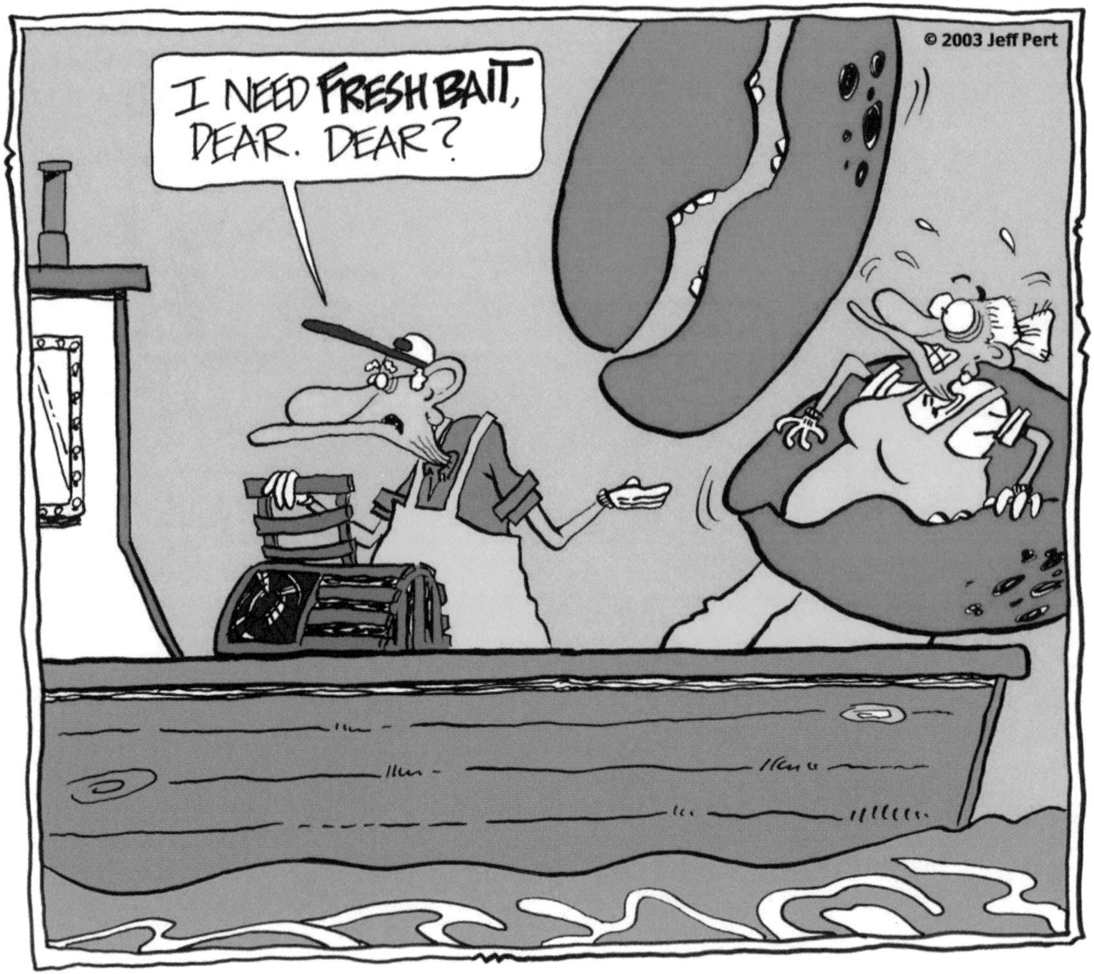
© 2003 Jeff Pert
I NEED FRESH BAIT, DEAR. DEAR?

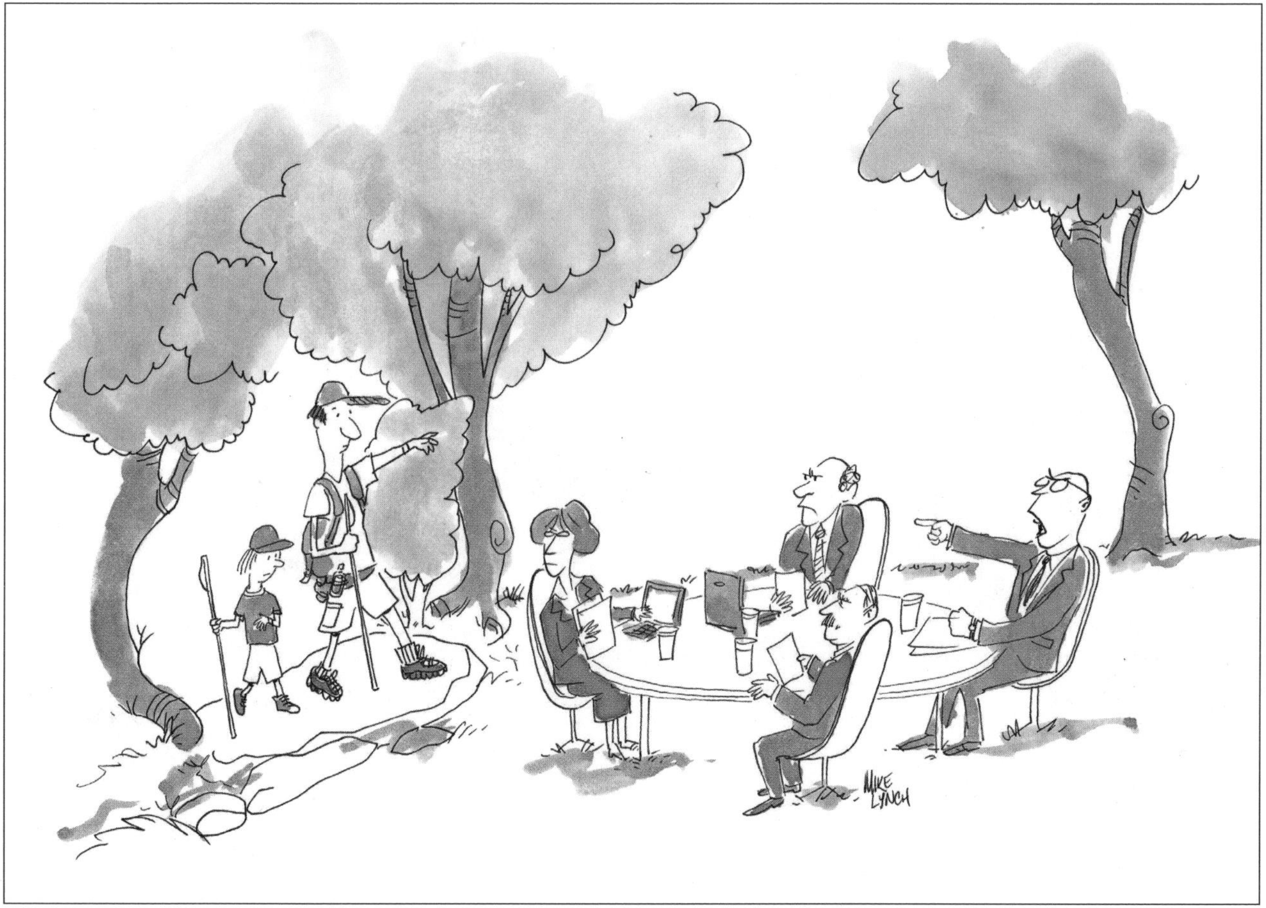
MIKE LYNCH

"This is a private, corporate retreat. No thru-hikers!"

"You knew I liked fishing when you said you'd marry me."

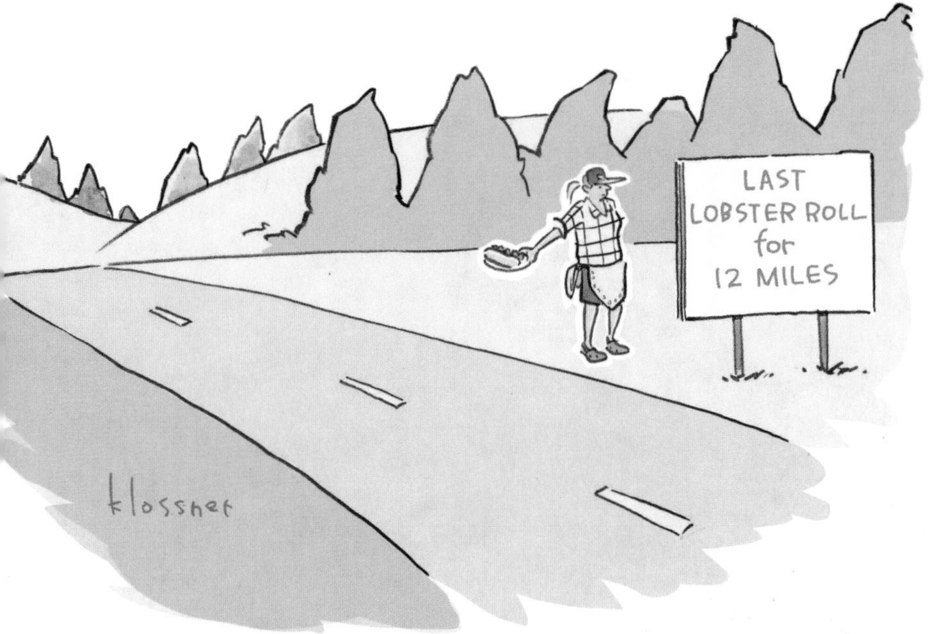
LAST
LOBSTER ROLL
for
12 MILES
klossner

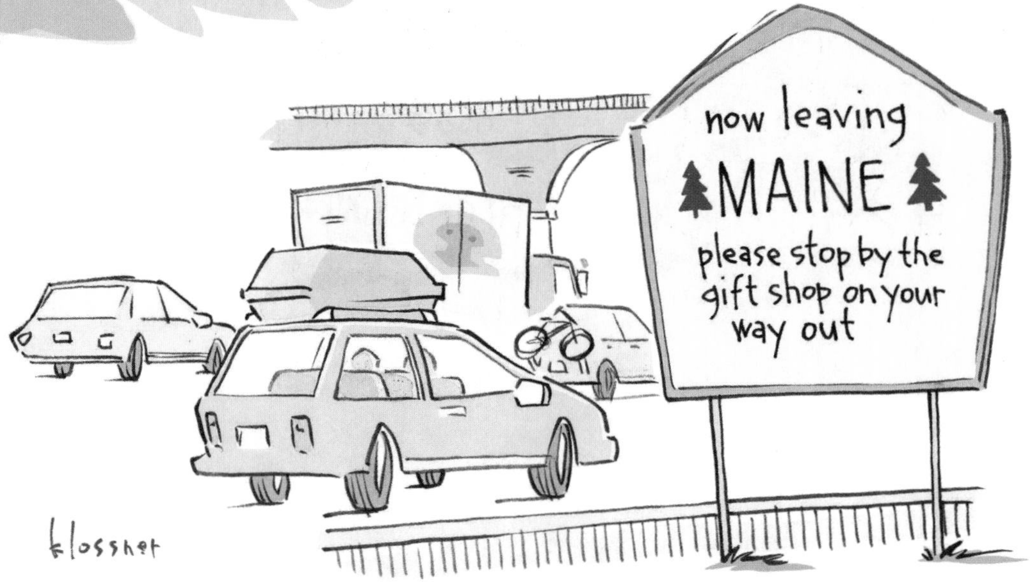
now leaving
MAINE
please stop by the
gift shop on your
way out
klossner

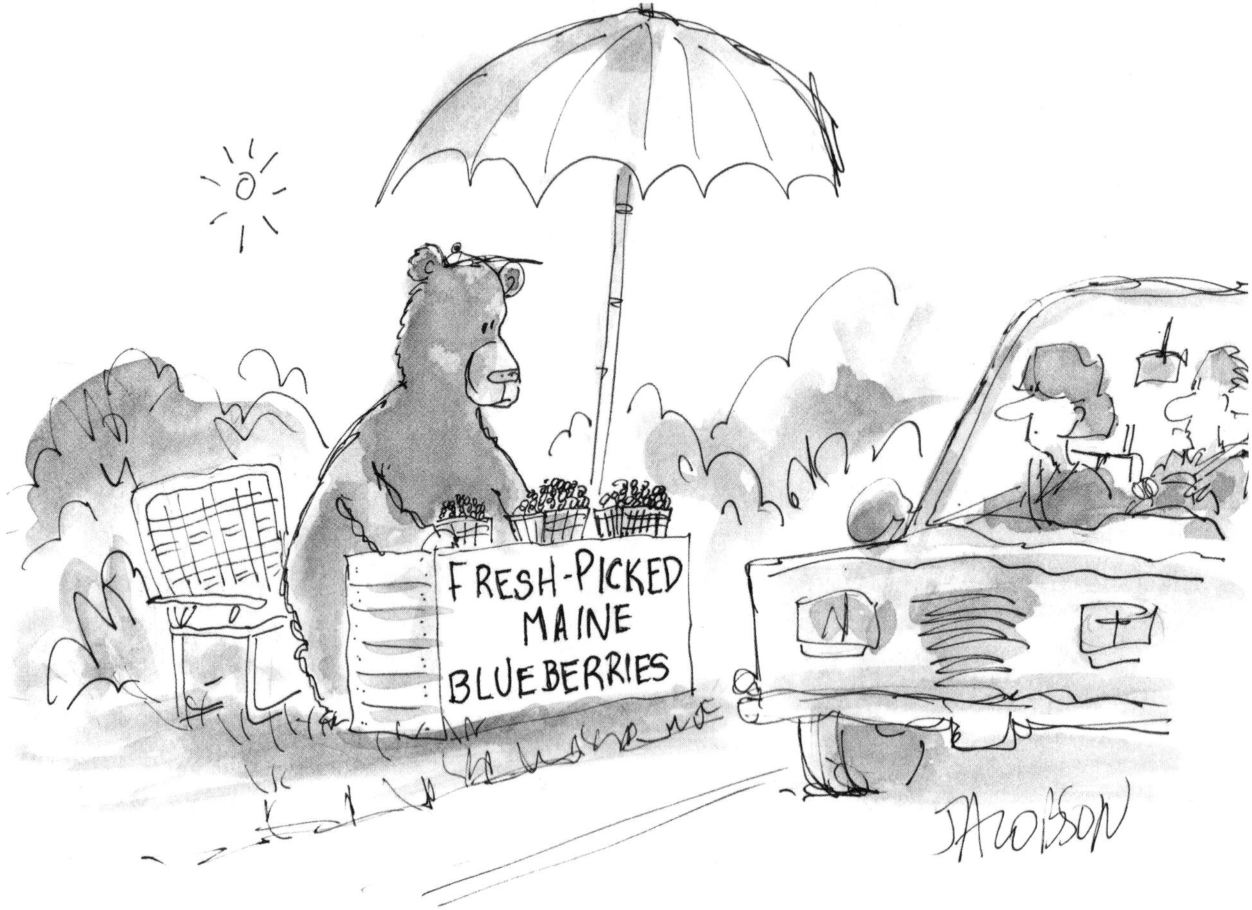
FRESH-PICKED
MAINE
BLUEBERRIES
JACOBSON

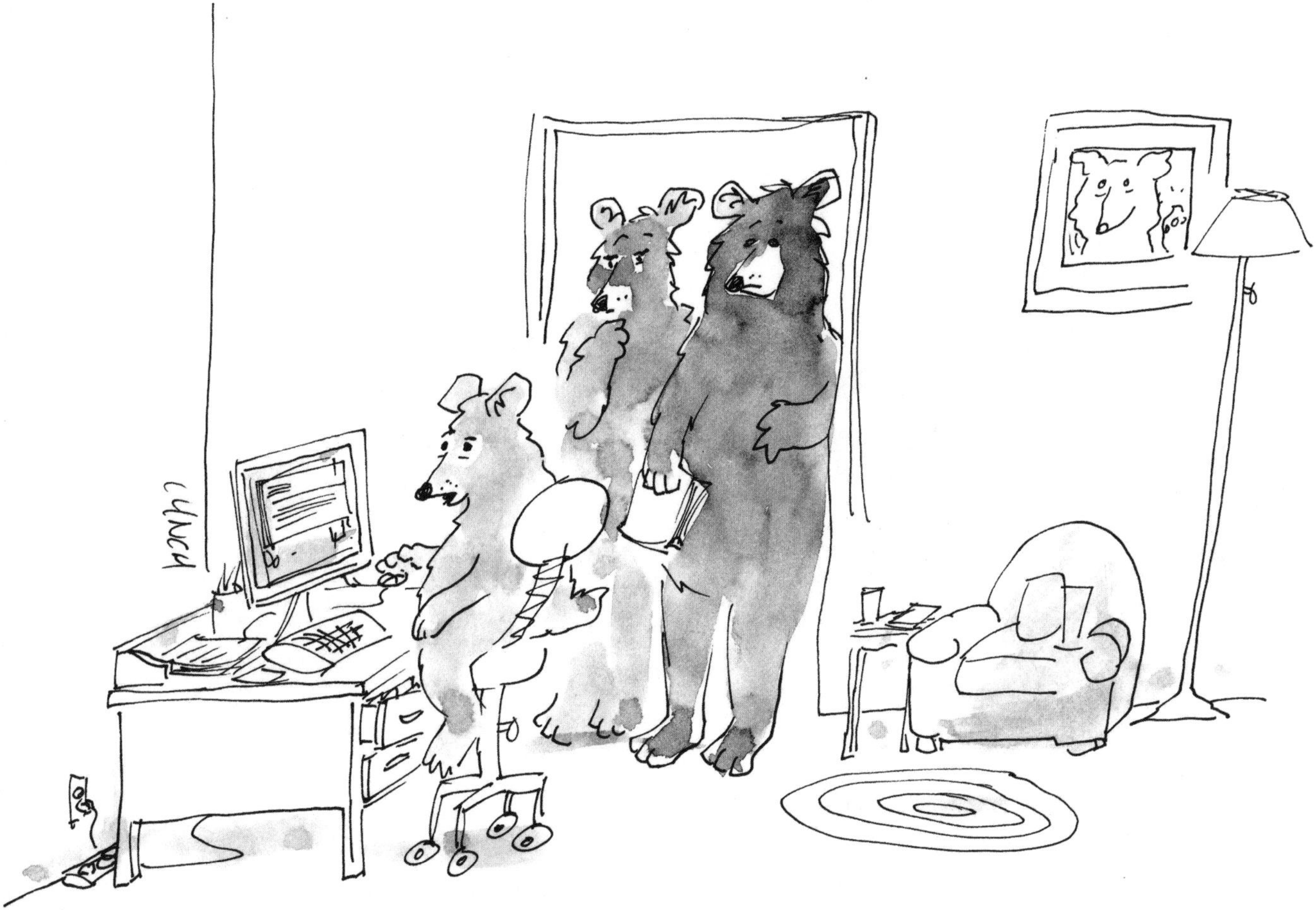

“The deal’s off. Goldilocks found a bowl that’s ‘just right’ on eBay.”

"I had no idea clam digging could be so difficult."

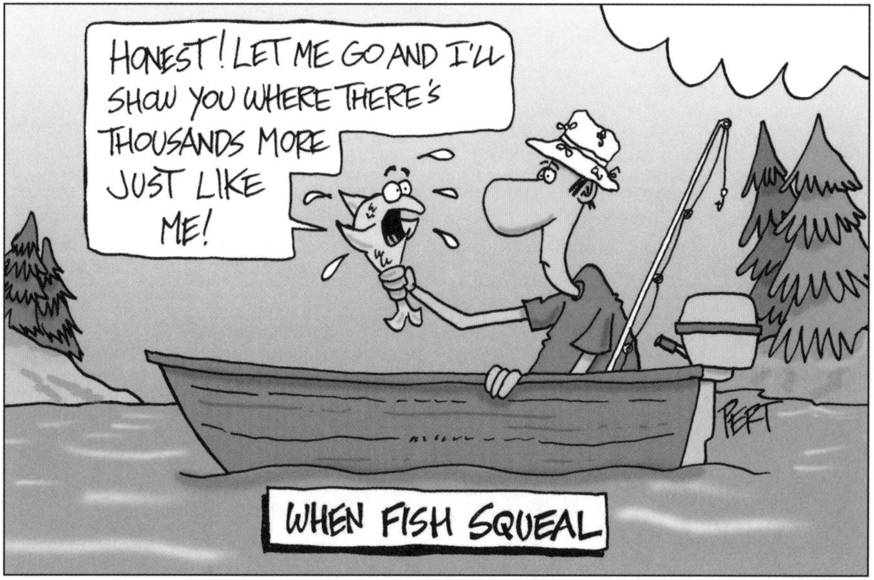
HONEST! LET ME GO AND I'LL SHOW YOU WHERE THERE'S THOUSANDS MORE JUST LIKE ME!
PERT
WHEN FISH SQUEAL

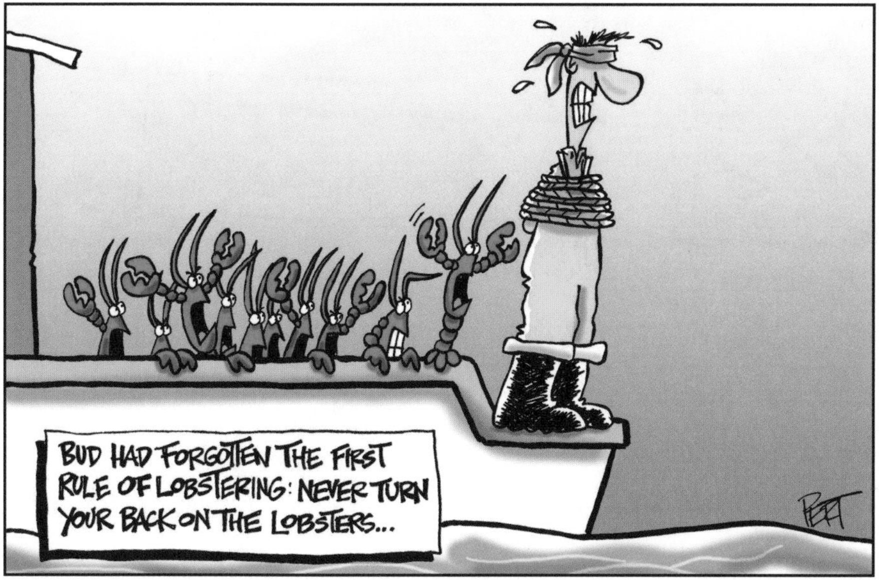
BUD HAD FORGOTTEN THE FIRST RULE OF LOBSTERING: NEVER TURN YOUR BACK ON THE LOBSTERS...
PERT

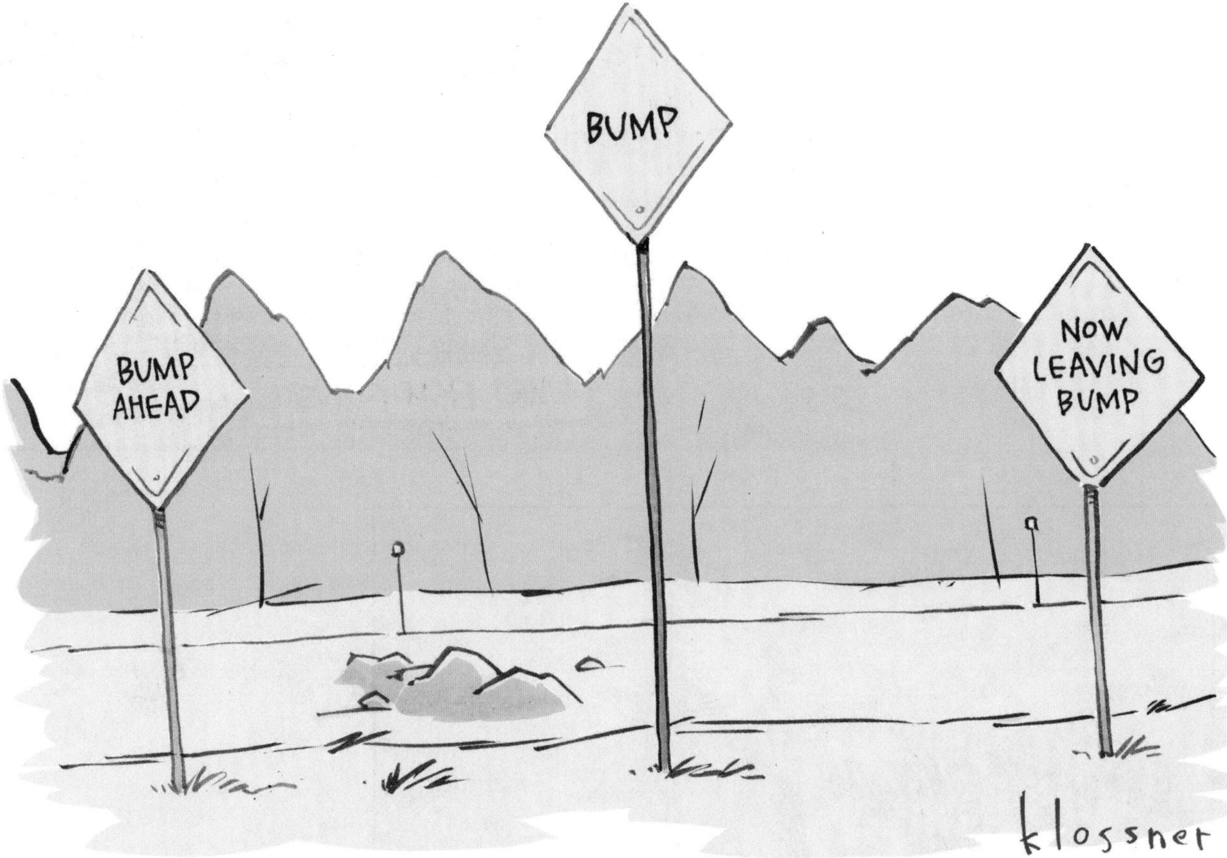
BUMP AHEAD
BUMP
NOW LEAVING BUMP
klossner

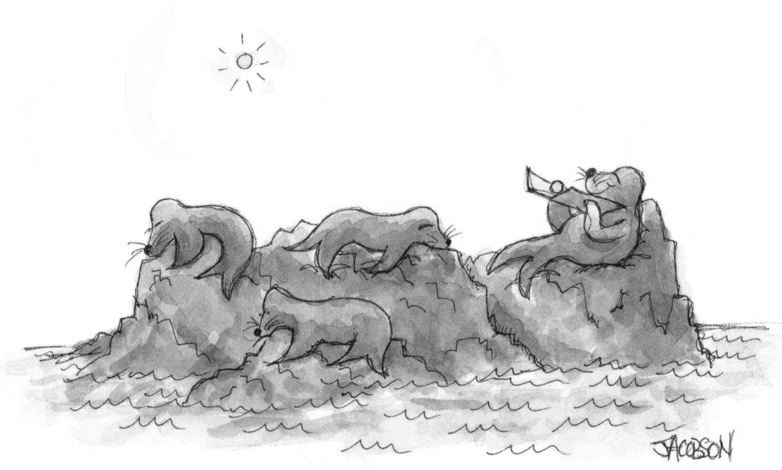
JACOBSON

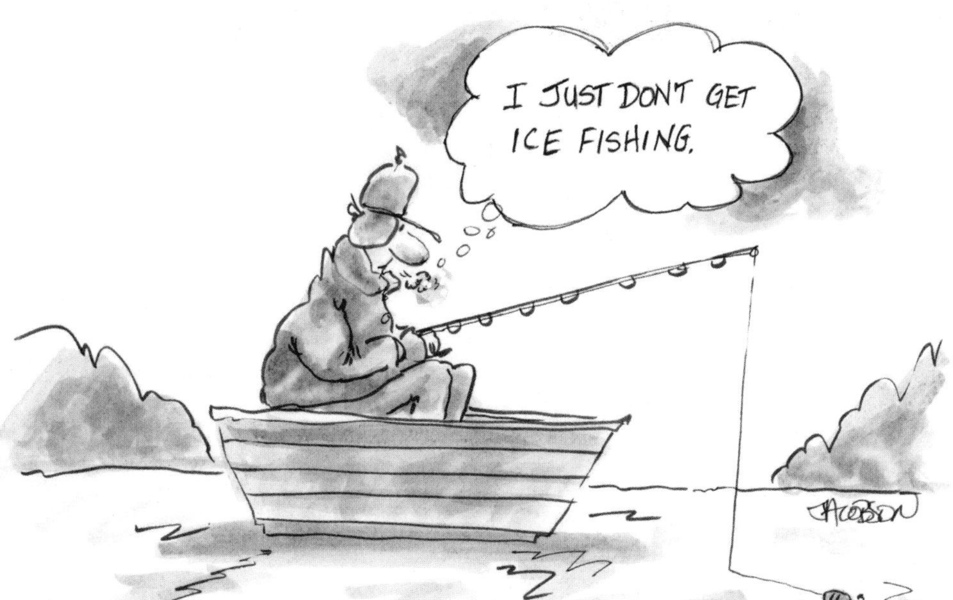
I JUST DON'T GET ICE FISHING.
JACOBSON

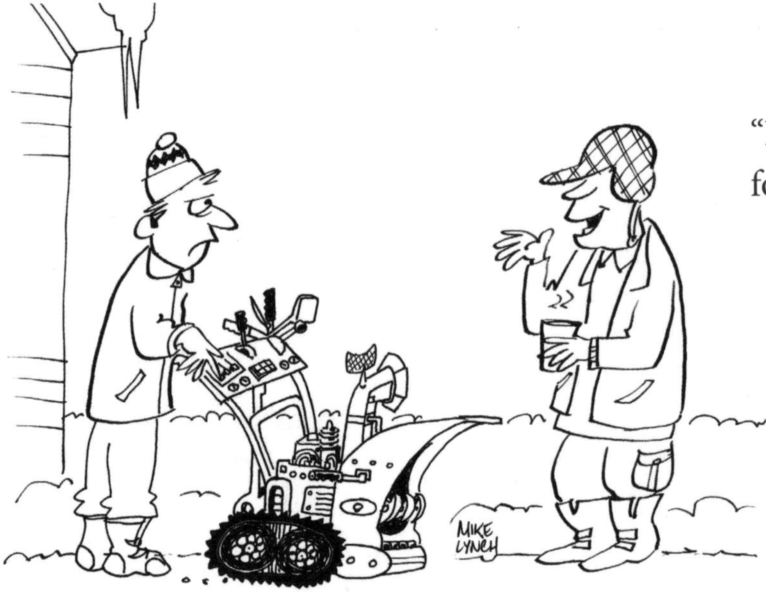
MIKE LYNCH

"Hey, Phil. How long does it take for your pre-flight check prep?"

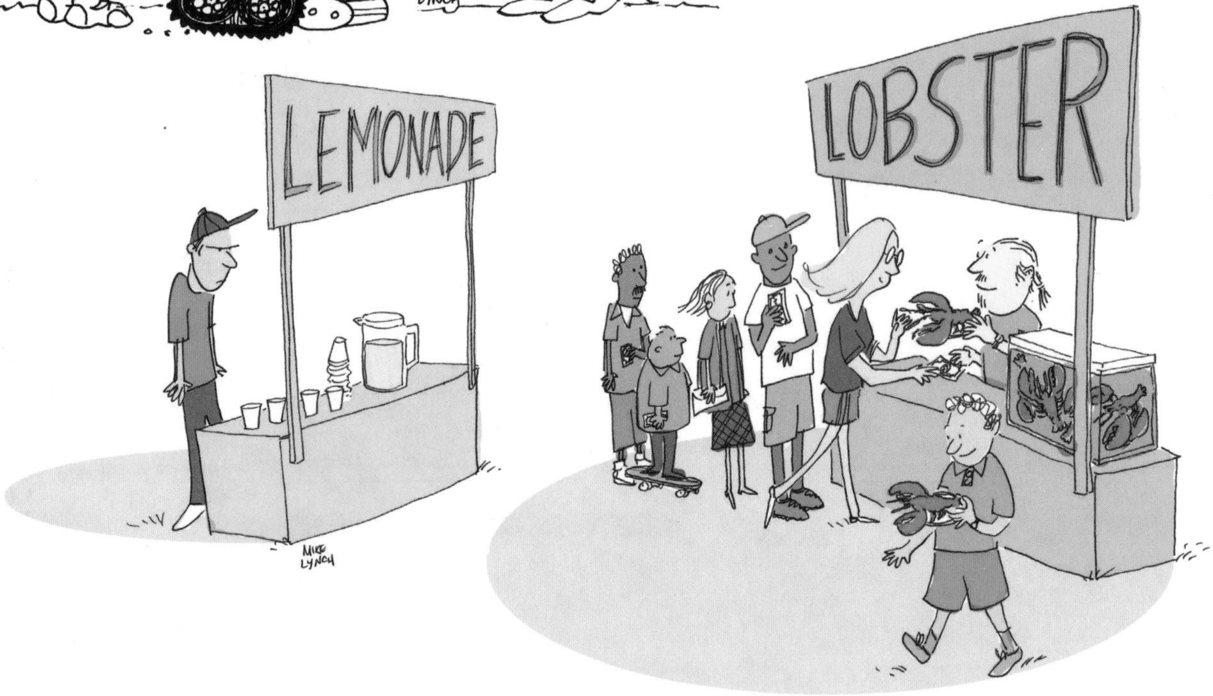
LEMONADE
LOBSTER
MIKE LYNCH

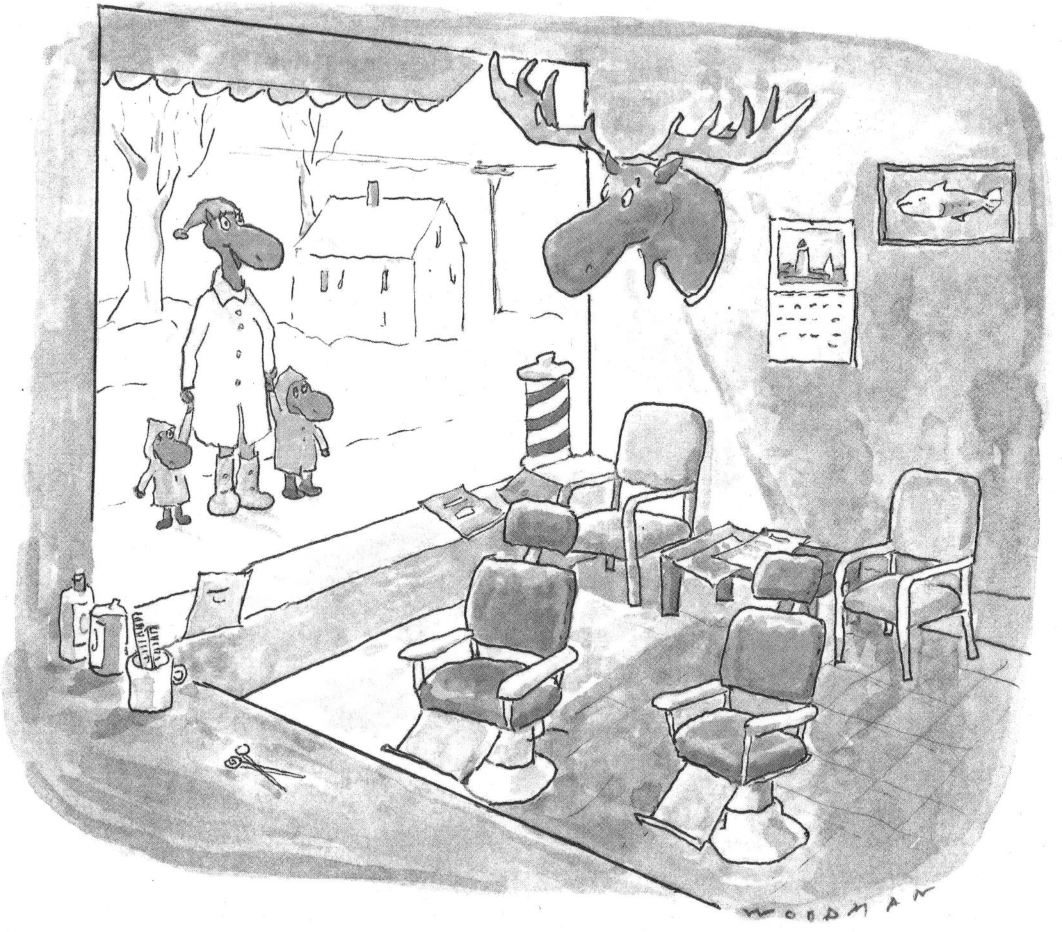
WOODMAN

“The kids wanted to see where you work.”

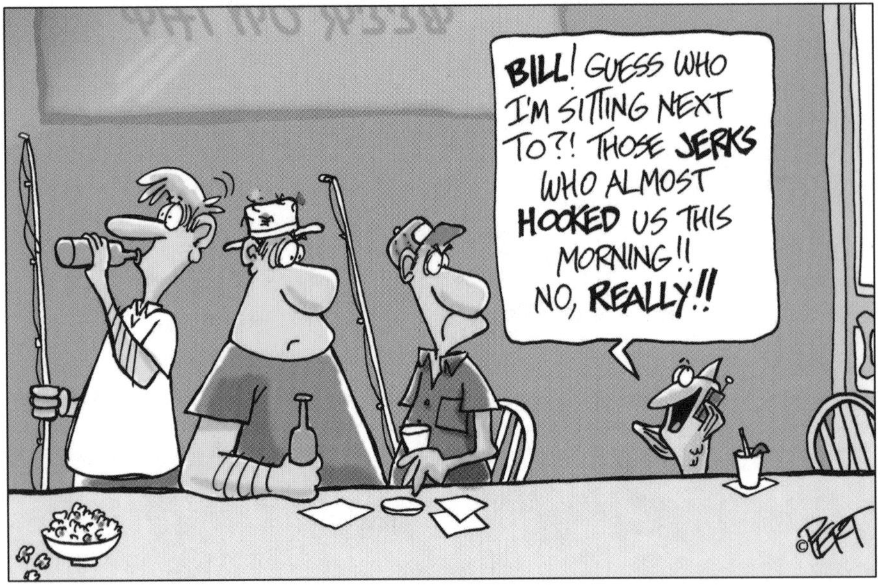
BILL! GUESS WHO I'M SITTING NEXT TO?! THOSE JERKS WHO ALMOST HOOKED US THIS MORNING!! NO, REALLY!!
©PERT

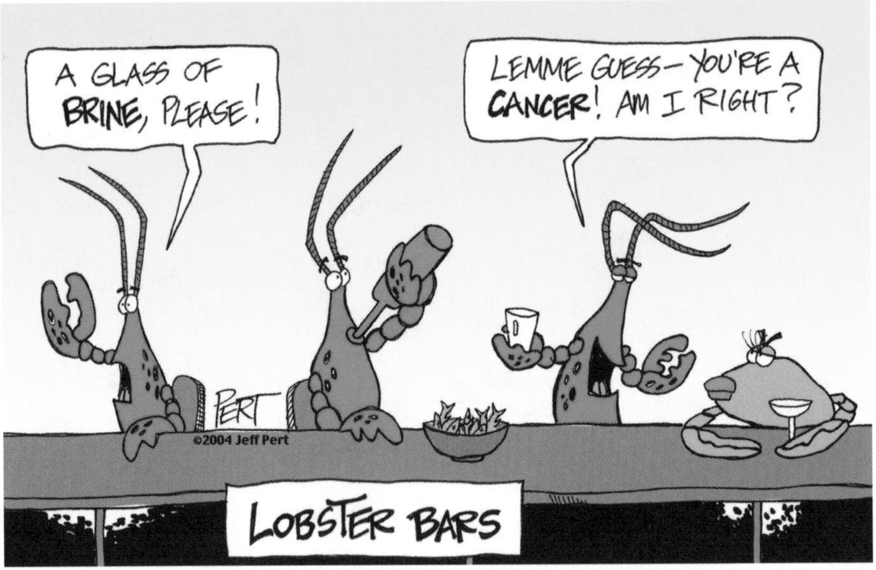
A GLASS OF BRINE, PLEASE!
LEMME GUESS— YOU'RE A CANCER! AM I RIGHT?
PERT
©2004 Jeff Pert
LOBSTER BARS

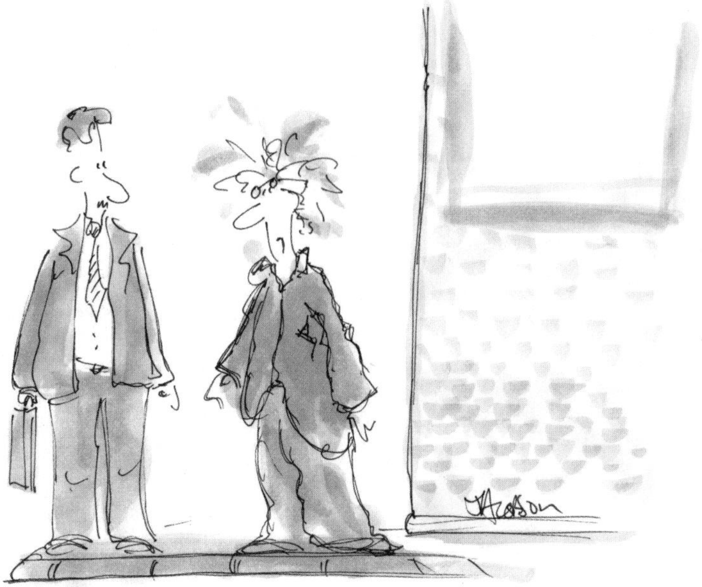

“Watch out for that wind farm back there.”

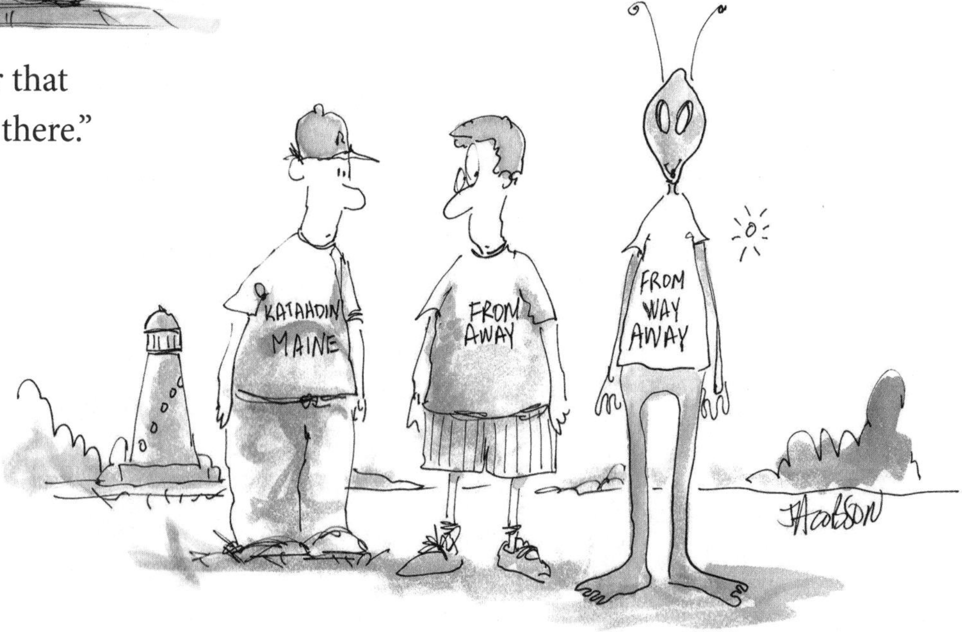
KATAHDIN
MAINE
FROM AWAY
FROM WAY AWAY

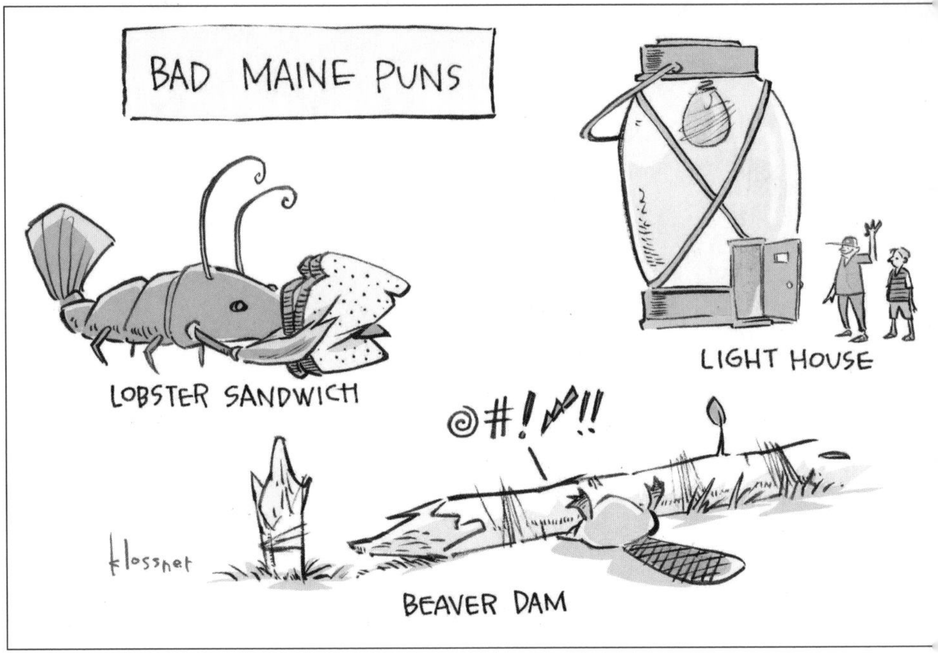
BAD MAINE PUNS
LOBSTER SANDWICH
LIGHT HOUSE
BEAVER DAM
klossner

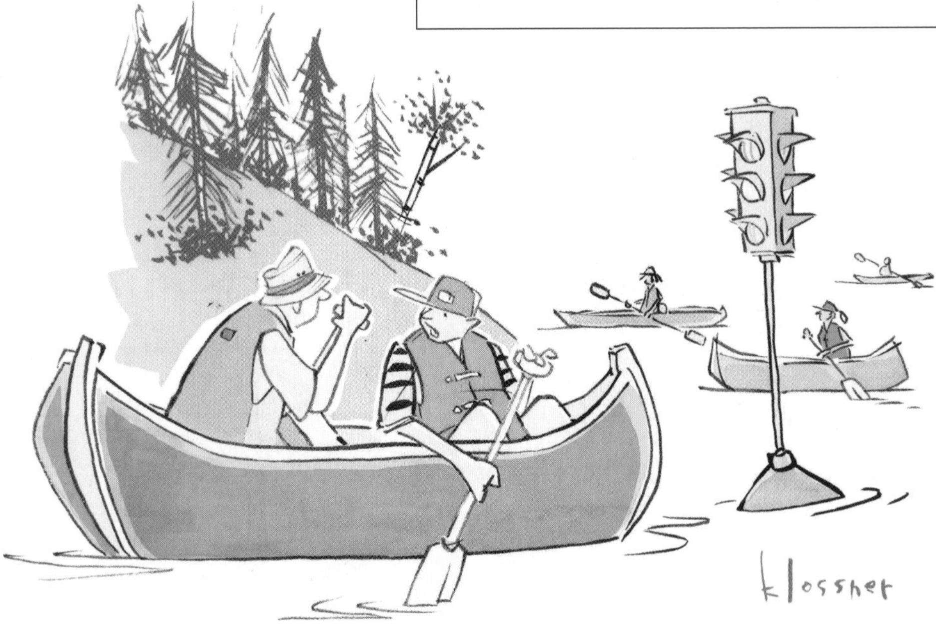
klossner

"Wilderness sure ain't what it used to be."

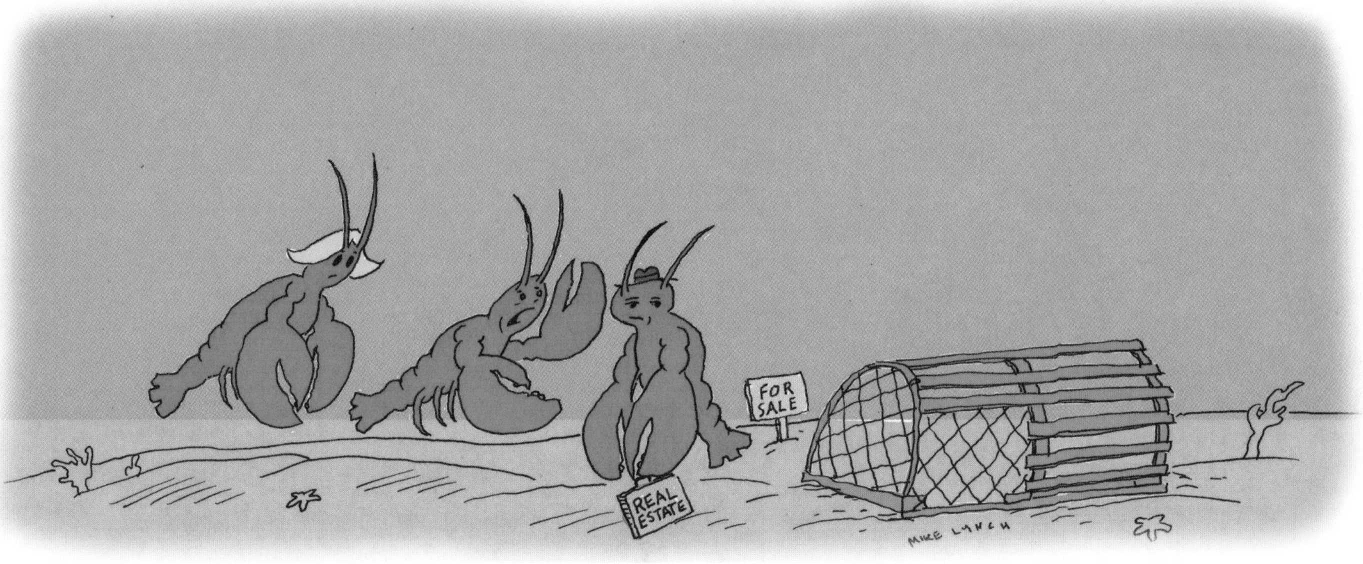
FOR SALE
REAL ESTATE
MIKE LYNCH

"We heard a rumor that the previous tenant died in the place."

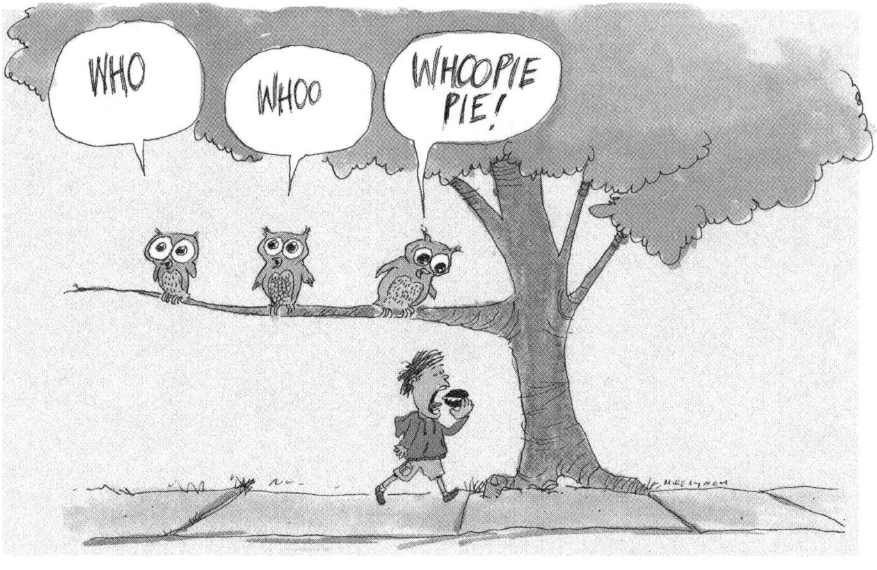
WHO
WHOO
WHOOPIE PIE!

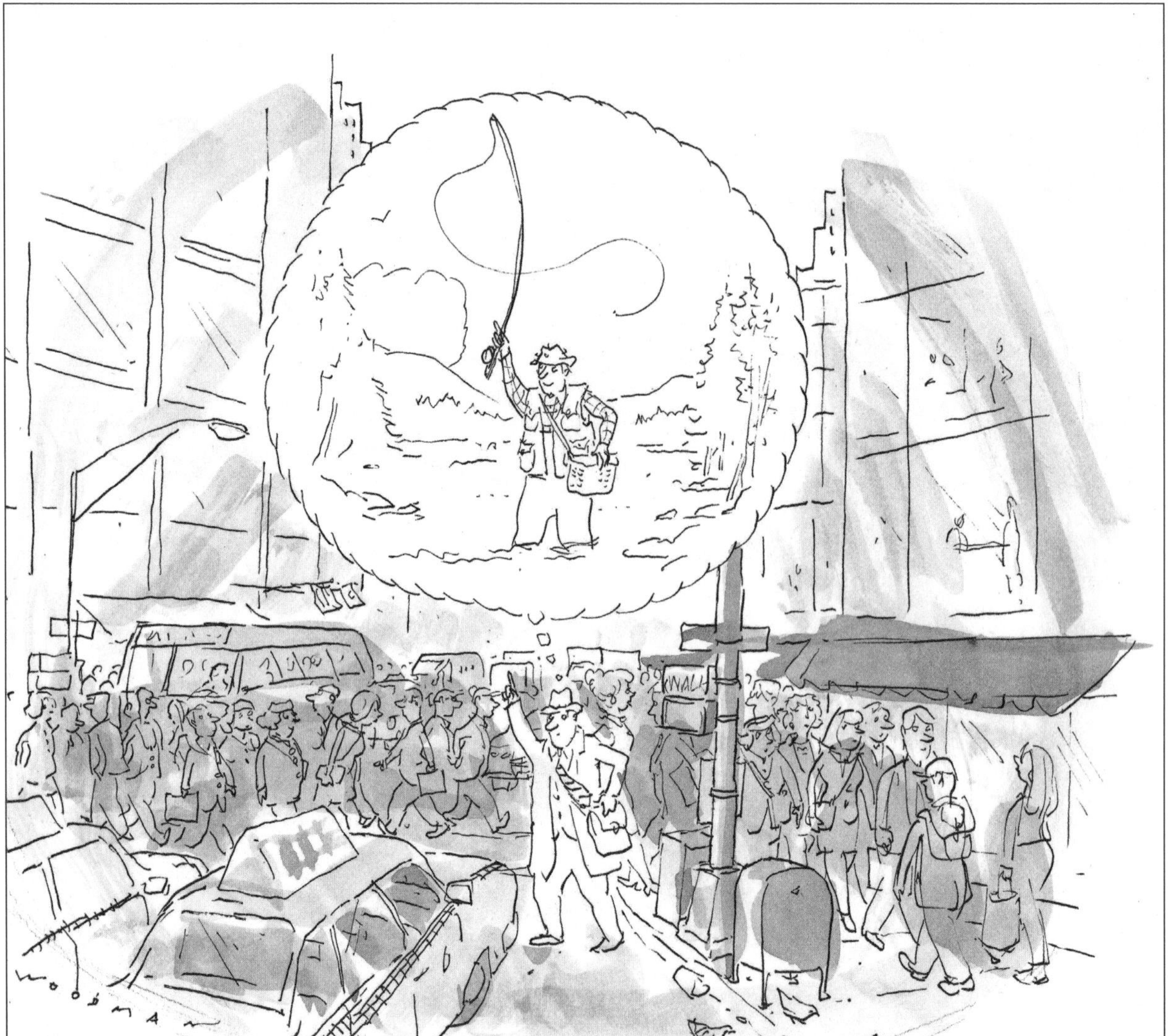
WOODMAN

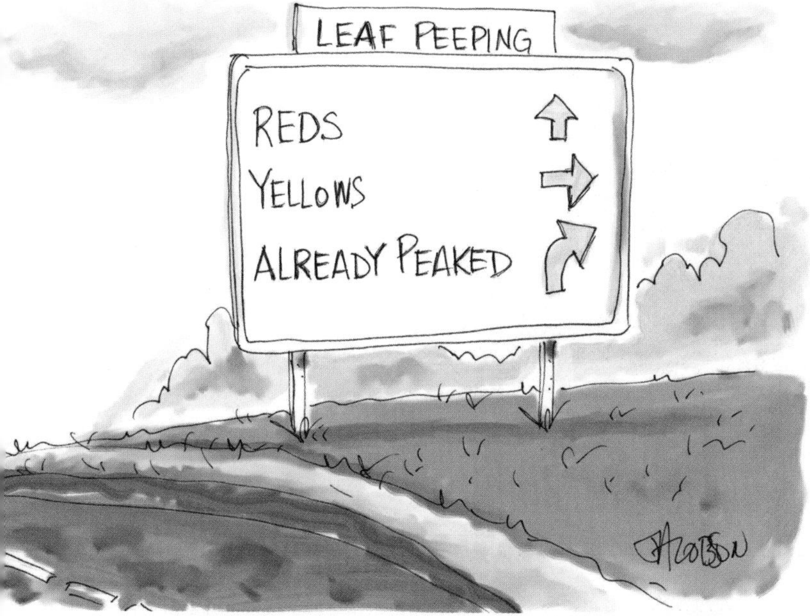
LEAF PEEPING
REDS
YELLOWS
ALREADY PEAKED

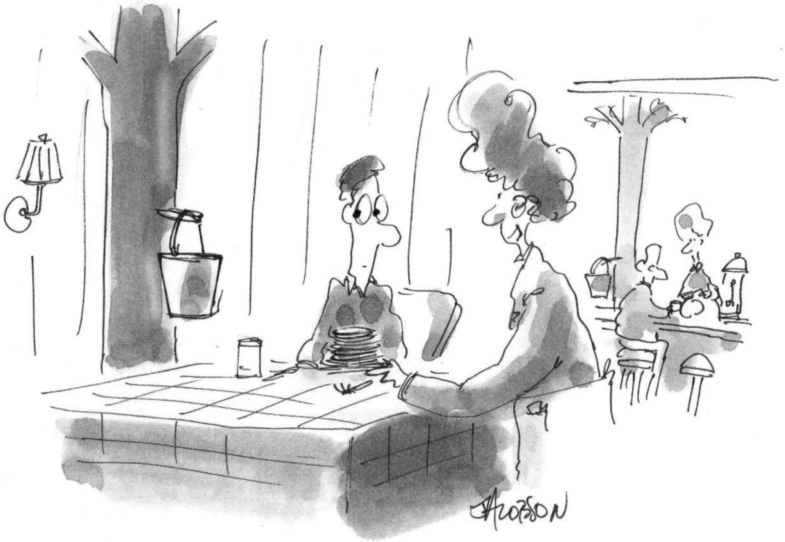

"We make our own maple syrup."

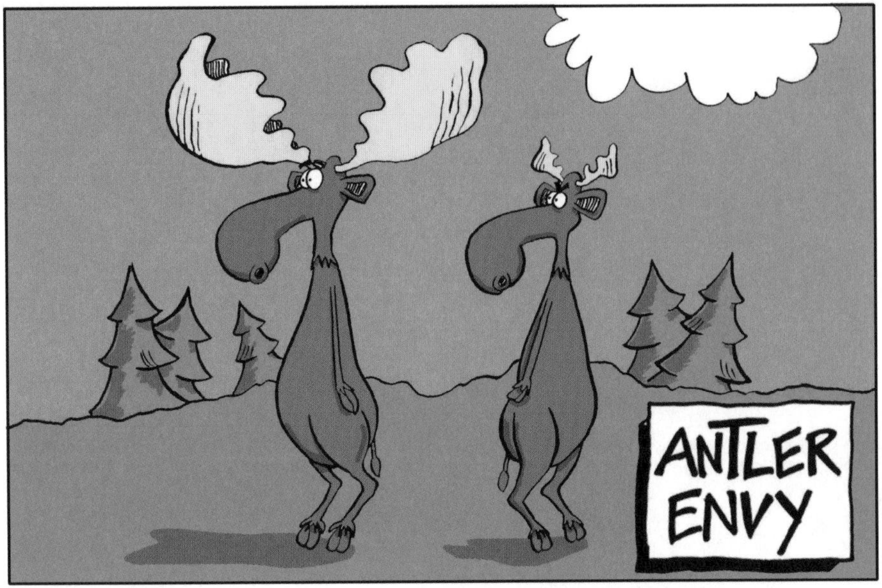
ANTLER ENVY

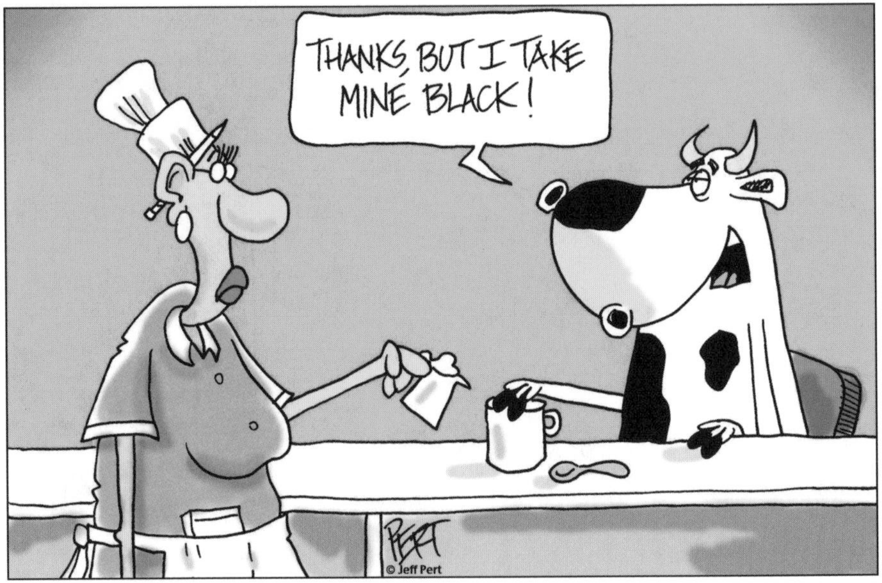
THANKS, BUT I TAKE MINE BLACK!
PERT
© Jeff Pert

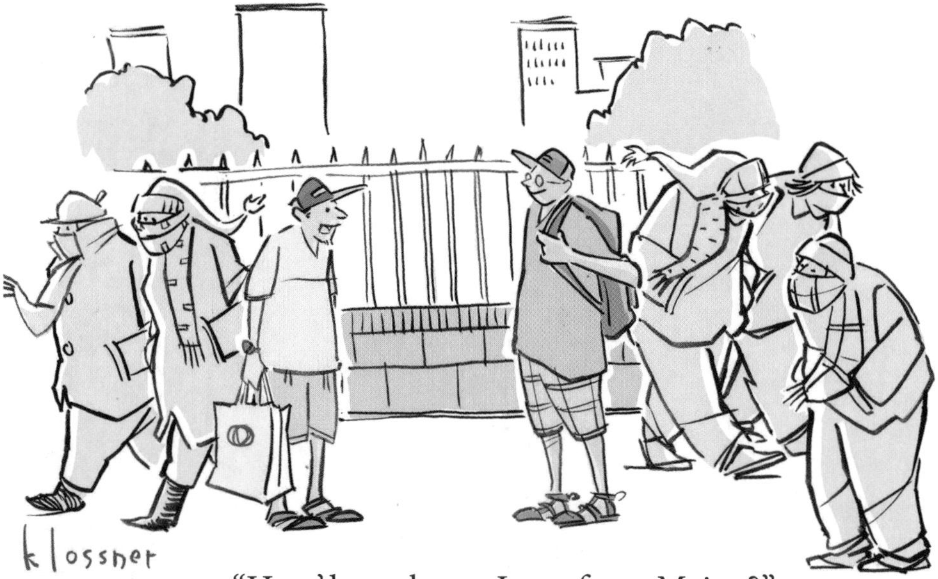
klossner

"How'd you know I was from Maine?"

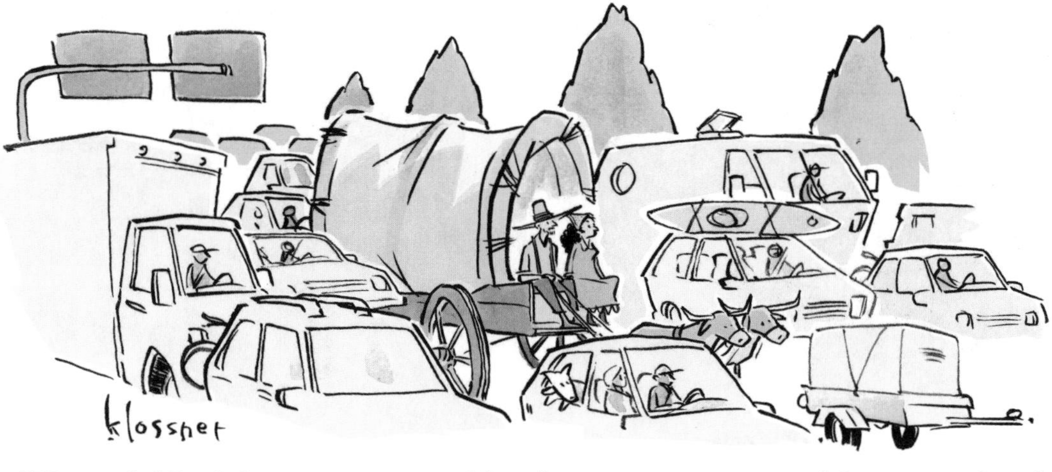
klossner

"He said, 'Go West, young man,' but he never mentioned I-95 on a Sunday."

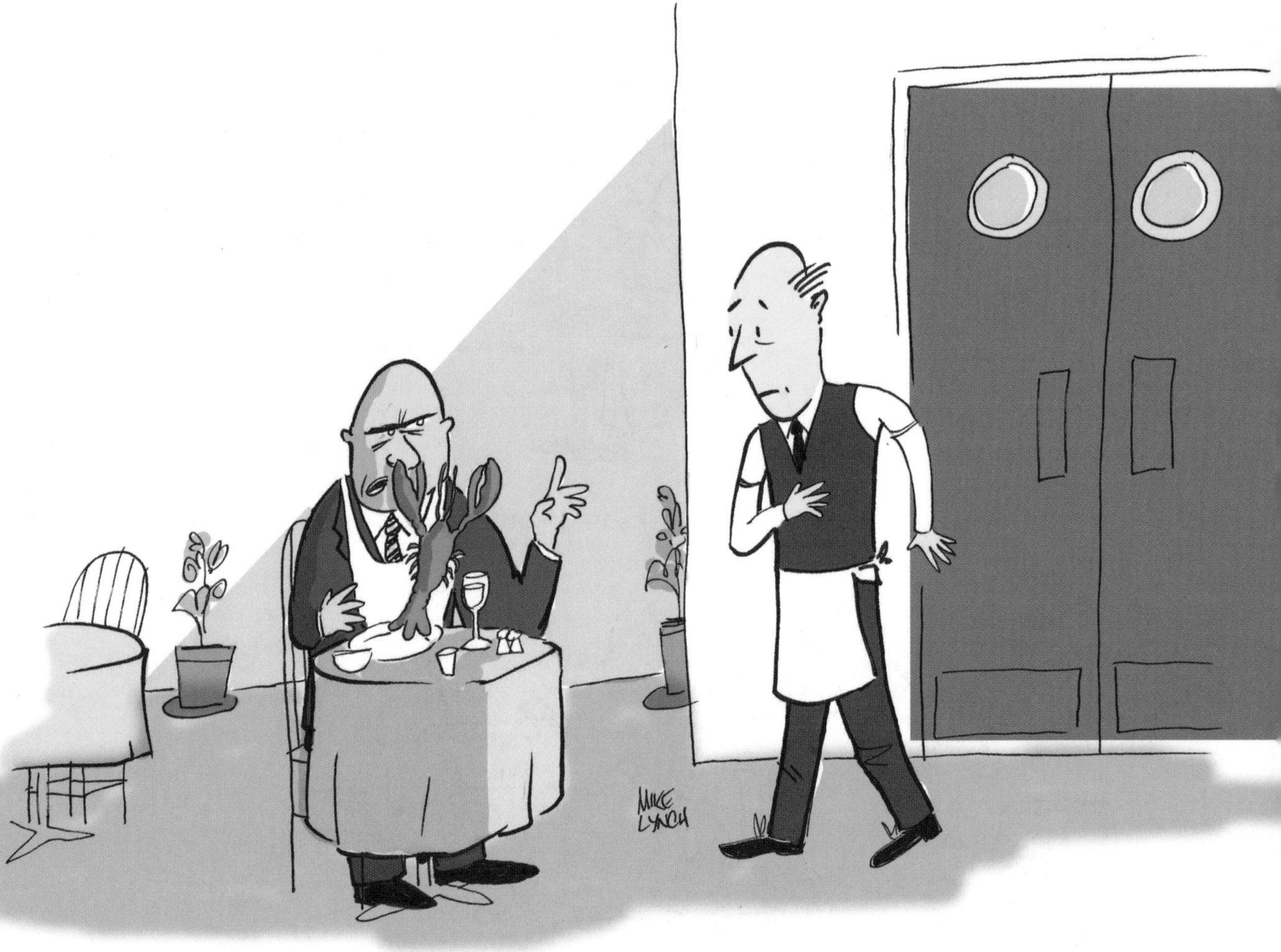
MIKE
LYNCH

"A word with the chef, if you please."

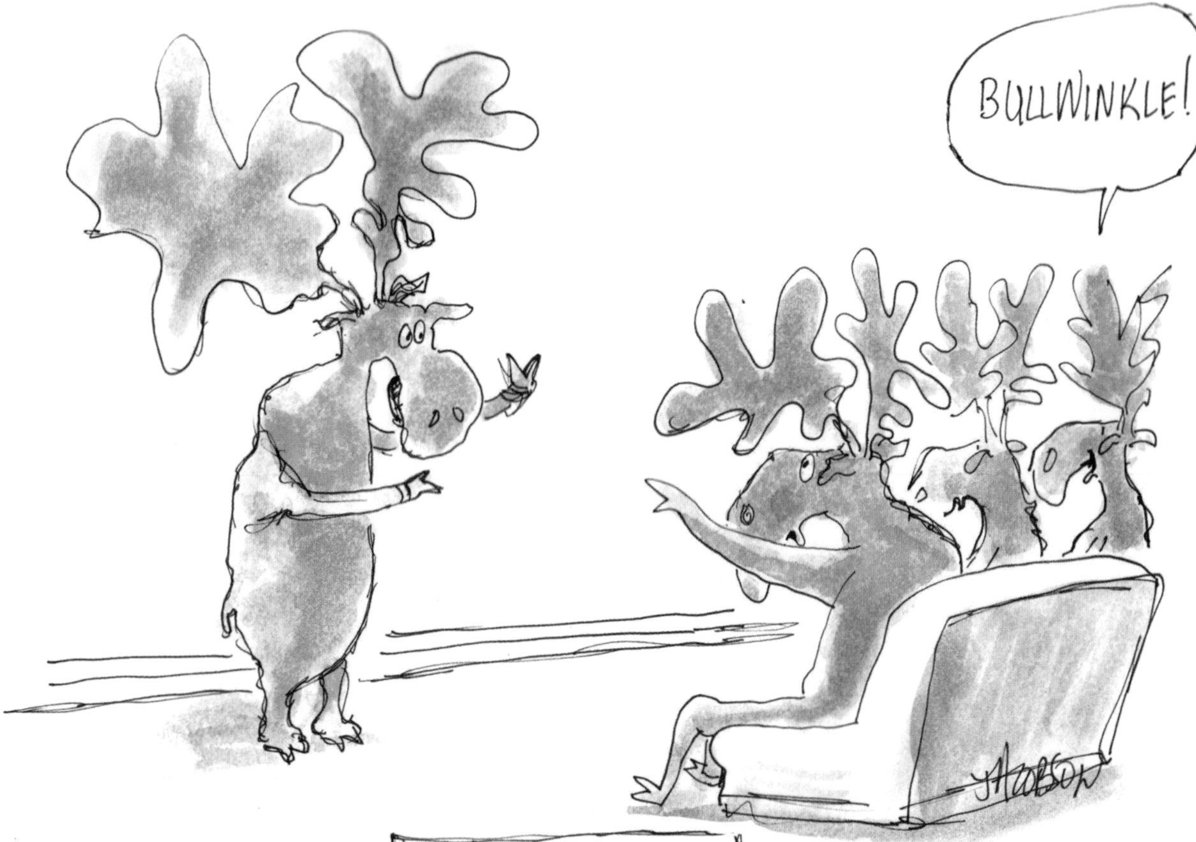
BULLWINKLE!

MOOSE CHARADES!

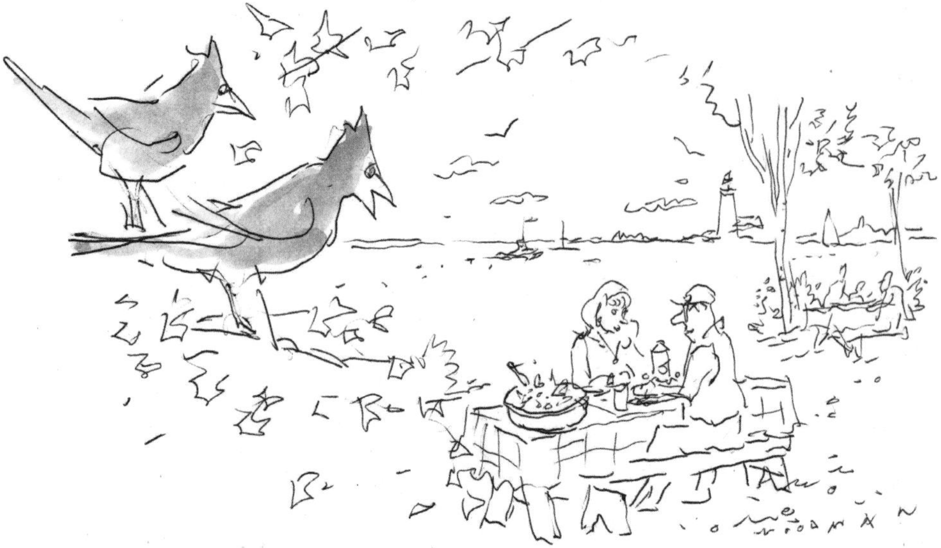
WOODMAN

"Wow! That's one good looking homemade bean salad."

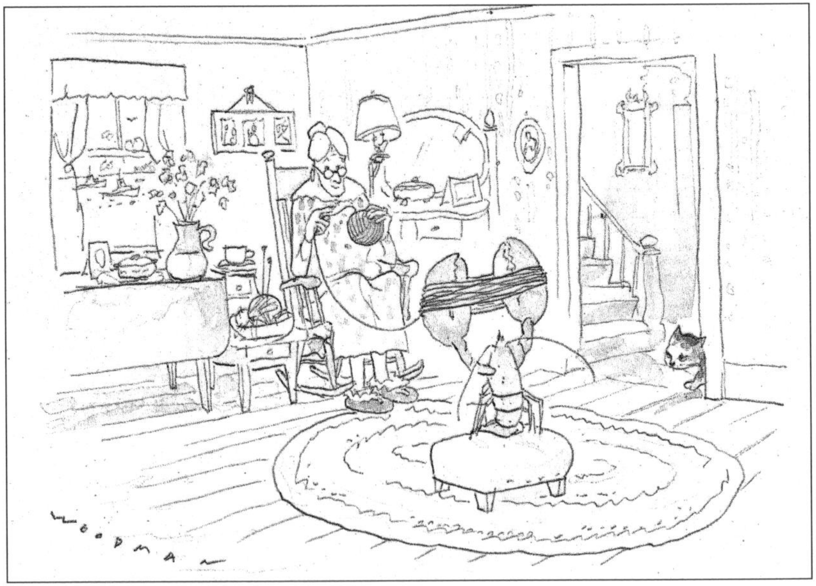
WOODMAN

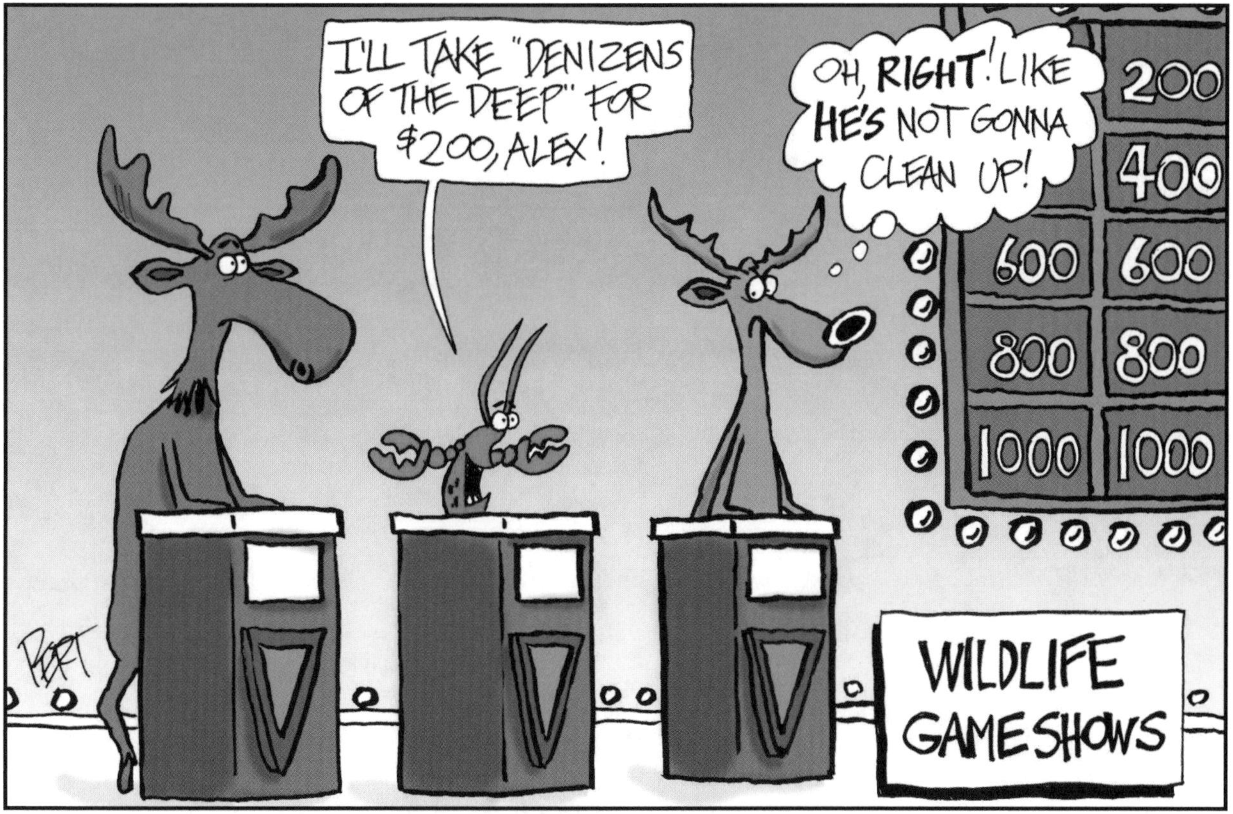
I'LL TAKE "DENIZENS OF THE DEEP" FOR $200, ALEX!
OH, RIGHT! LIKE HE'S NOT GONNA CLEAN UP!
200
400
600 600
800 800
1000 1000
BERT
WILDLIFE GAME SHOWS

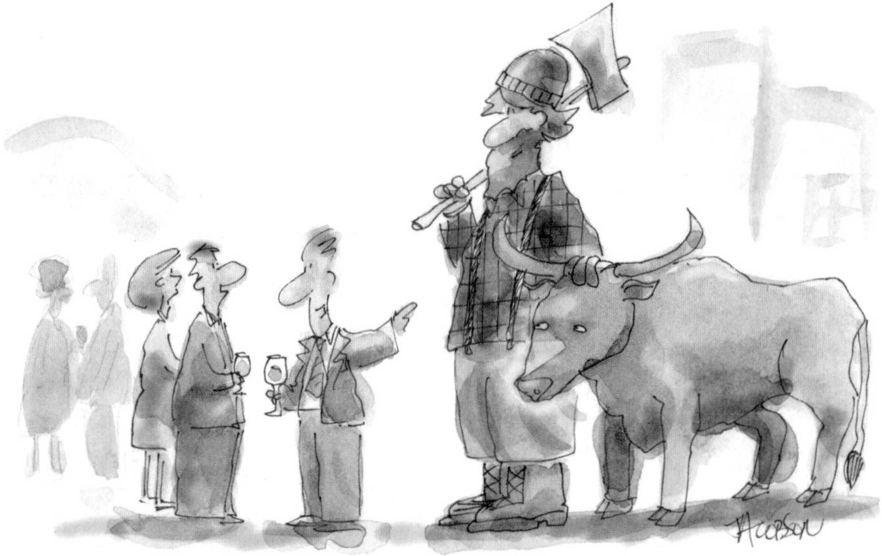
JACOBSON

"Paul works in wood."

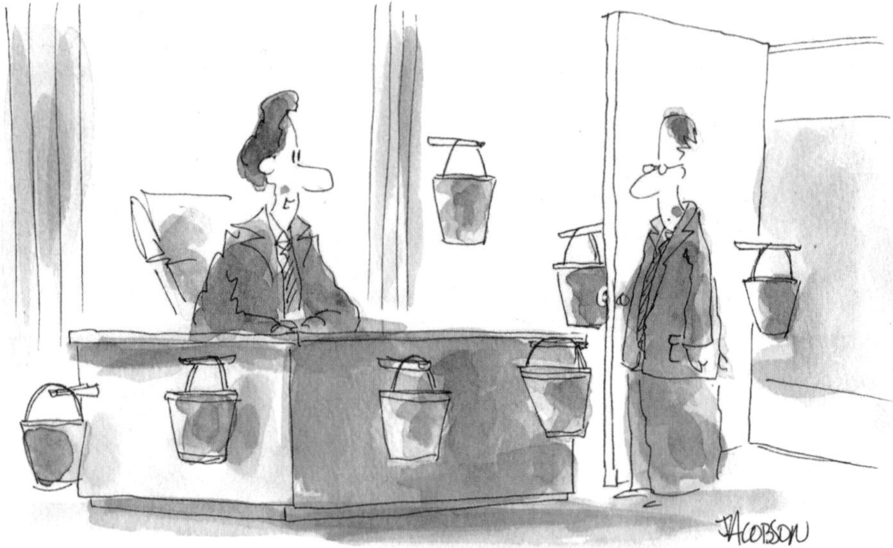
JACOBSON

"With these warm days and cool nights, the sap is really running."

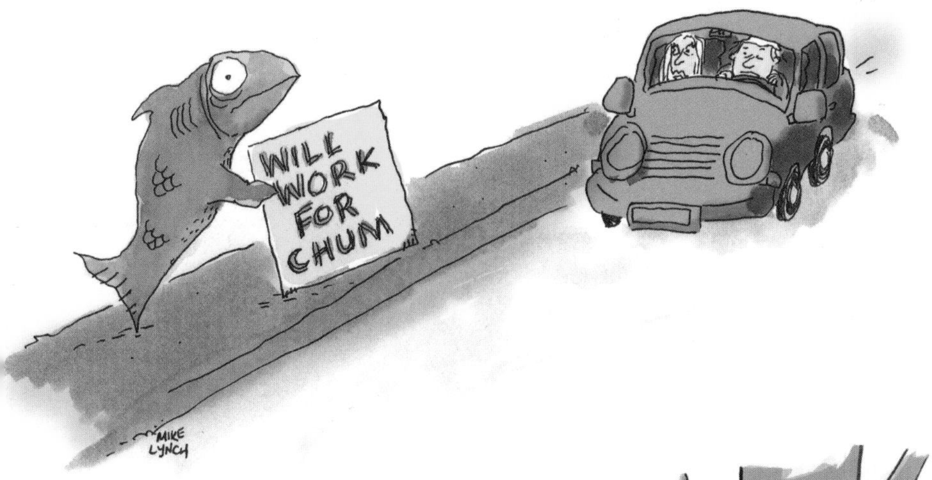
WILL WORK FOR CHUM
MIKE LYNCH

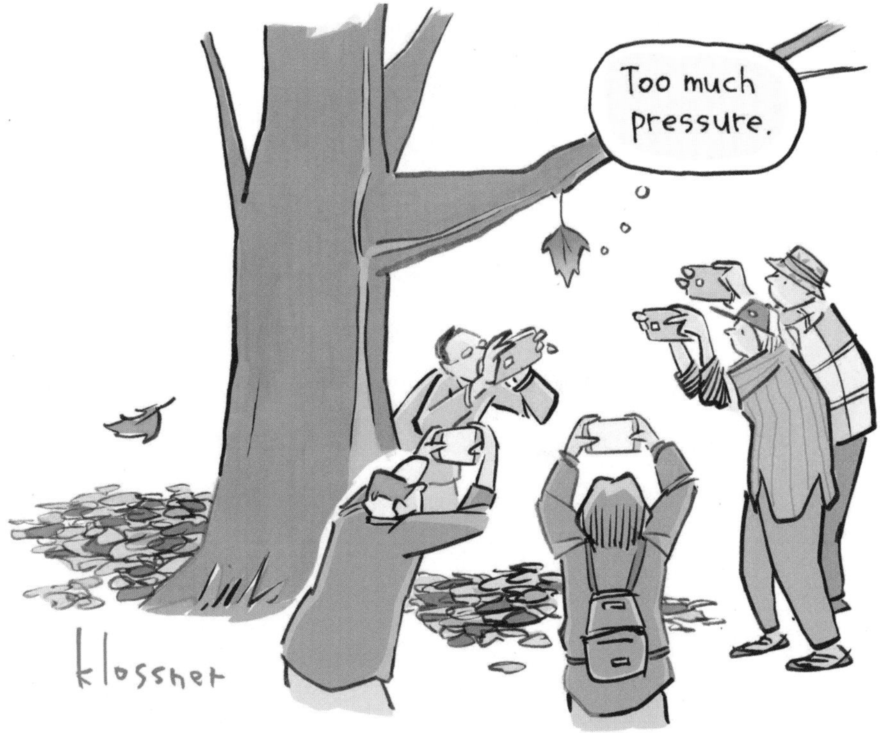
Too much pressure.
klossner

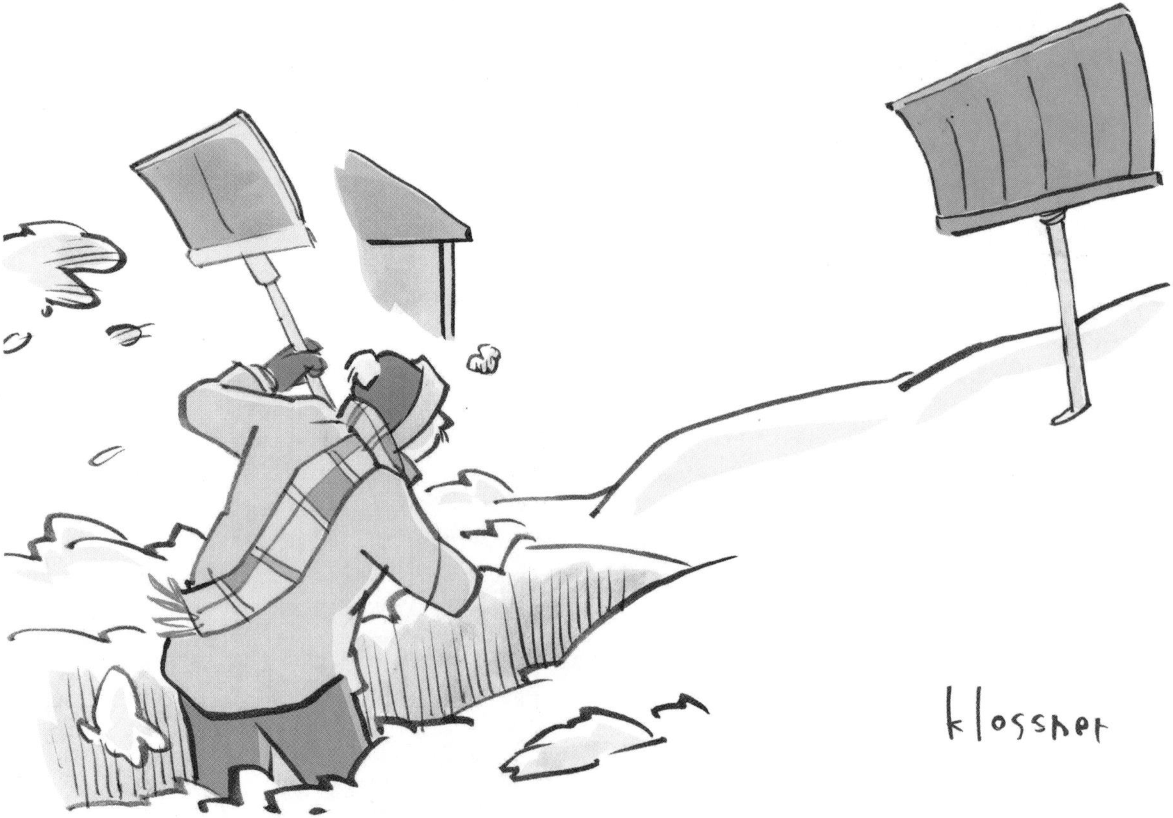
klossner

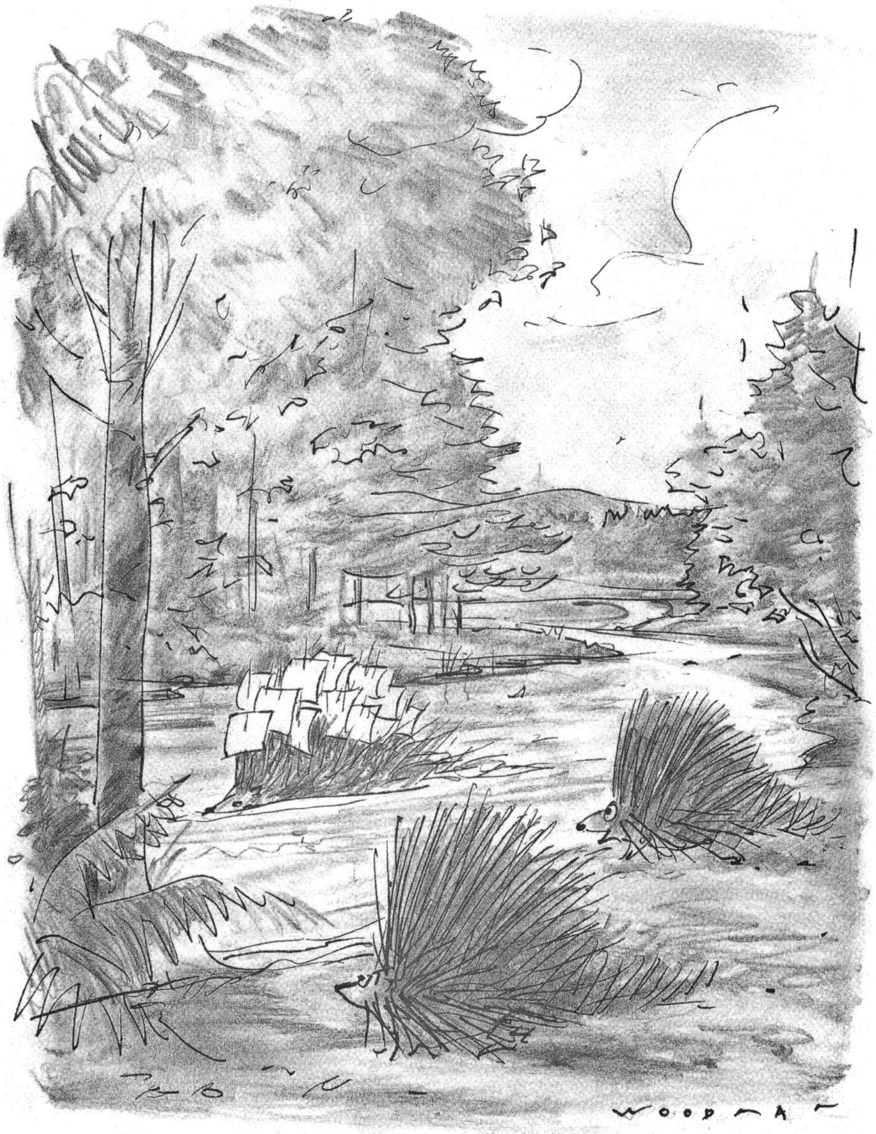

"Gee, why didn't I think of that?"

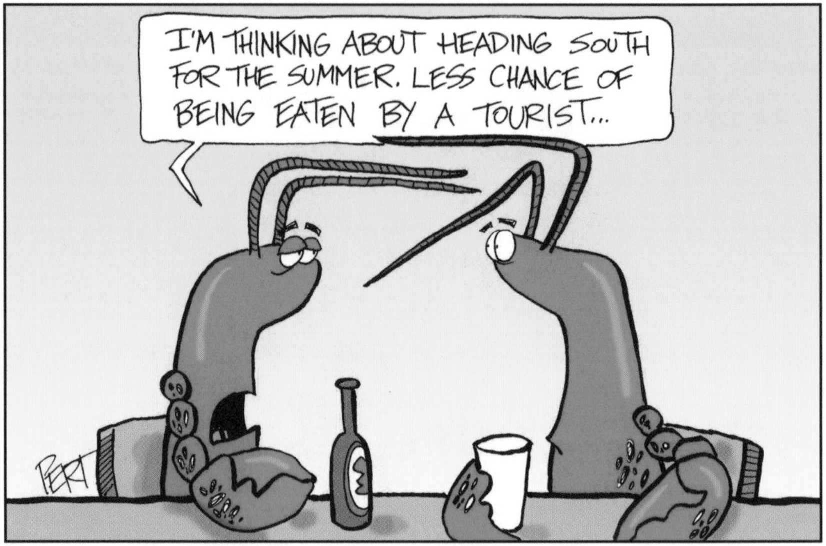
I'M THINKING ABOUT HEADING SOUTH FOR THE SUMMER. LESS CHANCE OF BEING EATEN BY A TOURIST...
PERT

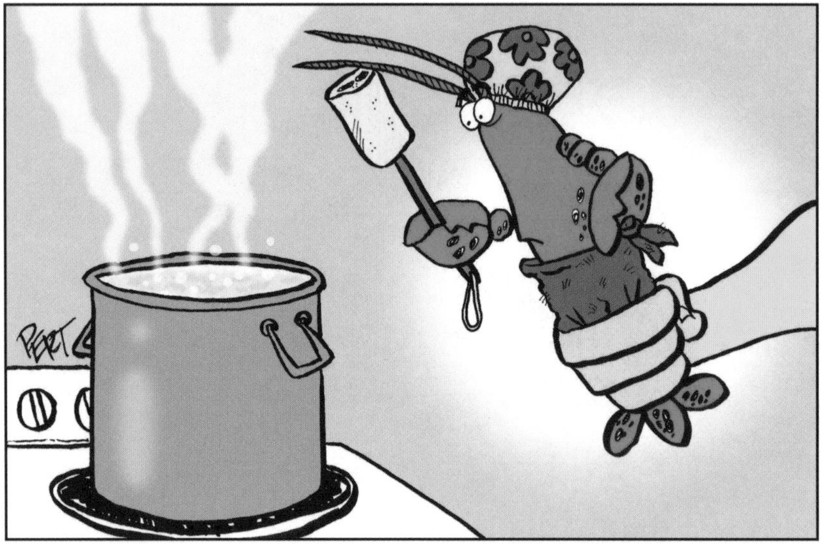
PERT

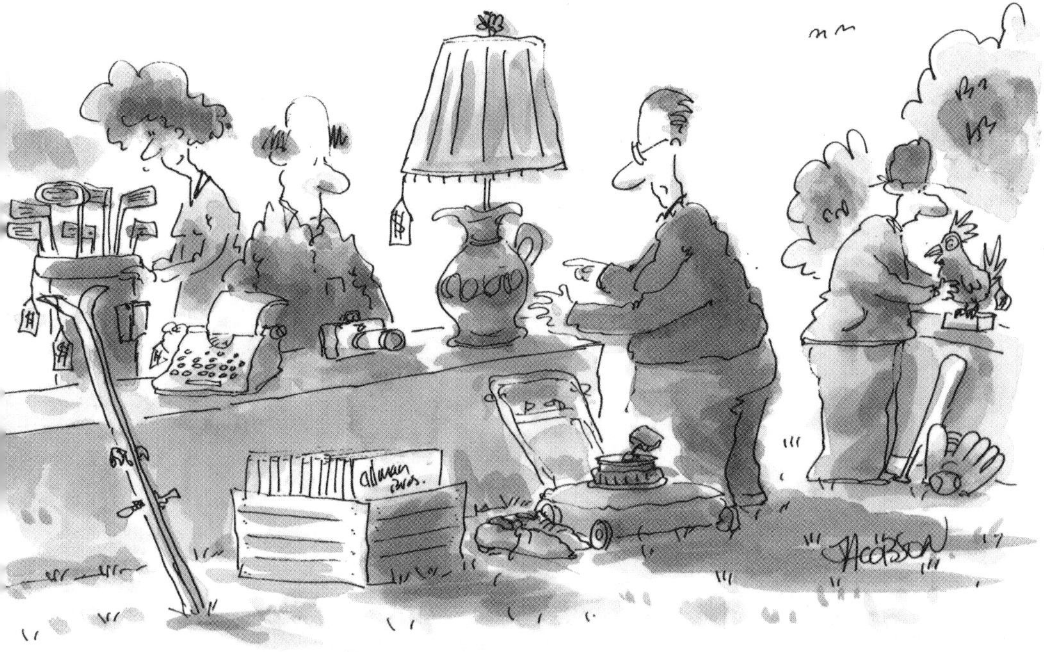
JACOBSON

"Didn't you buy that from me at my yard sale?"

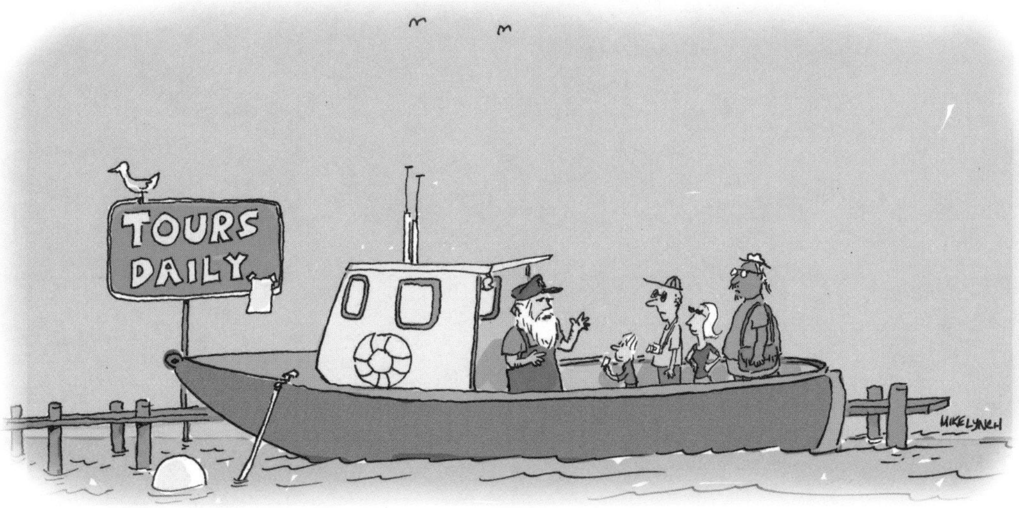
TOURS
DAILY
MIKE LYNCH

"Oh, it was a tempestuous storm. Lightning, thunder, and, worst of all, the complimentary wi-fi had gone dead . . ."

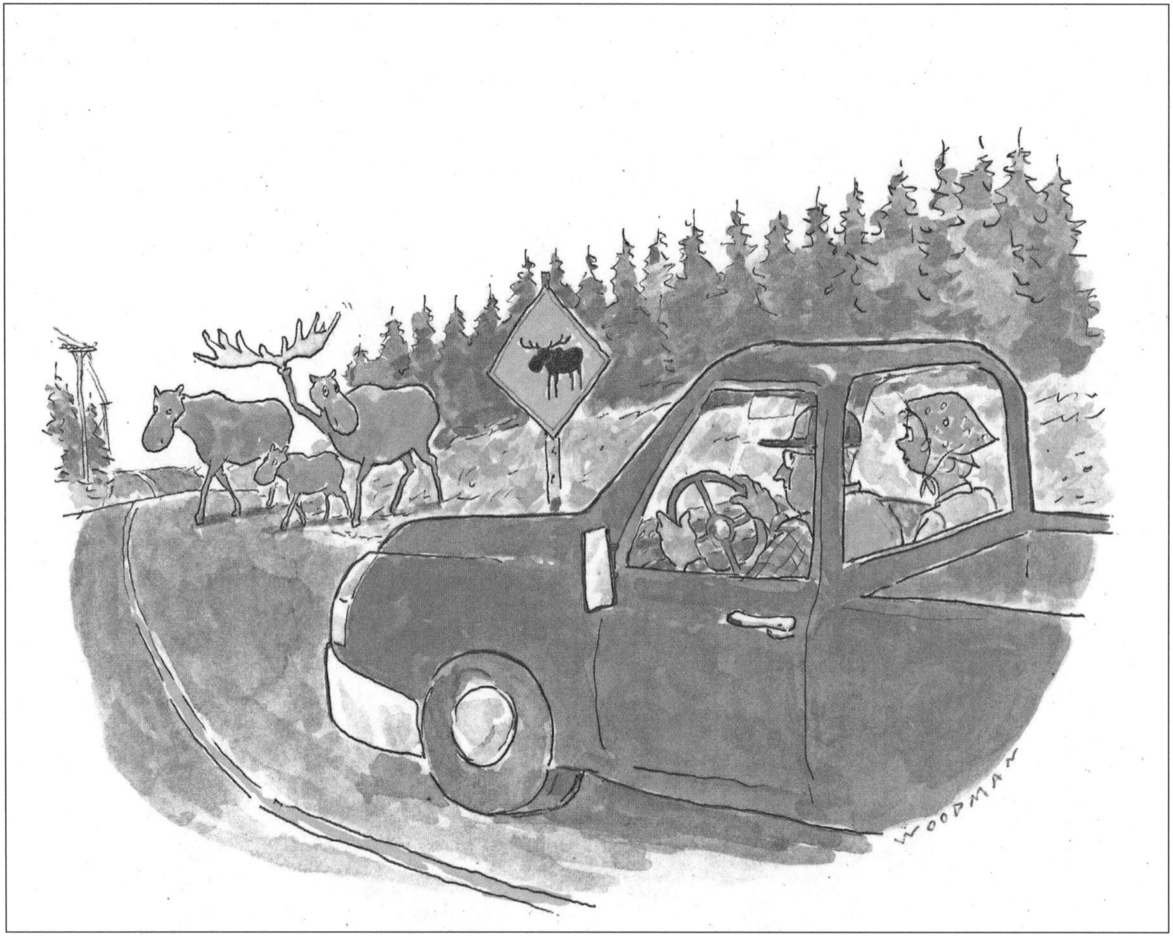
WOODMAN

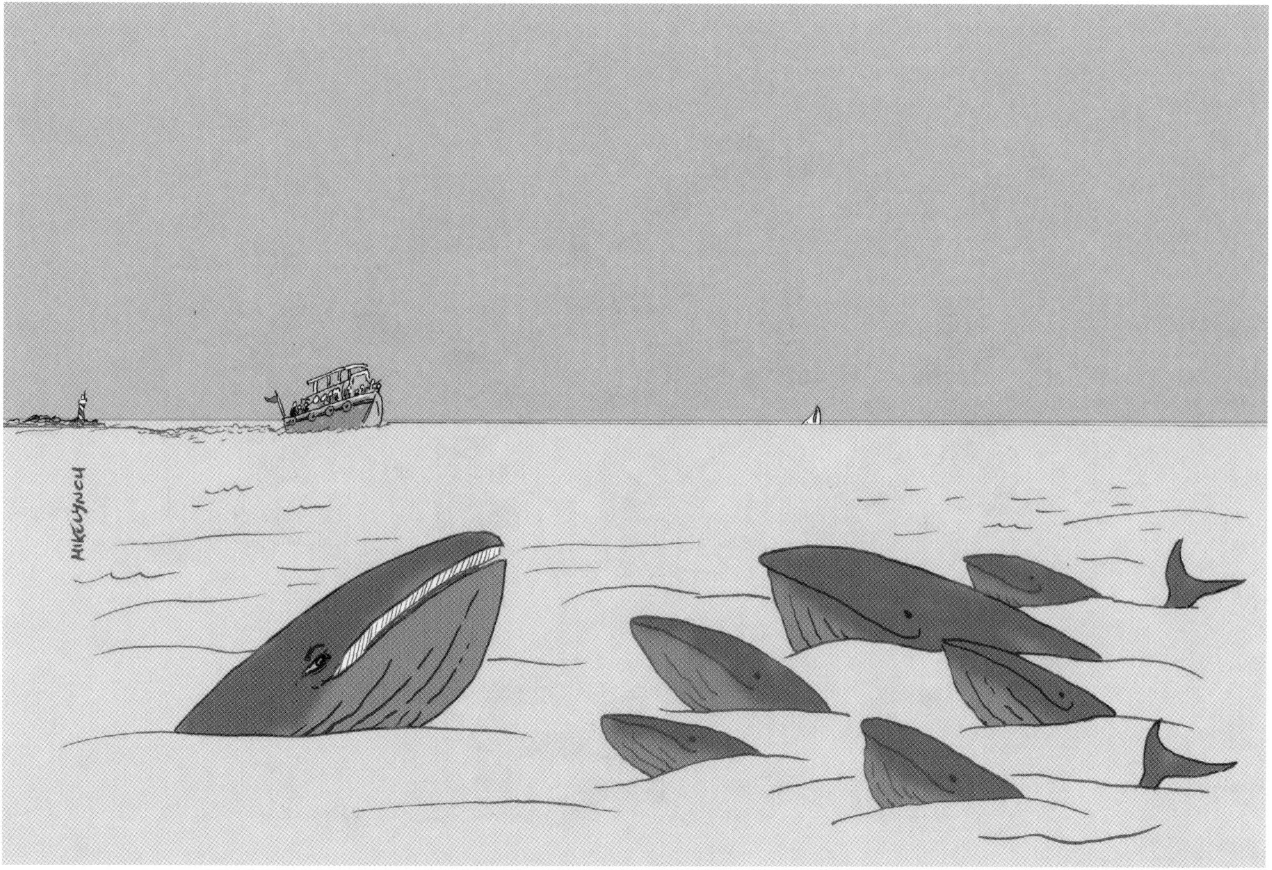
MIKELYNCH

"This is the best spot for people watching. If we're lucky, they'll put on quite a show."

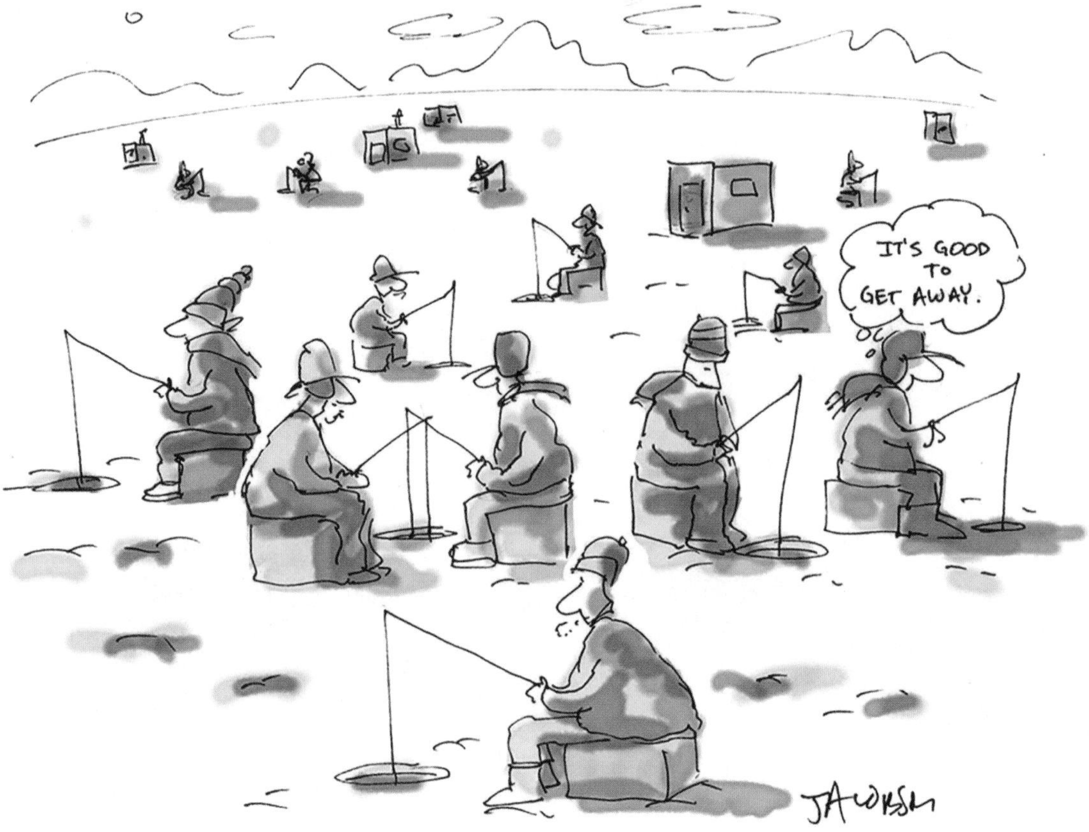
IT'S GOOD TO GET AWAY.
JACOBSON

fwoomph!!

Maine Climate Change

klossner

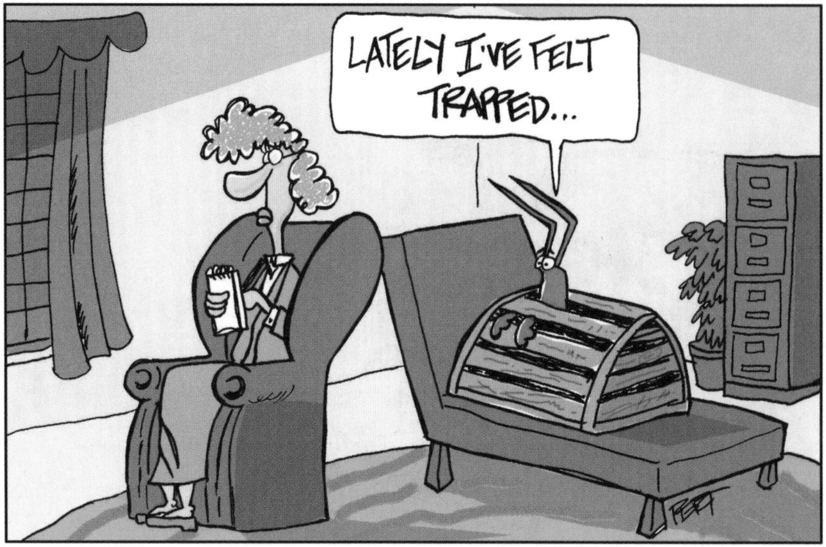
LATELY I'VE FELT TRAPPED...
PEET

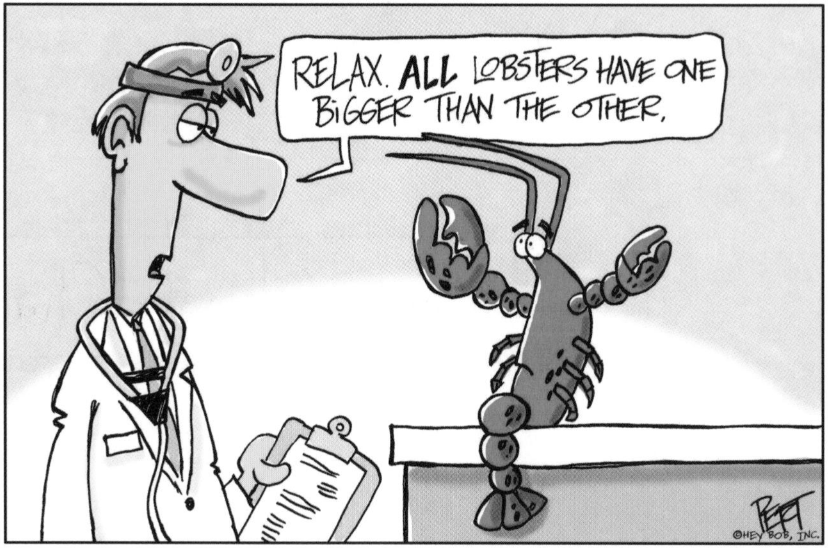
RELAX. **ALL** LOBSTERS HAVE ONE BIGGER THAN THE OTHER.
PEET
©HEY BOB, INC.

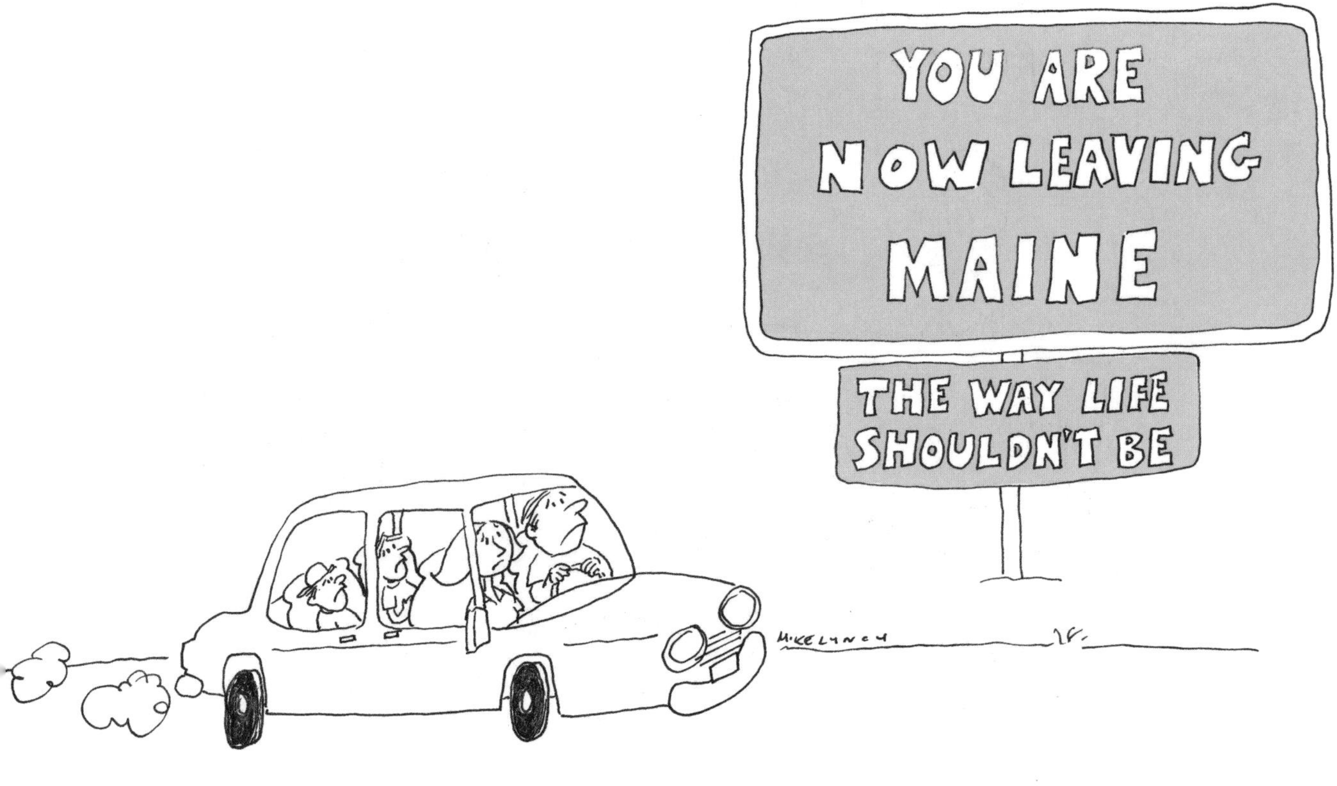
YOU ARE NOW LEAVING MAINE
THE WAY LIFE SHOULDN'T BE
MIKELYNCH

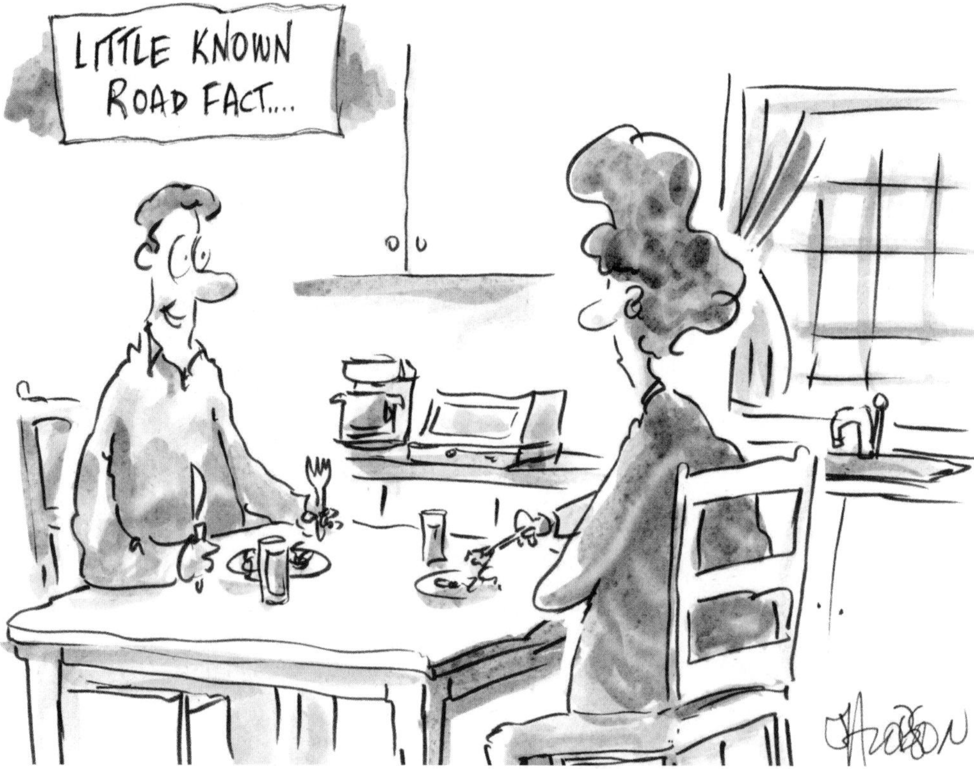
LITTLE KNOWN
ROAD FACT....

"If you take 495, subtract 295, and divide by 95,
you get 2.10526."

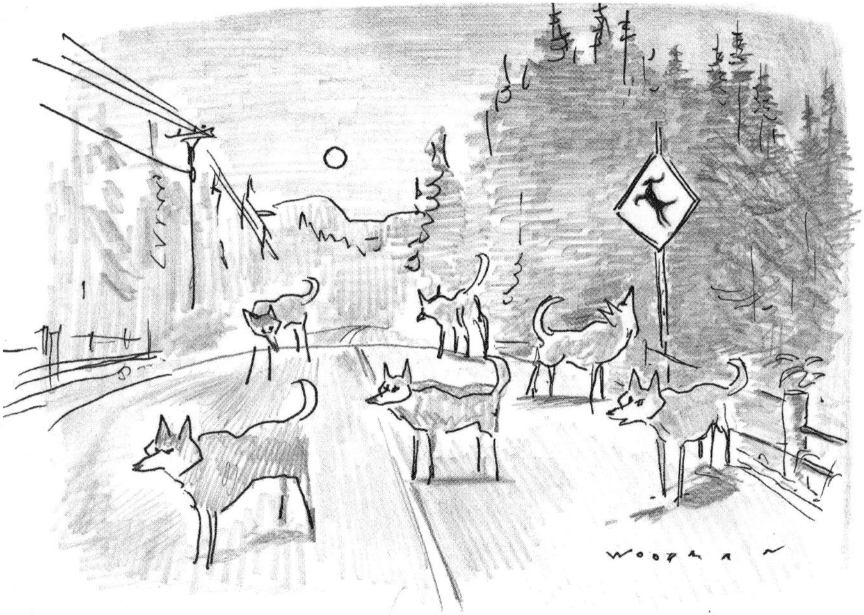

"Sign or no sign, I say we're wasting our time."

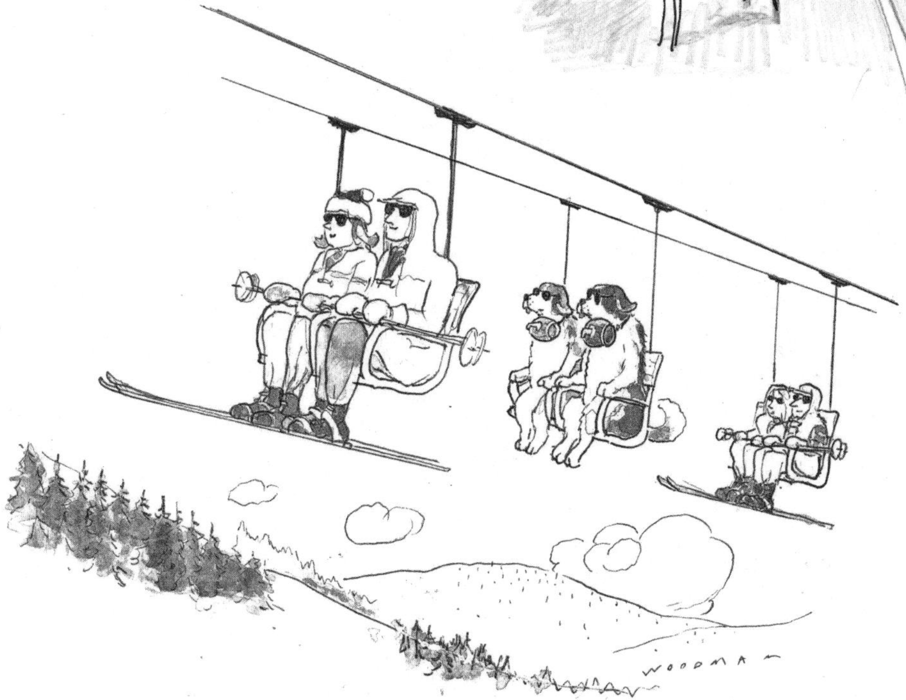

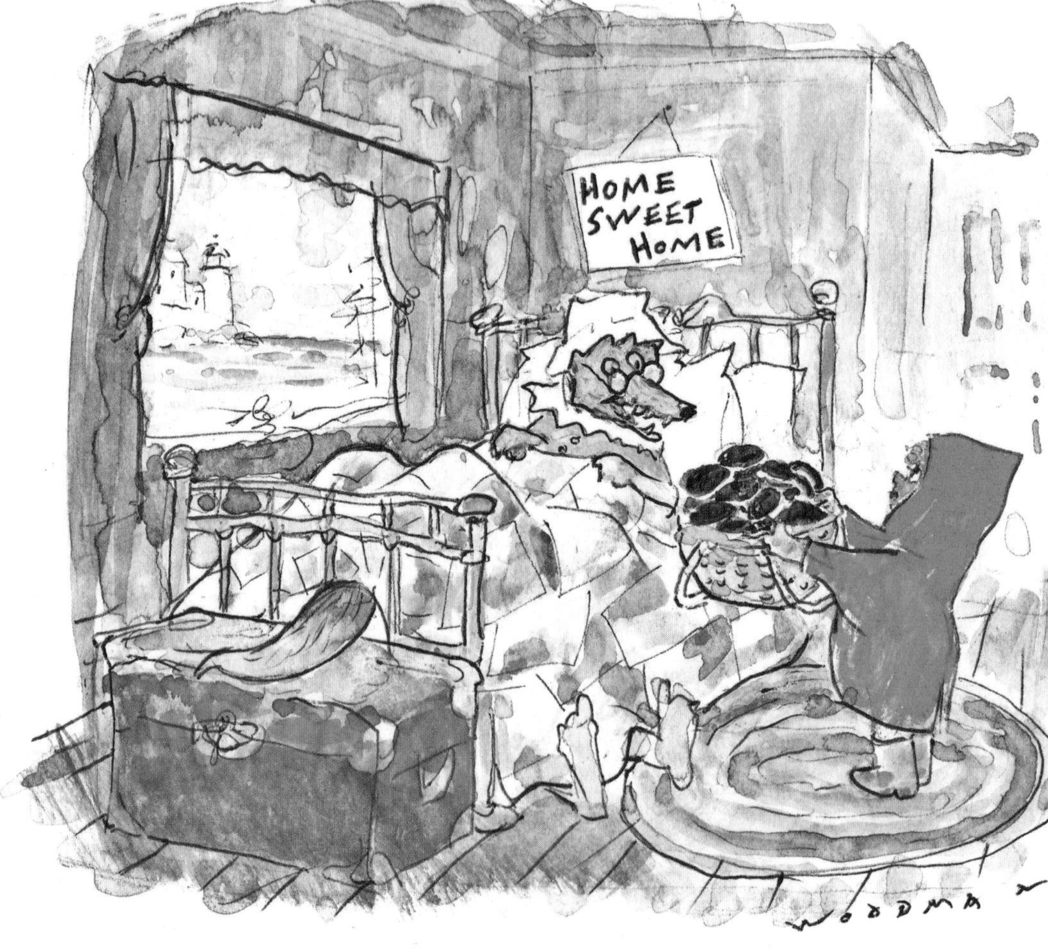
HOME
SWEET
HOME

"Whoopie pies! Why, thank you dear. I'll have them for dessert."

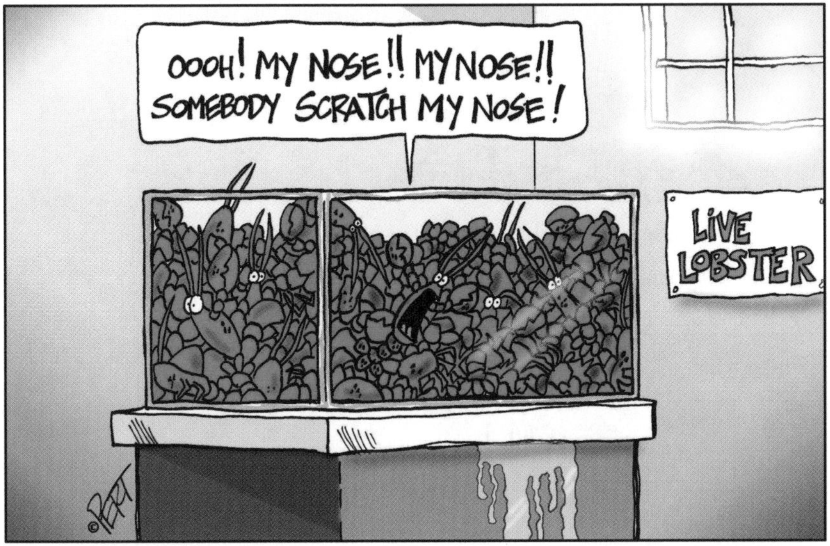
OOOH! MY NOSE!! MY NOSE!! SOMEBODY SCRATCH MY NOSE!
LIVE LOBSTER

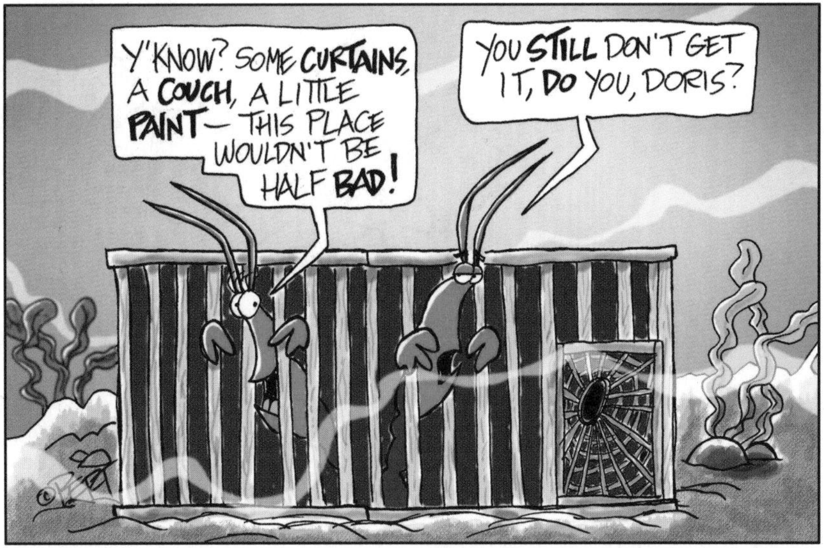
Y'KNOW? SOME CURTAINS, A COUCH, A LITTLE PAINT— THIS PLACE WOULDN'T BE HALF BAD!
YOU STILL DON'T GET IT, DO YOU, DORIS?

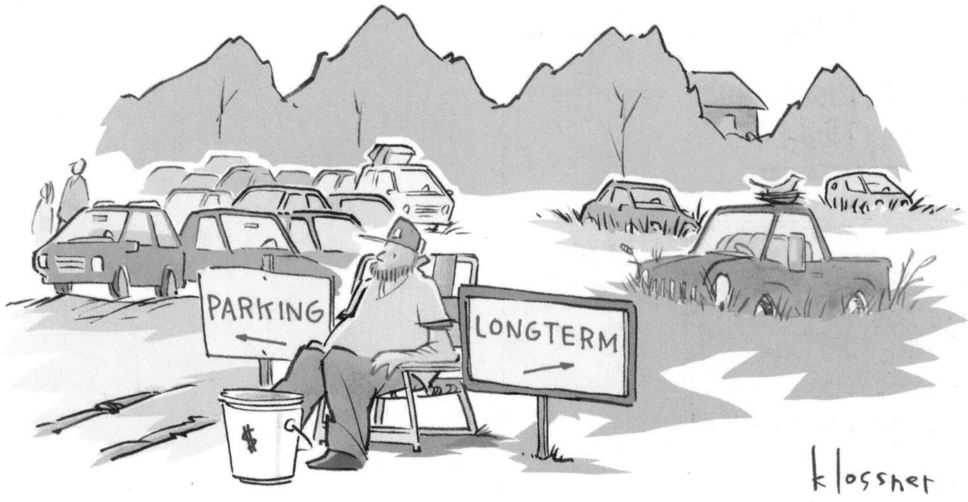
PARKING
LONGTERM
klossner

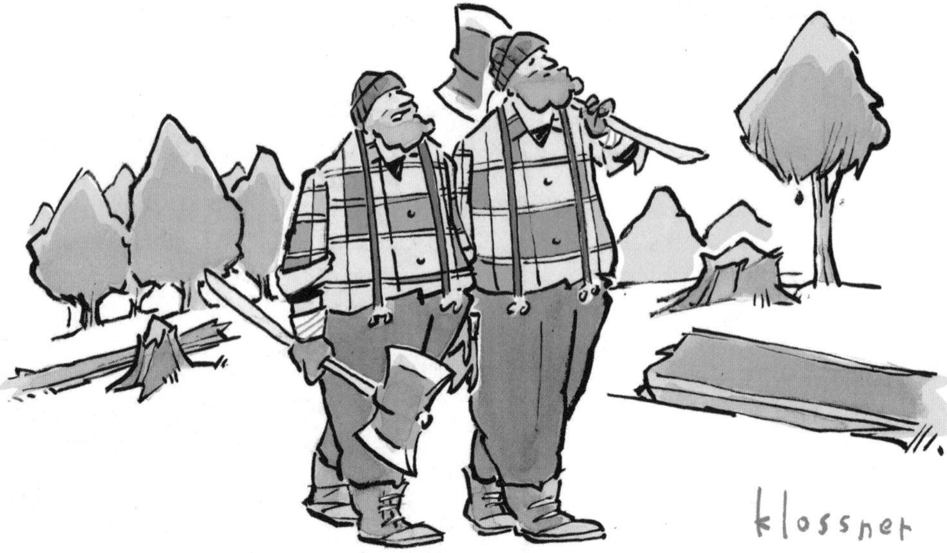
klossner

"I wish you had told me what you'd be wearing today."

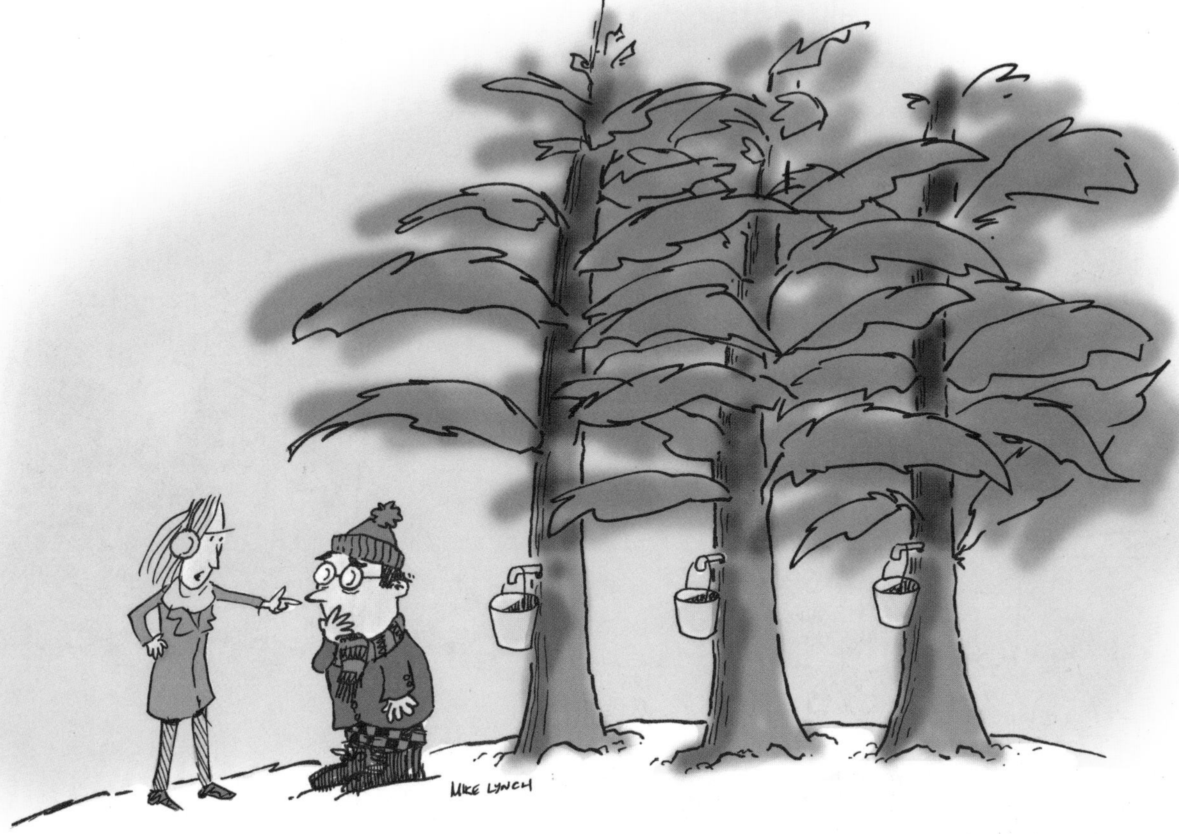
MIKE LYNCH

"That's it! I'm taking you to the optometrist! You've tapped the pine trees again!"

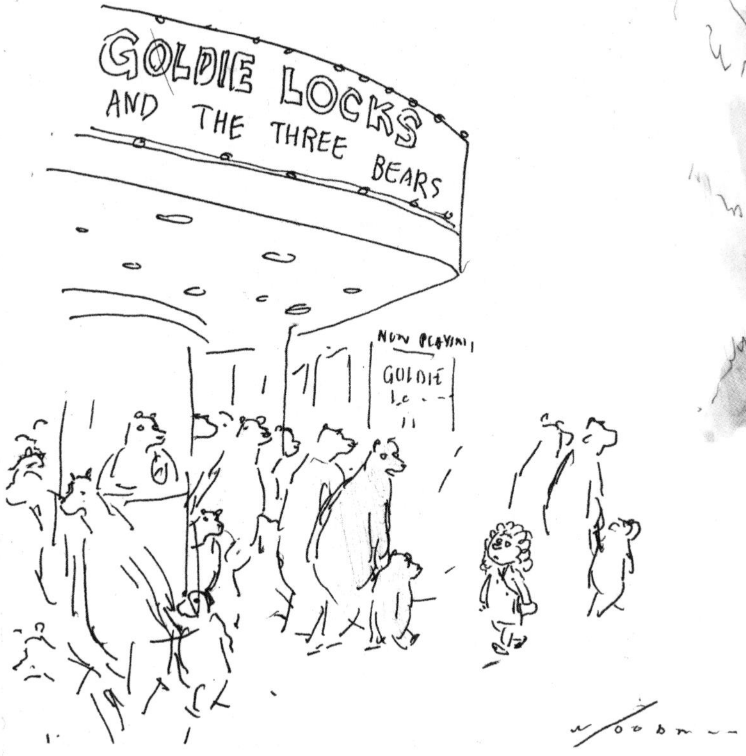
GOLDIE LOCKS
AND THE THREE BEARS
GOLDIE

"Bitch!"

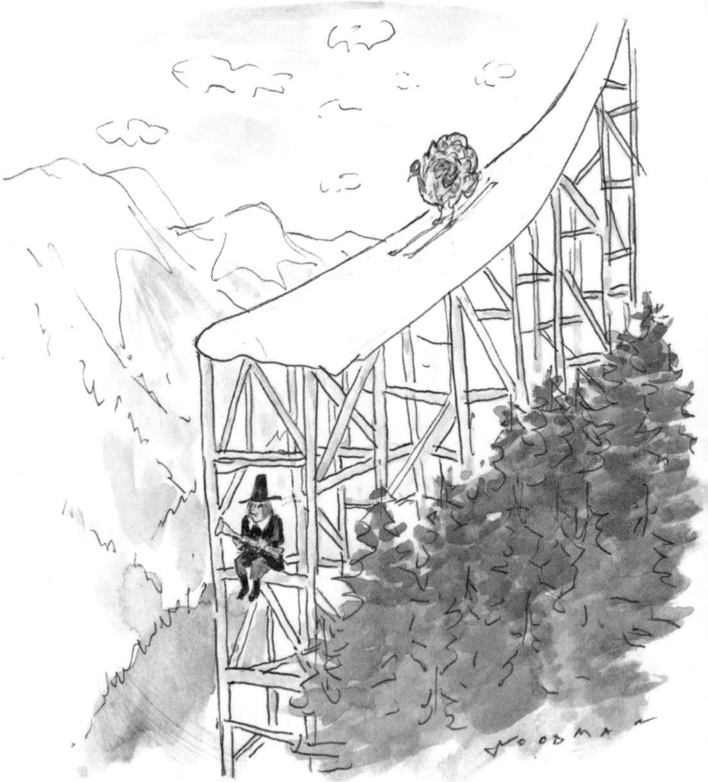

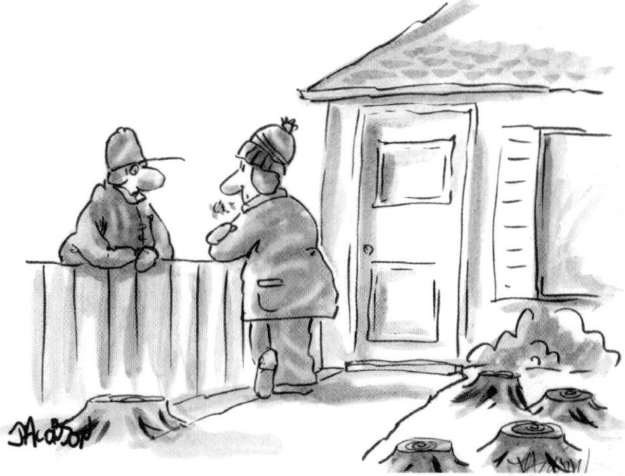
JACOBSON

"We do heat with wood."

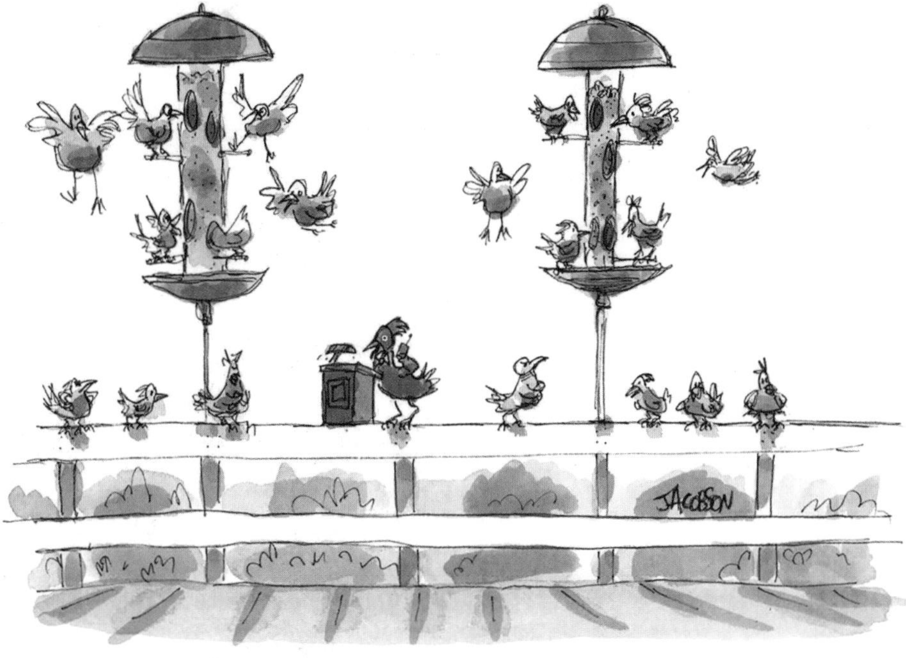
JACOBSON

"I can get you in next Thursday, at 5:30."

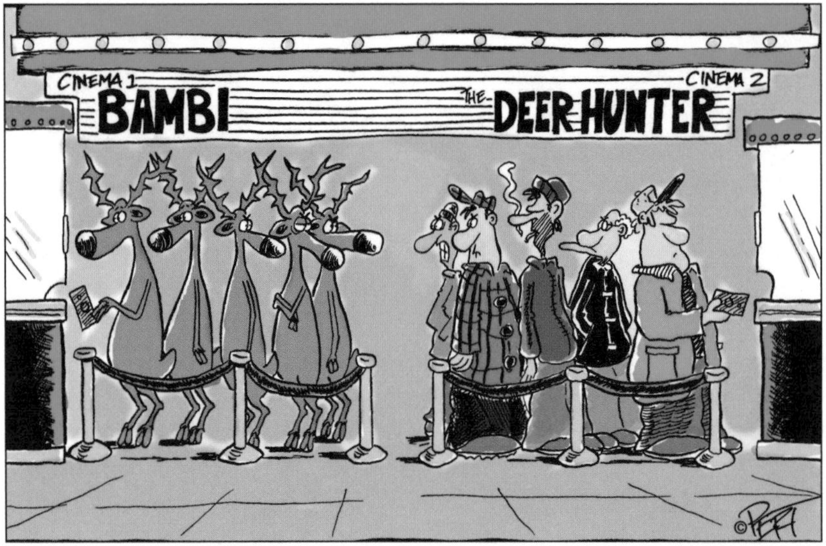
CINEMA 1
BAMBI
THE
DEER HUNTER
CINEMA 2
©PERI

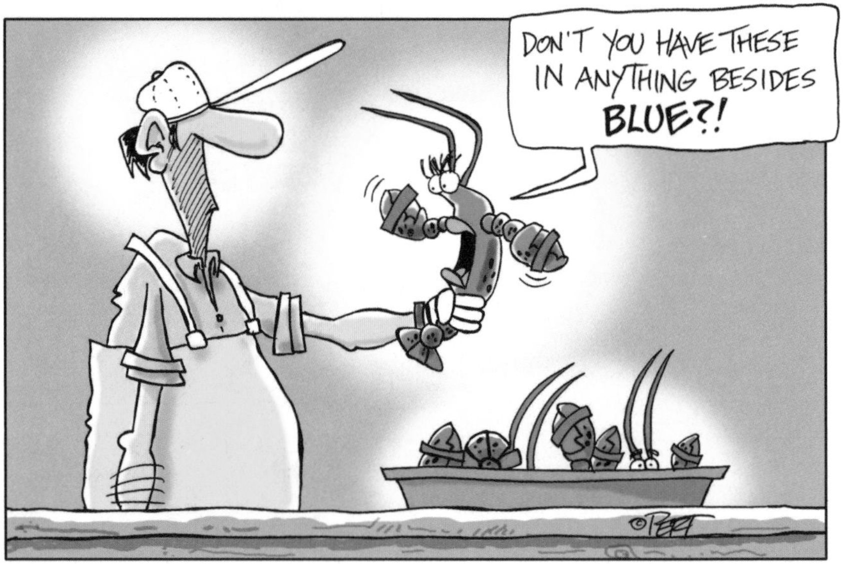
DON'T YOU HAVE THESE IN ANYTHING BESIDES BLUE?!
©PERI

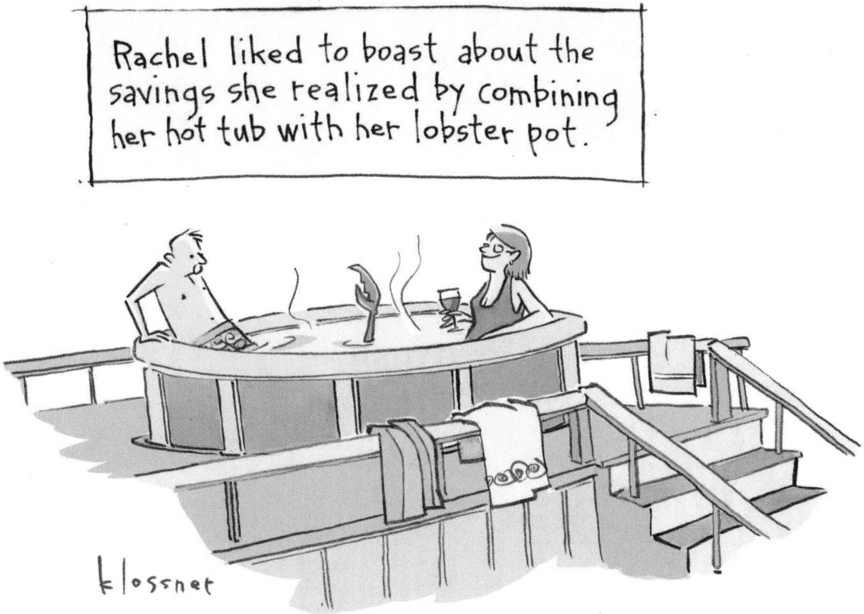
Rachel liked to boast about the savings she realized by combining her hot tub with her lobster pot.
klossner

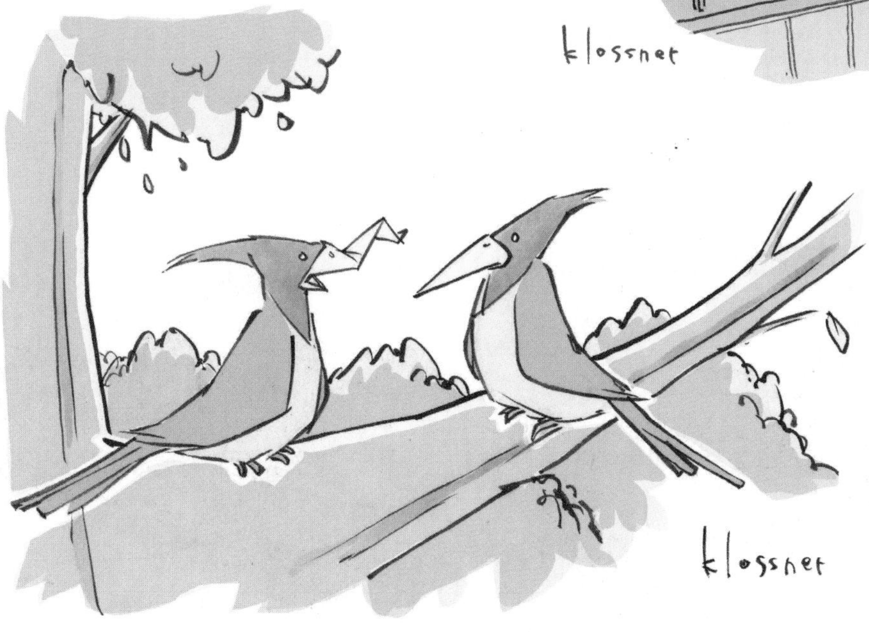
klossner

"How was I to know it was a camouflaged cell phone tower?"

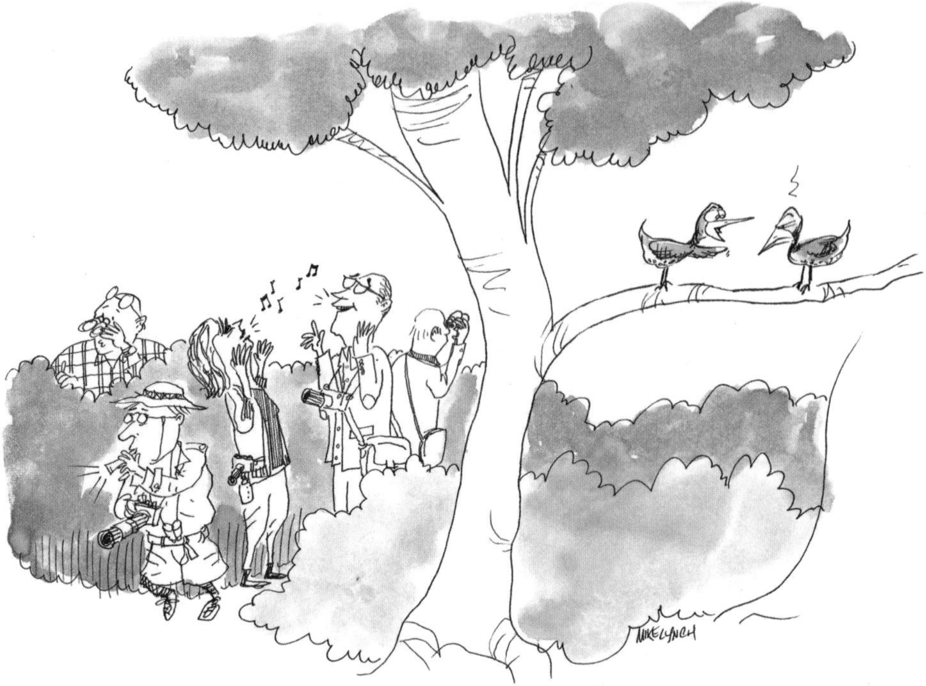
MIKE LYNCH

“Call for you.”

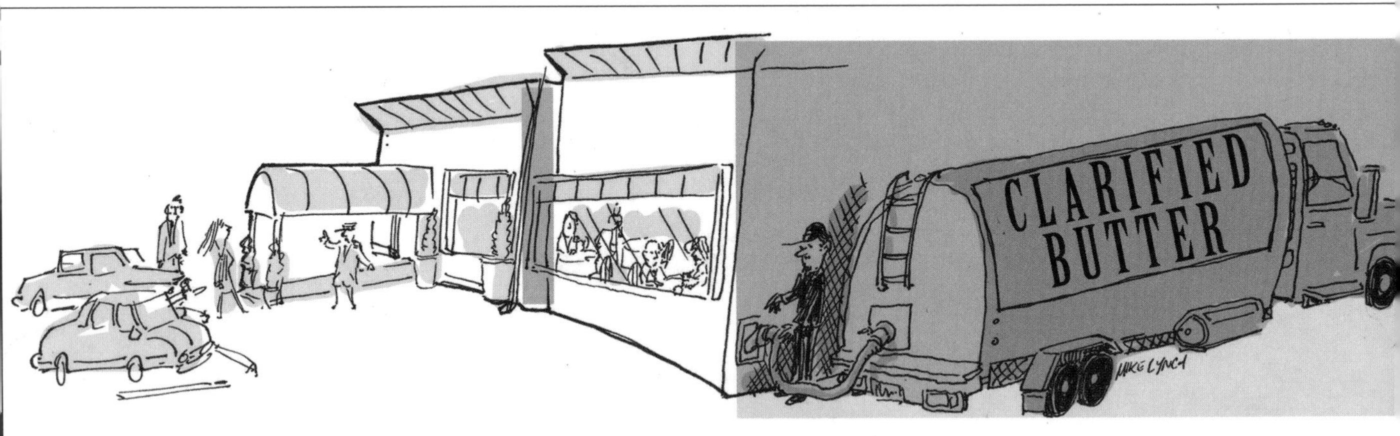
CLARIFIED
BUTTER
MIKE LYNCH

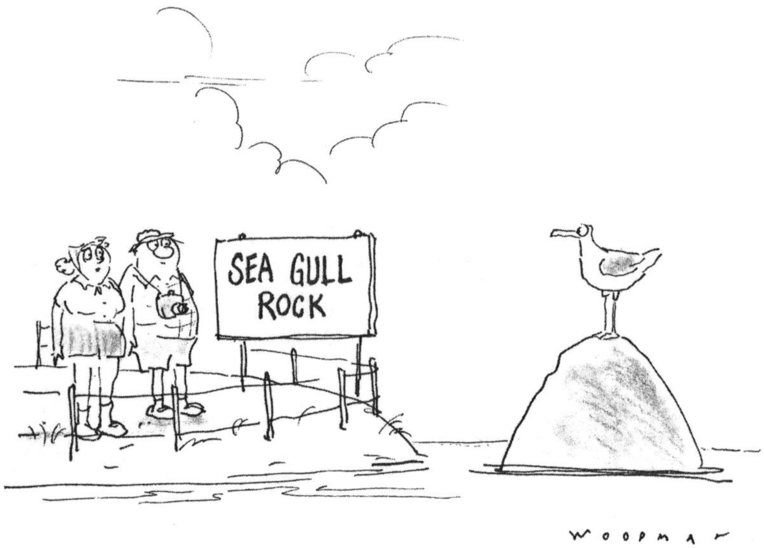
SEA GULL ROCK
WOODMAN

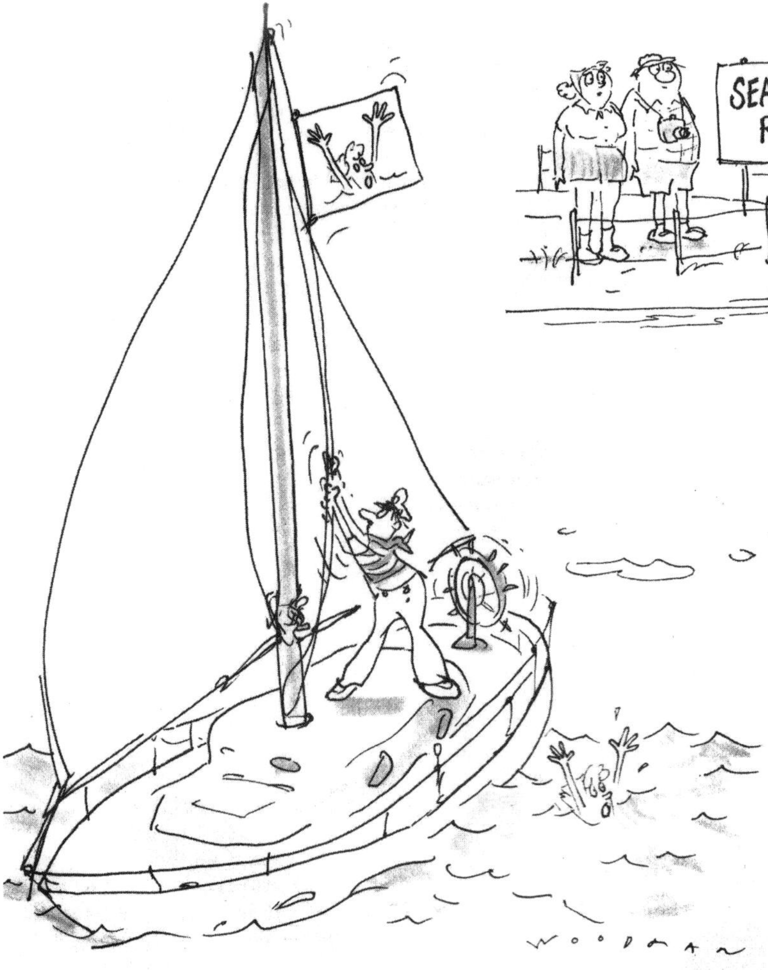
WOODMAN

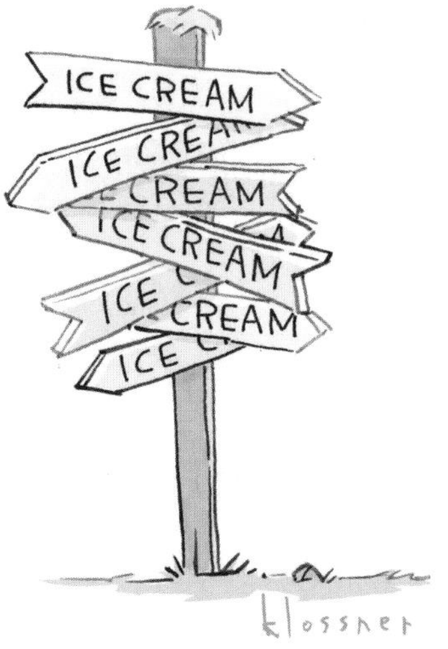
ICE CREAM
ICE CREAM
ICE CREAM
ICE CREAM
ICE CREAM
ICE CREAM
ICE CREAM
klossner

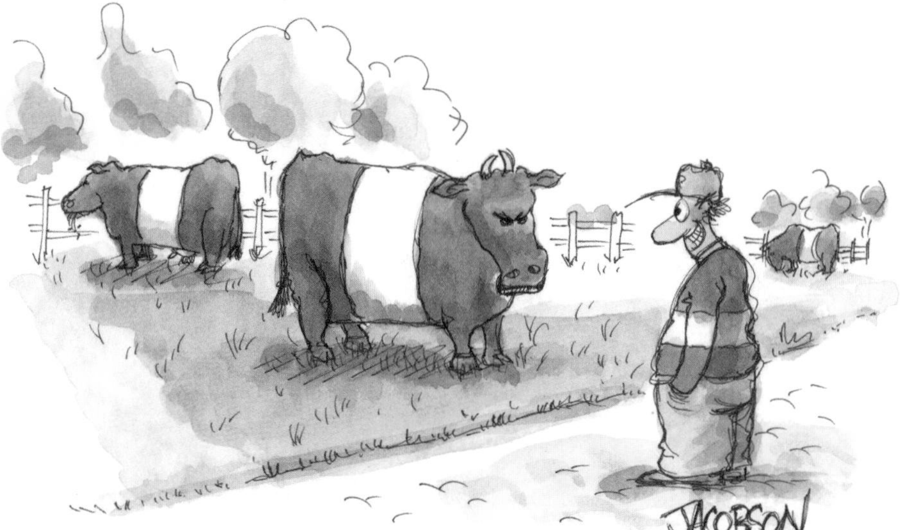
JACOBSON

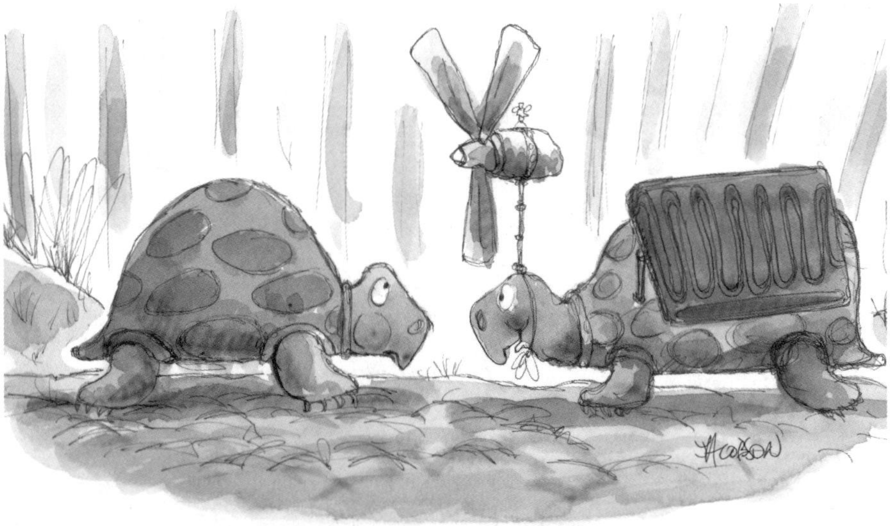
JACOBSON

"I'm completely off the grid."

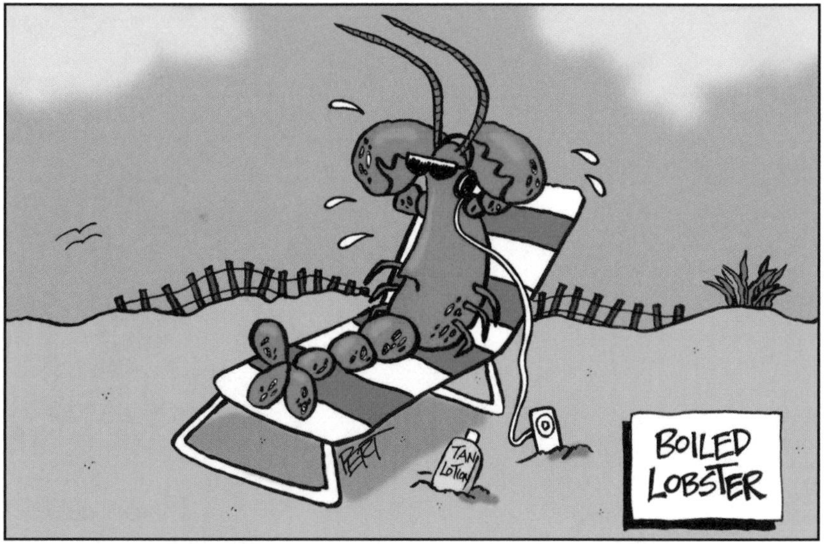
TAN LOTION
PERT
BOILED LOBSTER

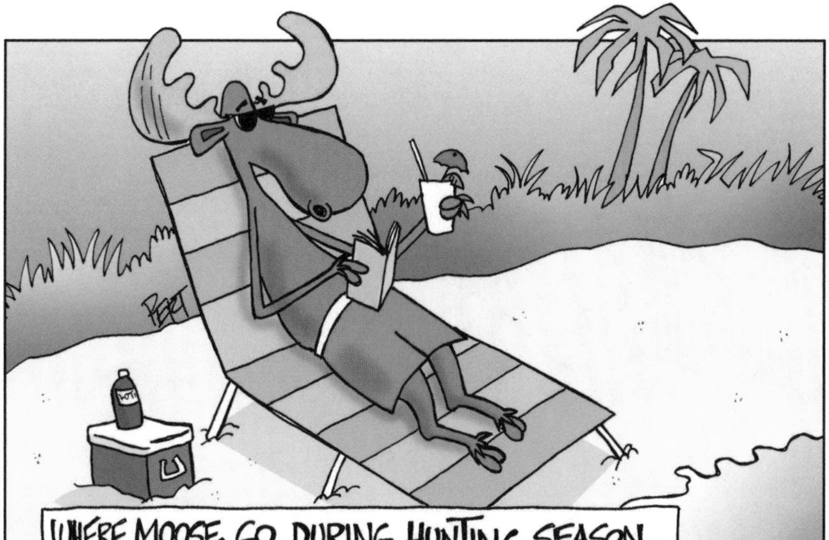
PERT
WHERE MOOSE GO DURING HUNTING SEASON...

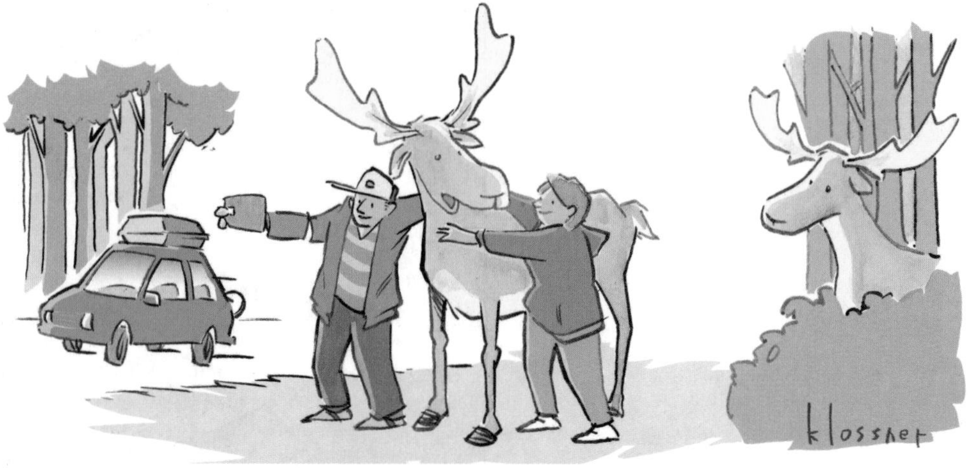
klossner

"If you can't beat 'em, sell to them."

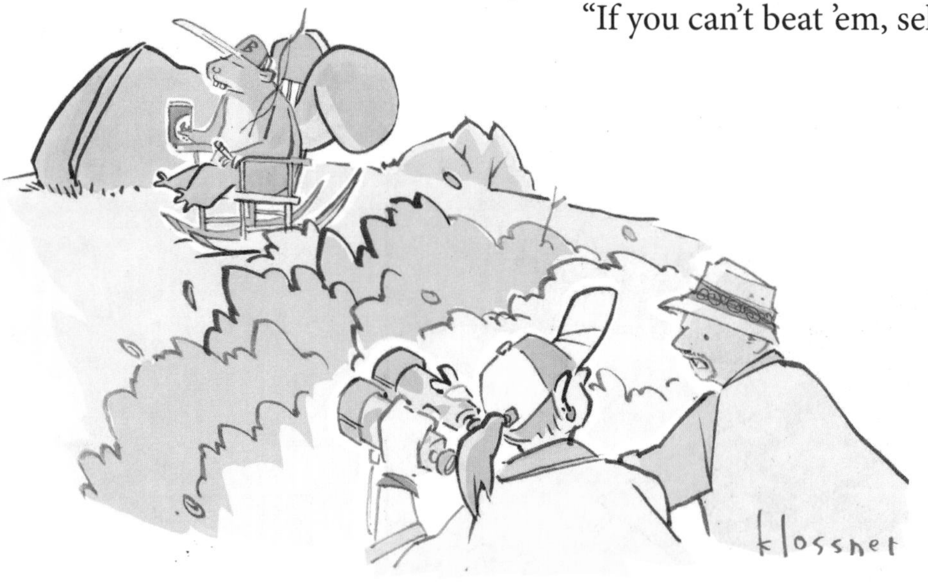
klossner

"This species is a little too native for me."

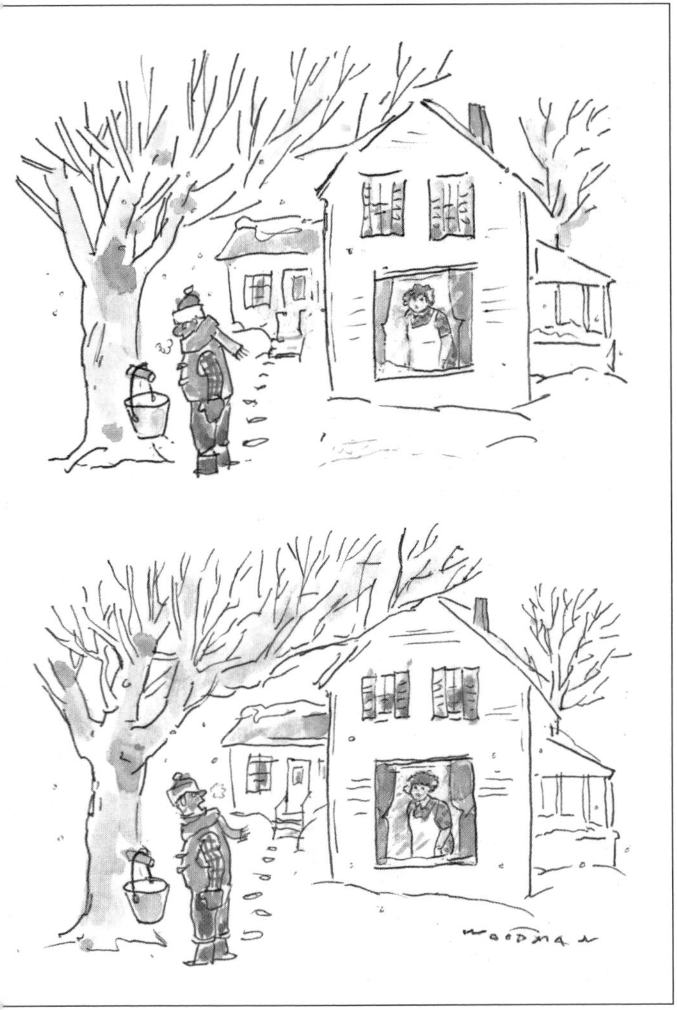
WOODMAN

"Nothing yet."

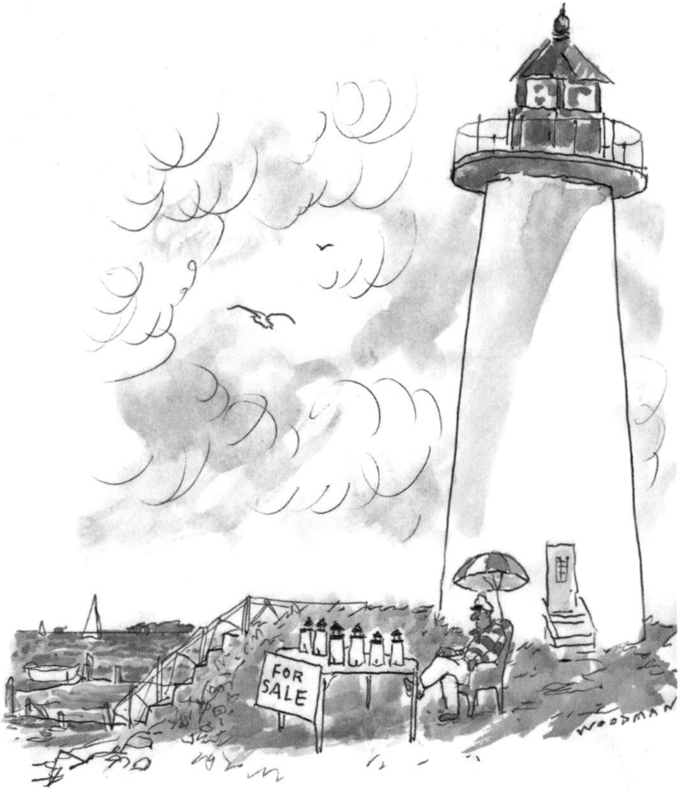
FOR SALE
WOODMAN

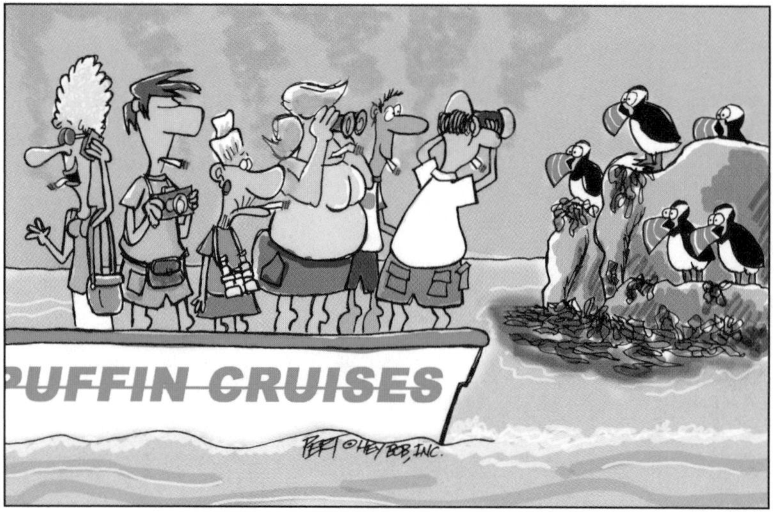
PUFFIN CRUISES
PEET ©HEY BOB, INC.

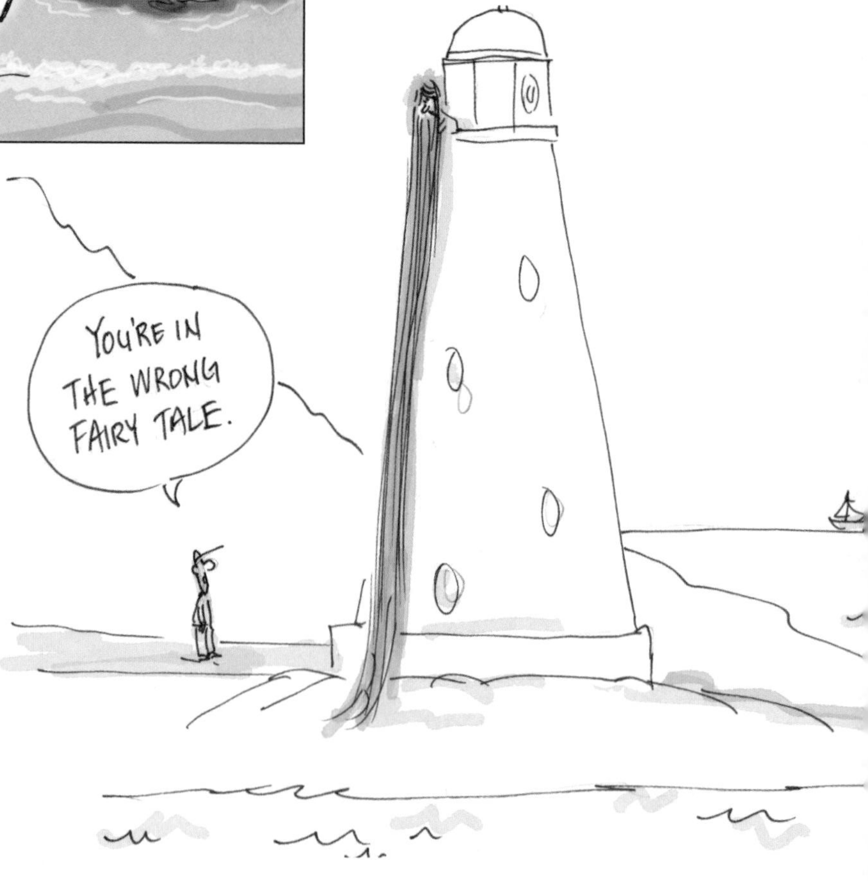
YOU'RE IN THE WRONG FAIRY TALE.

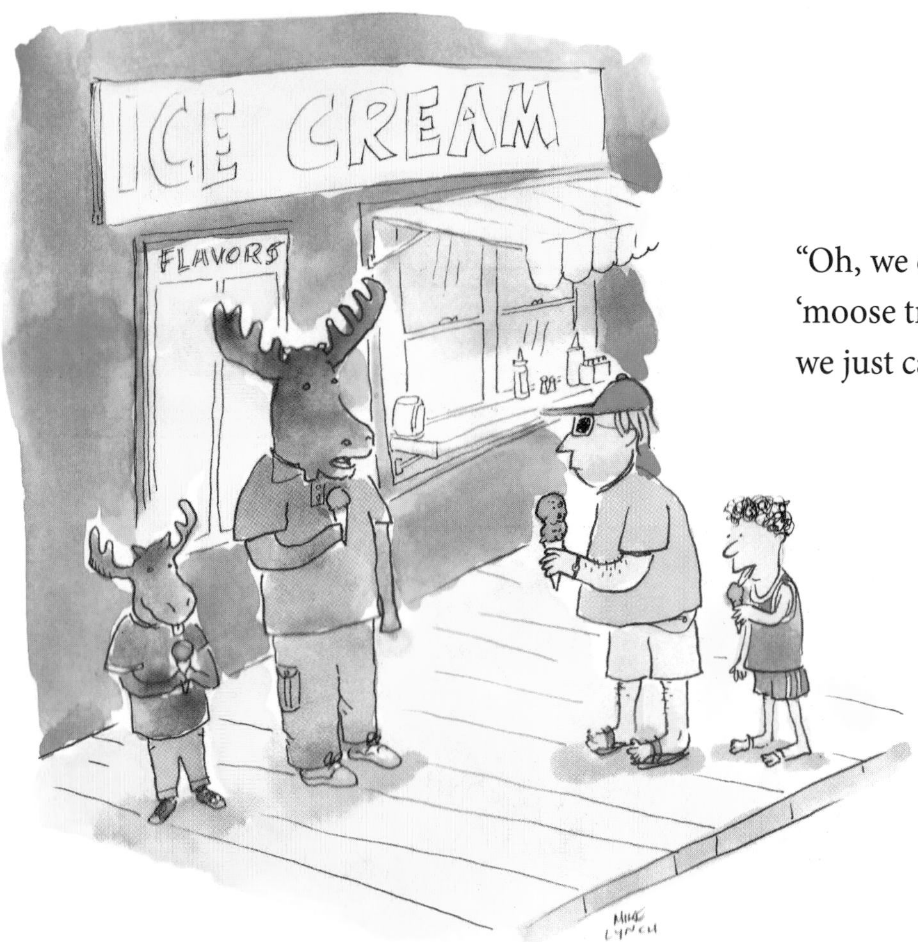
ICE CREAM
FLAVORS

"Oh, we don't call it 'moose tracks' ice cream, we just call it 'tracks.'"

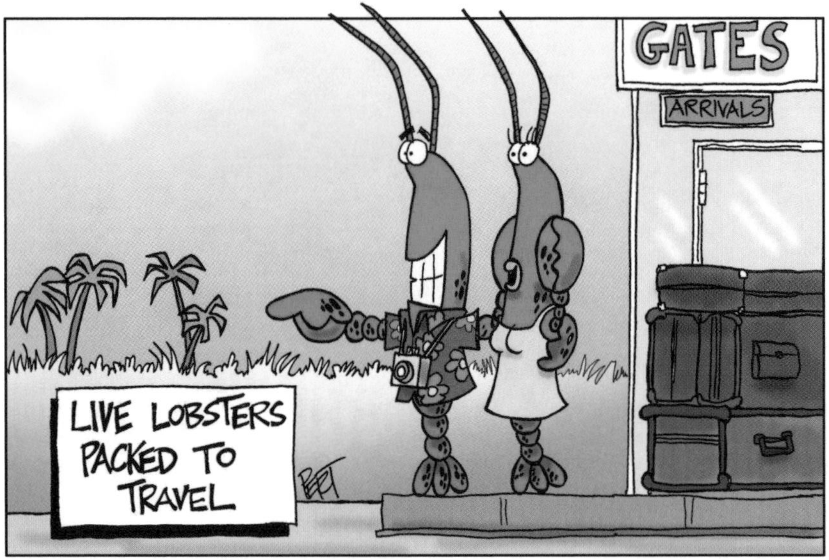
GATES
ARRIVALS
LIVE LOBSTERS PACKED TO TRAVEL

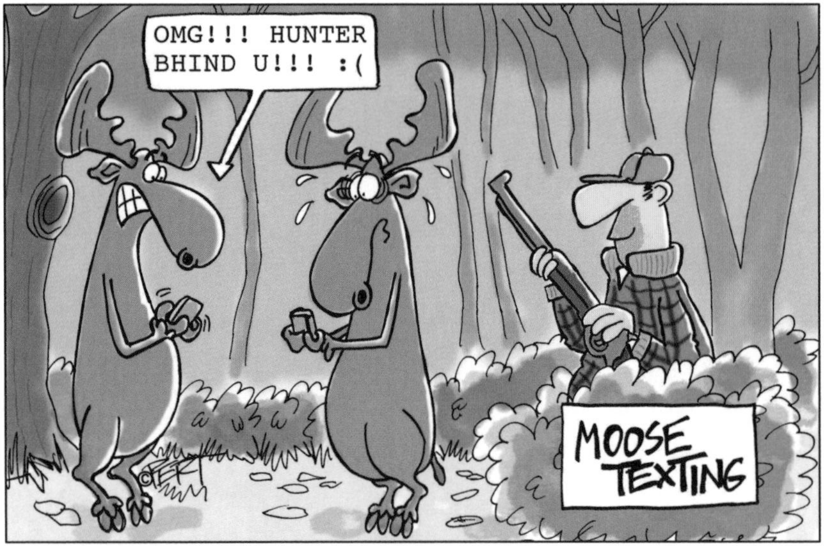
OMG!!! HUNTER
BHIND U!!! :(
MOOSE TEXTING

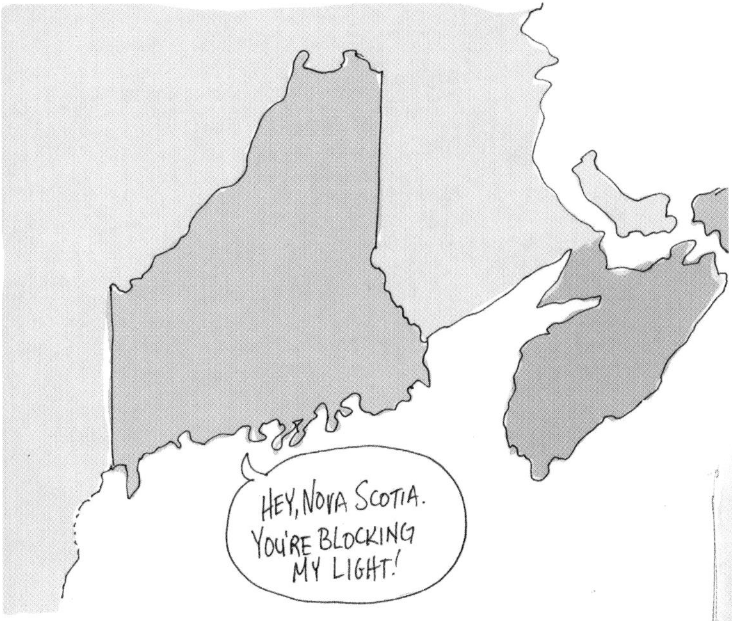
HEY, NOVA SCOTIA. YOU'RE BLOCKING MY LIGHT!

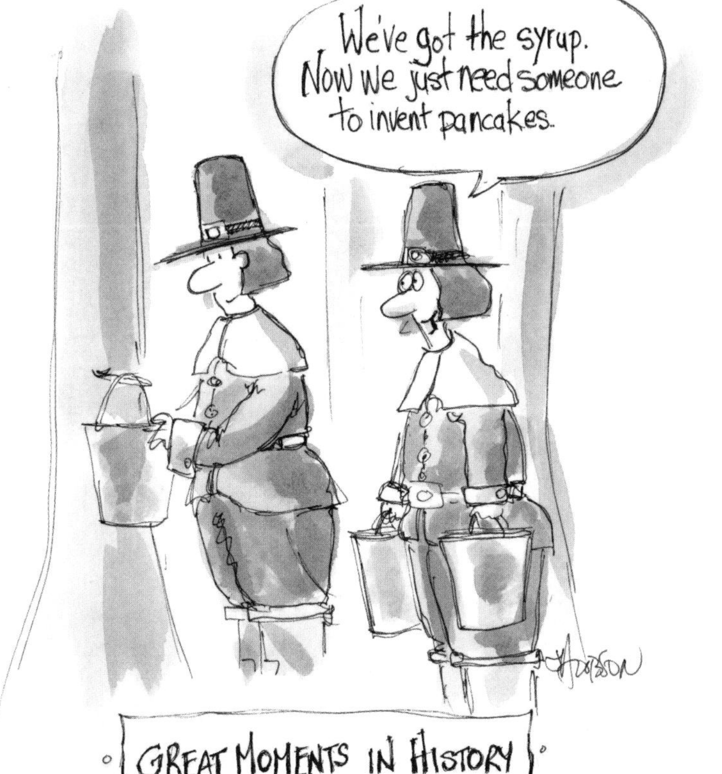
We've got the syrup. Now we just need someone to invent pancakes.
GREAT MOMENTS IN HISTORY

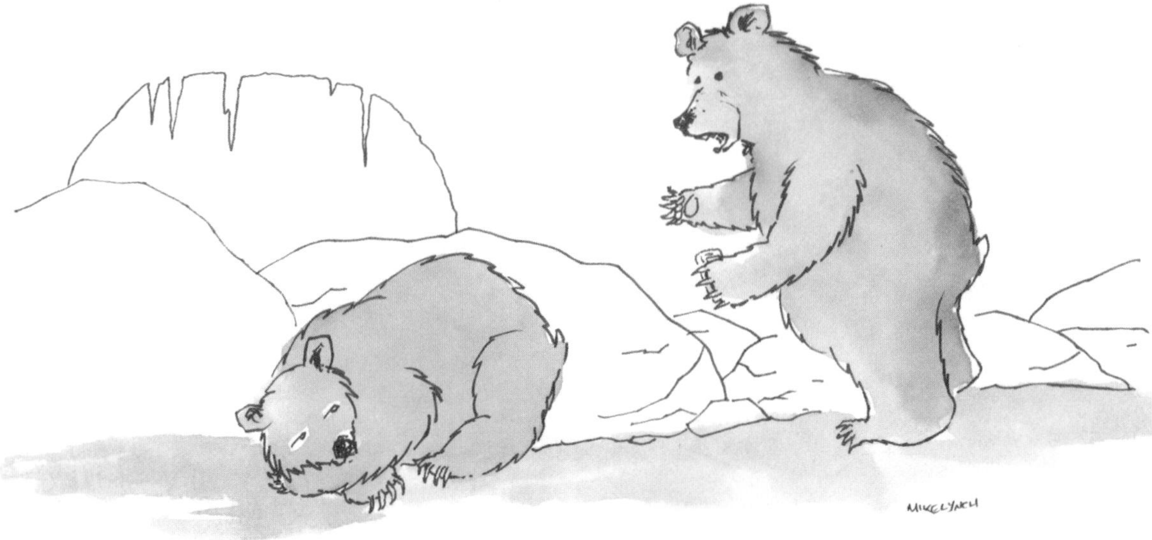
MIKE LYNCH

"Okay, hibernation is over. Time to catch up on our Twitter feed."

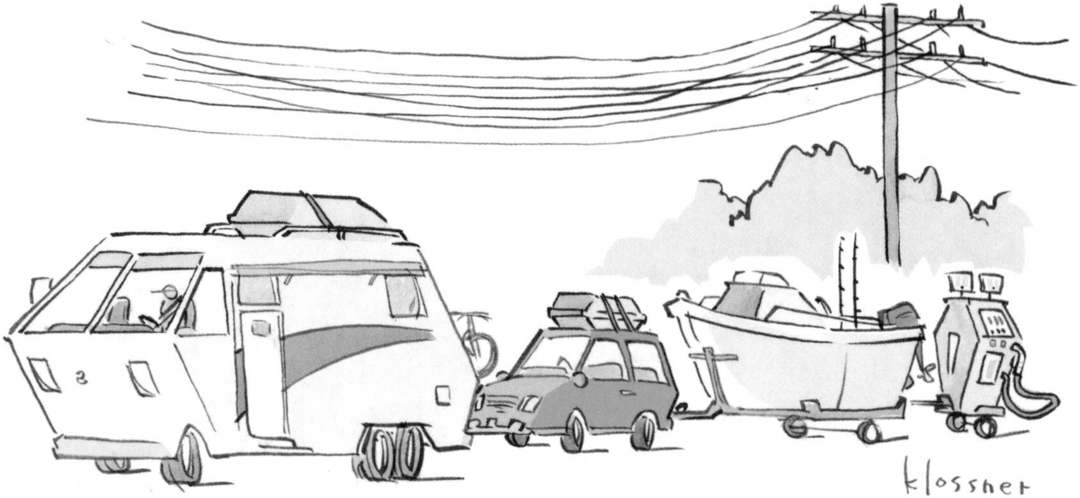
klossner

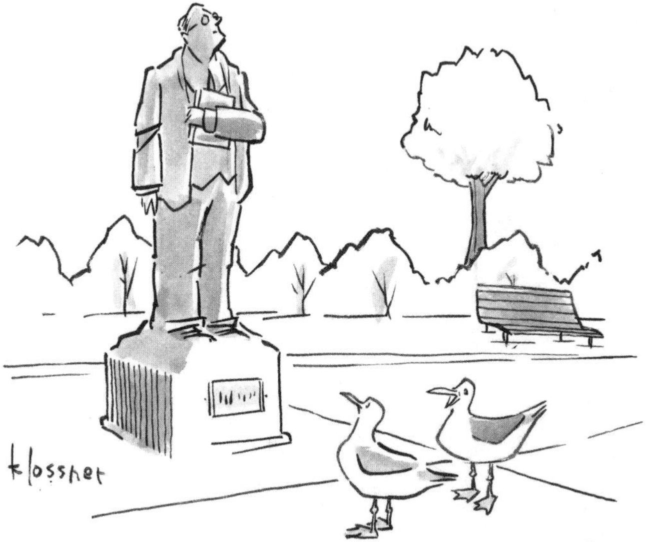
klossner

"He didn't do squat for sea gulls."

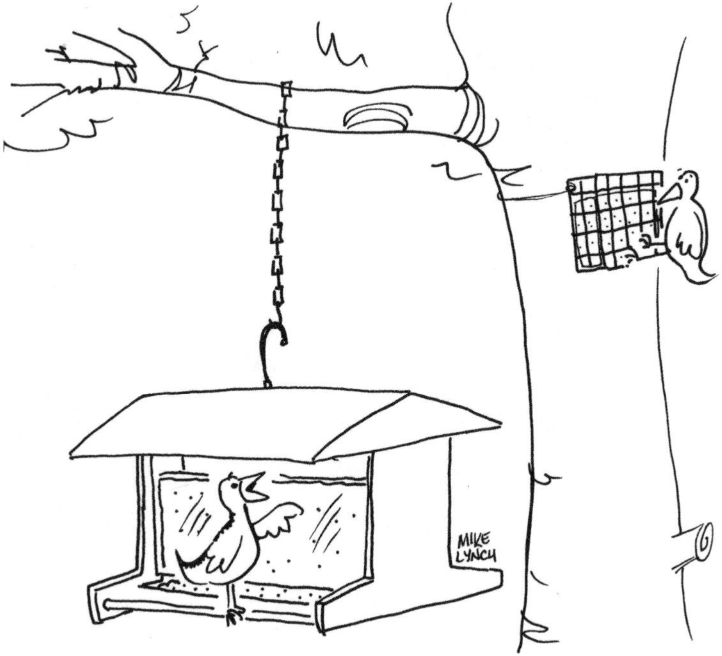
MIKE LYNCH

"No suet for me.
I'm watching my
cholesterol."

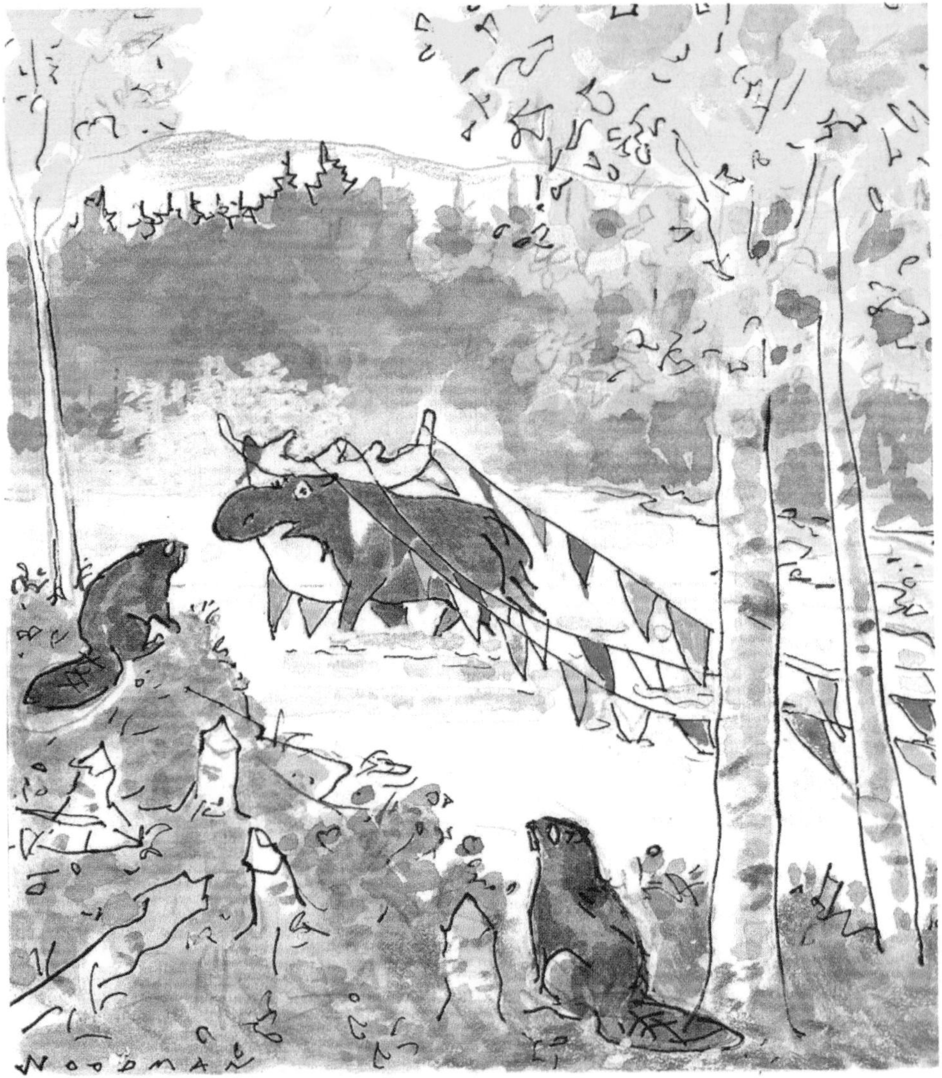

"There's a new car dealership over
where the old timber road used to be."

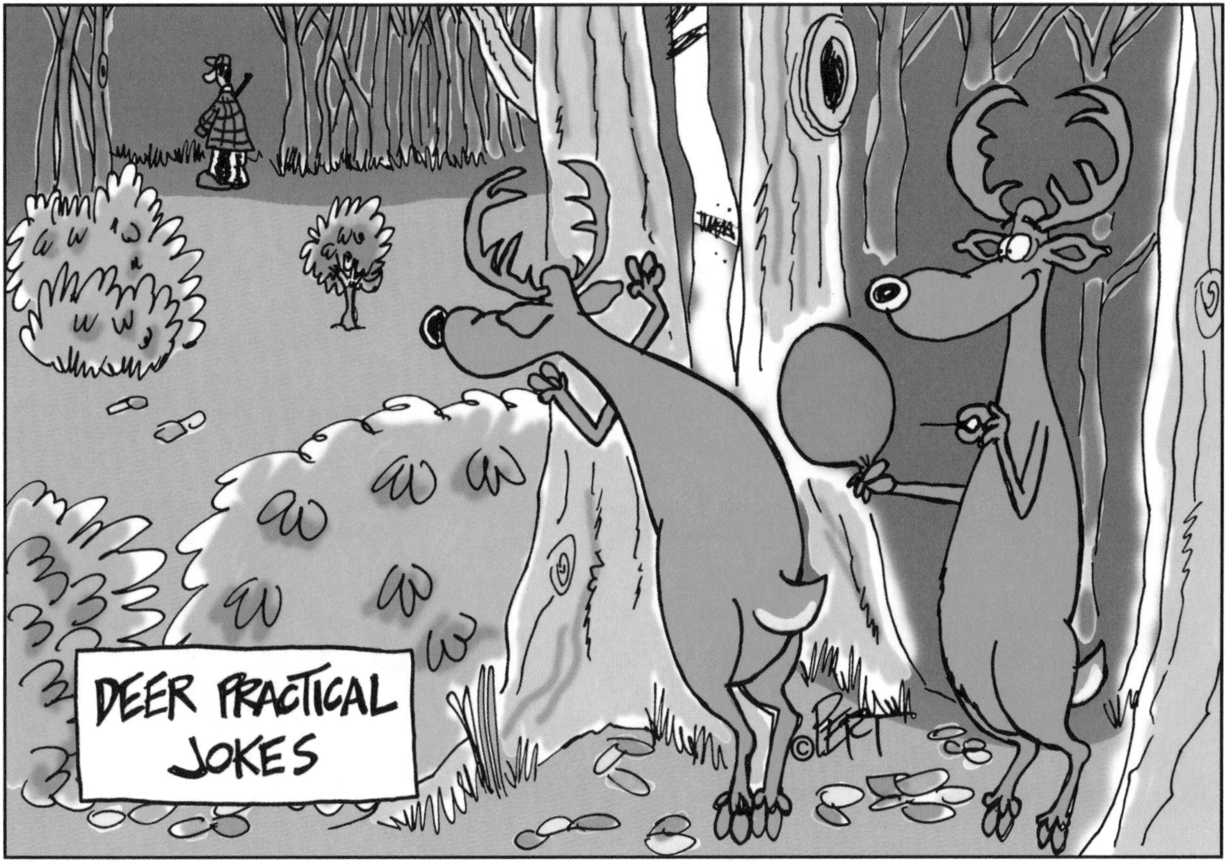
DEER PRACTICAL
JOKES

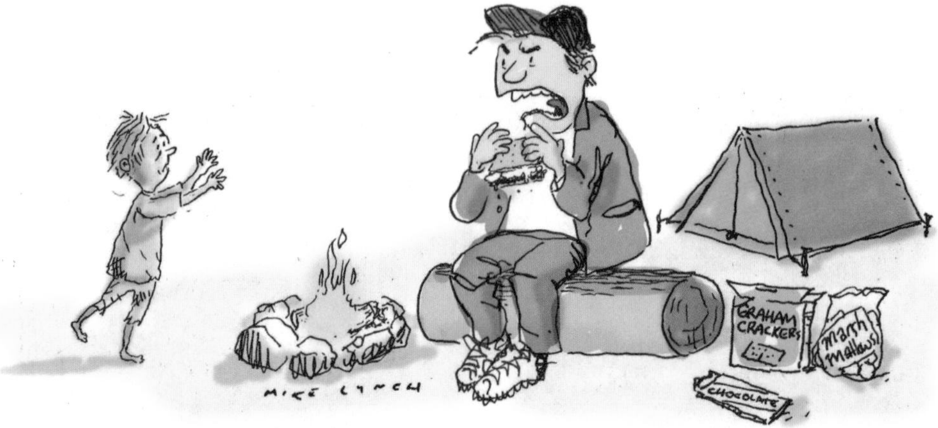
GRAHAM CRACKERS
Marsh Mallows
CHOCOLATE

"Oh, geez. It's that 'Please, sir, may I have s'more?' kid."

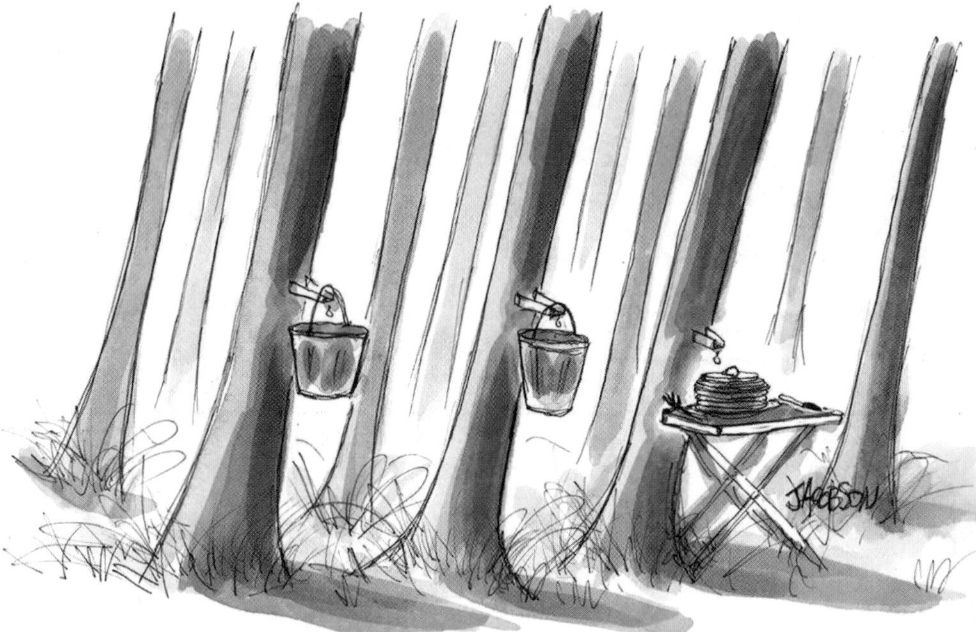

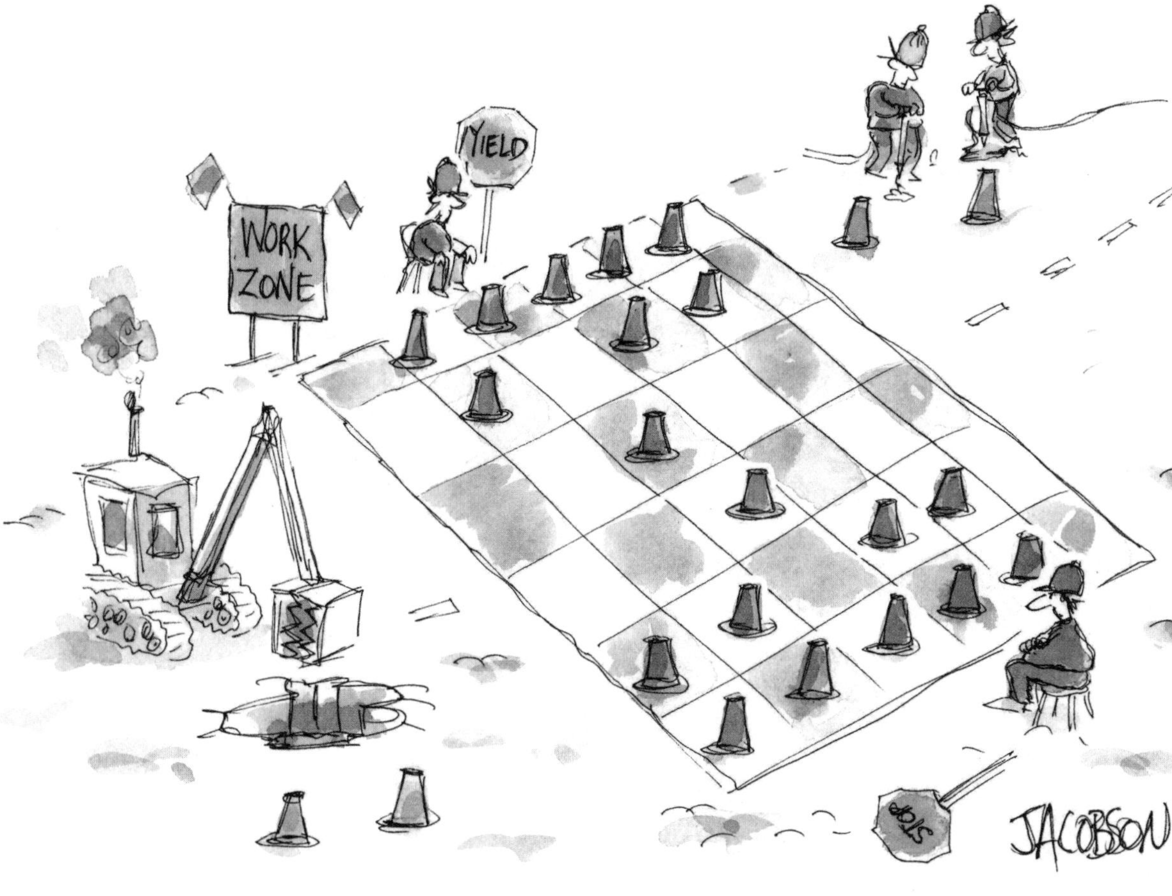

WORK ZONE
YIELD
JACOBSON

"It's a starter home."

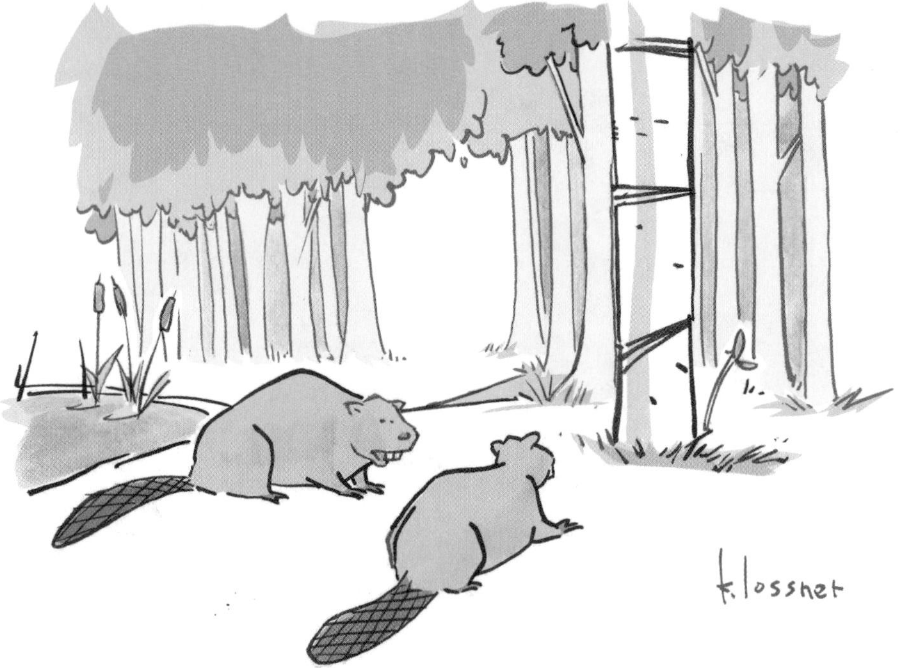
klossner

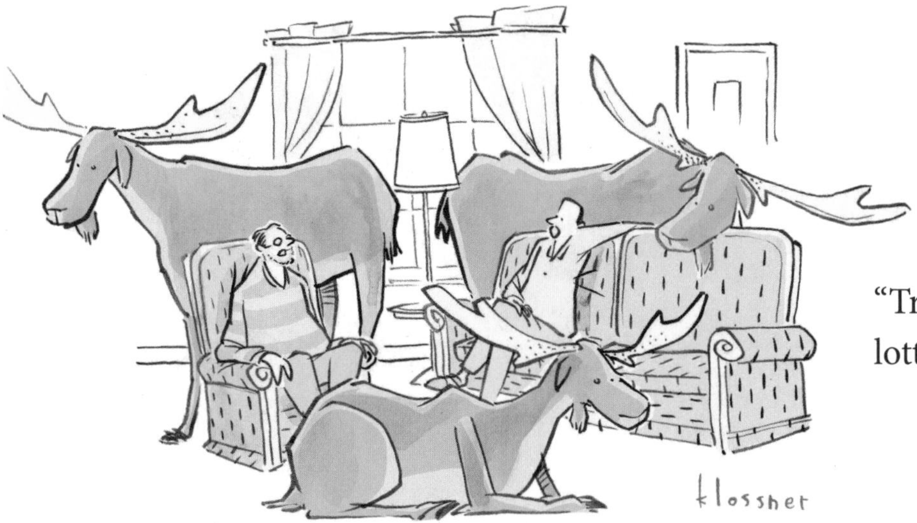
klossner

"Trust me; this is one moose lottery you don't want to win."

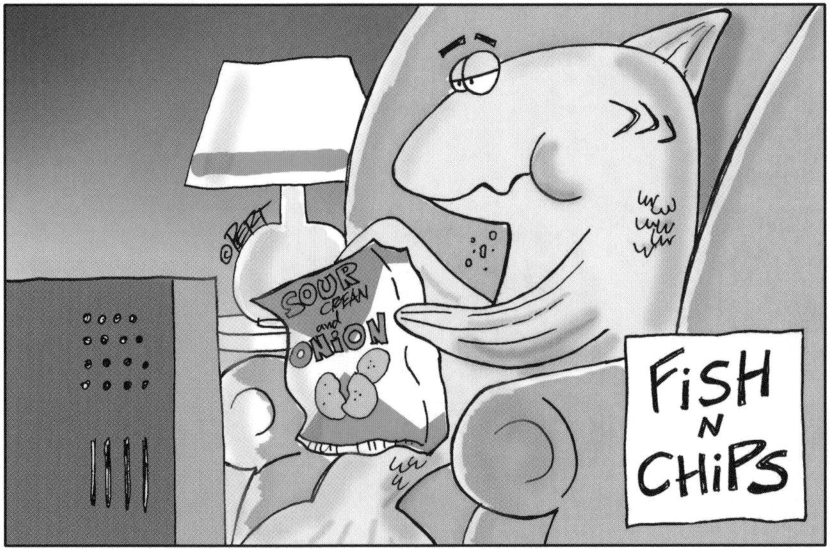
©PERT
SOUR CREAM and ONION
FISH N CHIPS

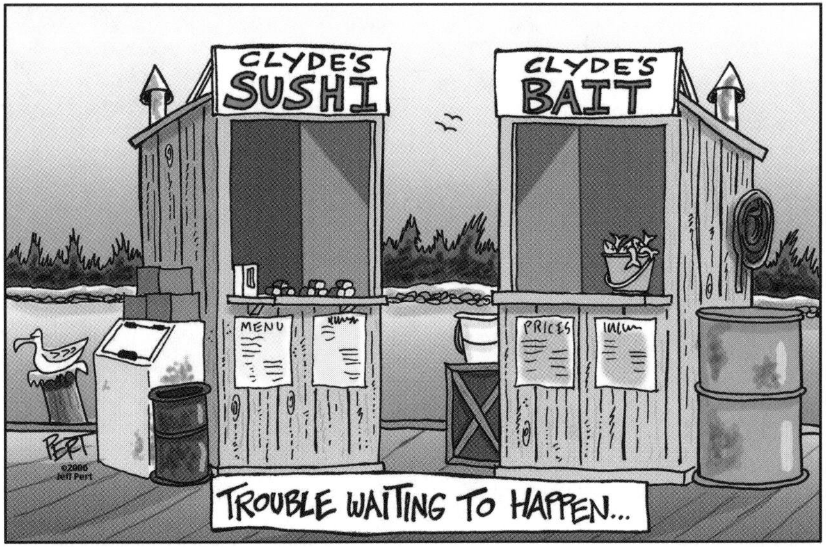
CLYDE'S SUSHI
CLYDE'S BAIT
MENU
PRICES
PERT
©2006 Jeff Pert
TROUBLE WAITING TO HAPPEN...

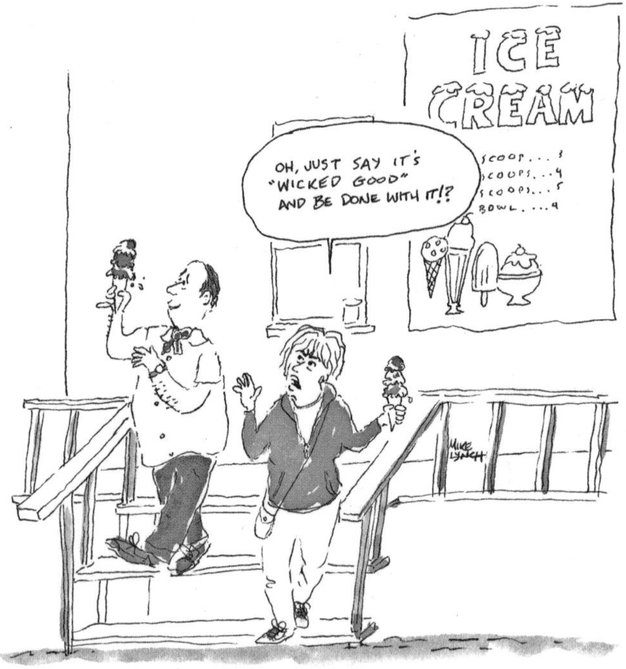
ICE CREAM
OH, JUST SAY IT'S "WICKED GOOD" AND BE DONE WITH IT!?
MIKE LYNCH

THE ROGETS ON VACATION

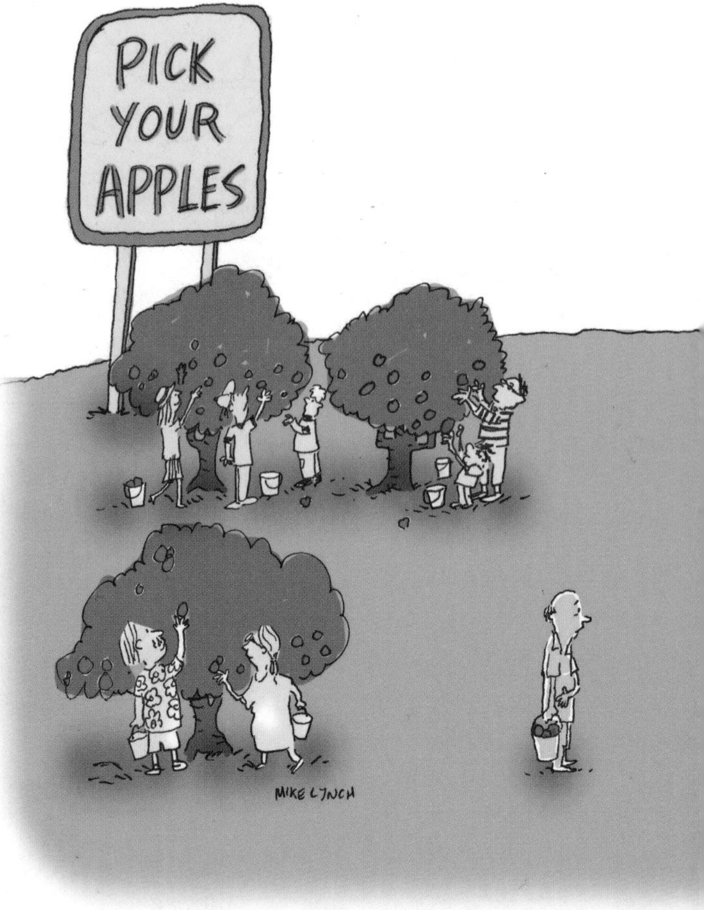
PICK YOUR APPLES
MIKE LYNCH

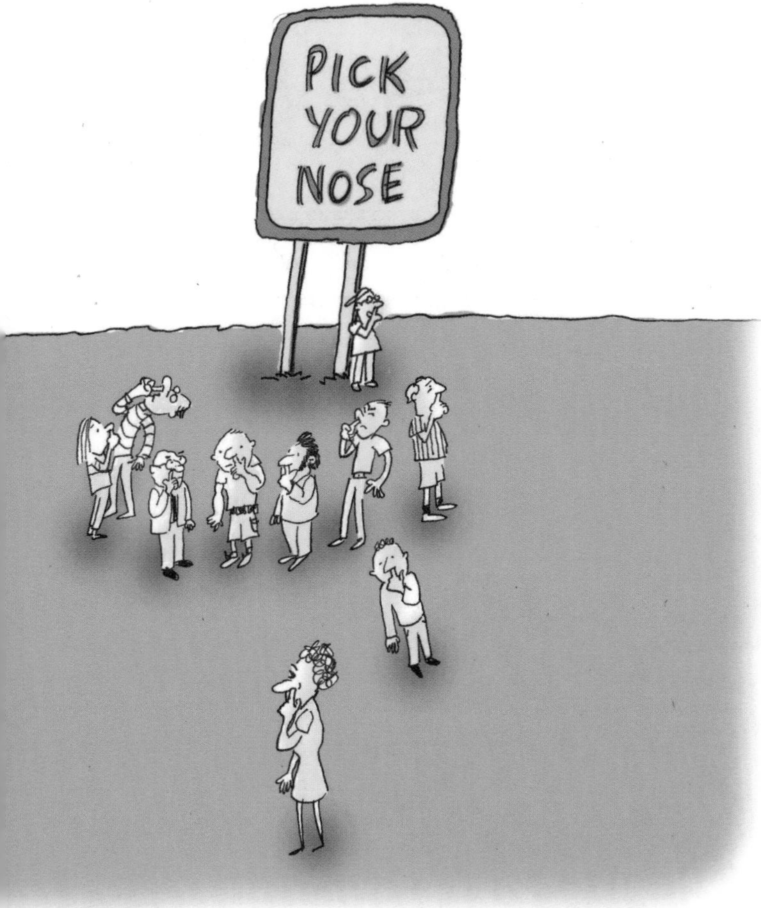
PICK
YOUR
NOSE

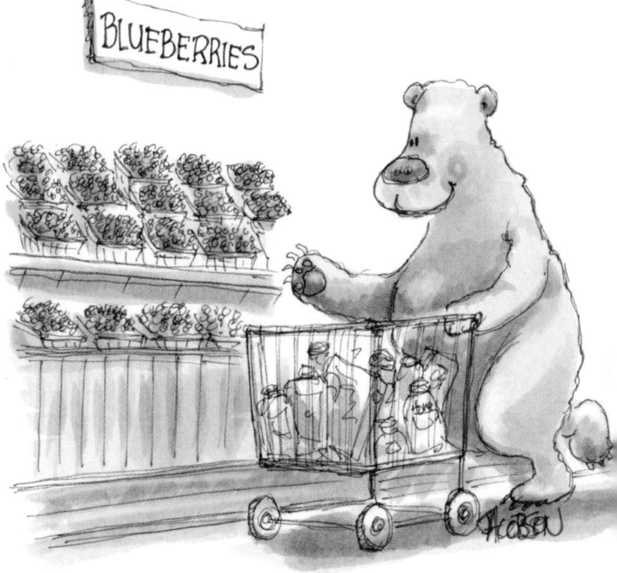
BLUEBERRIES

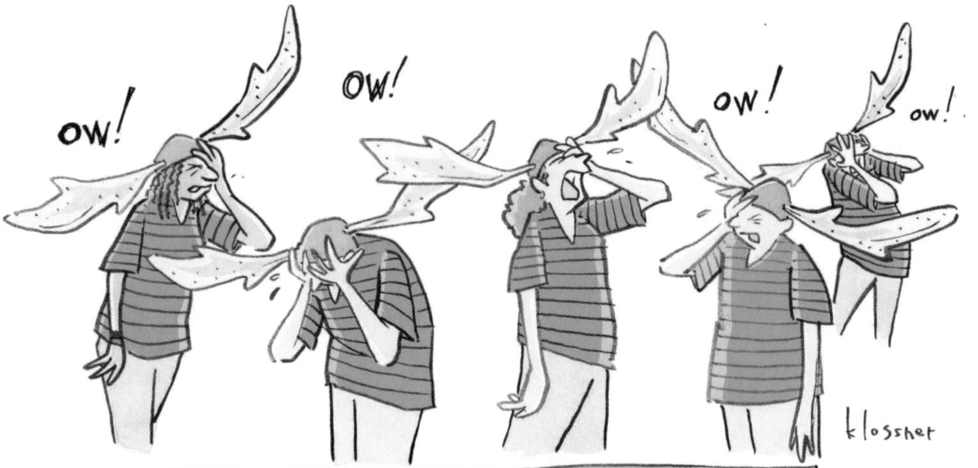
OW!
OW!
OW!
OW!
klossner

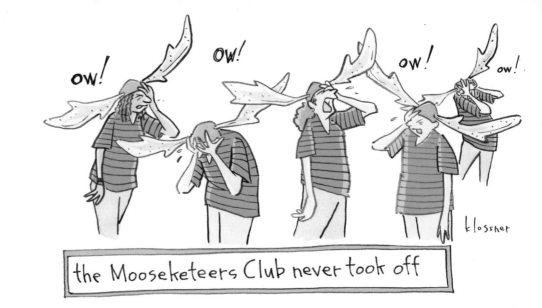

the Mooseketeers Club never took off

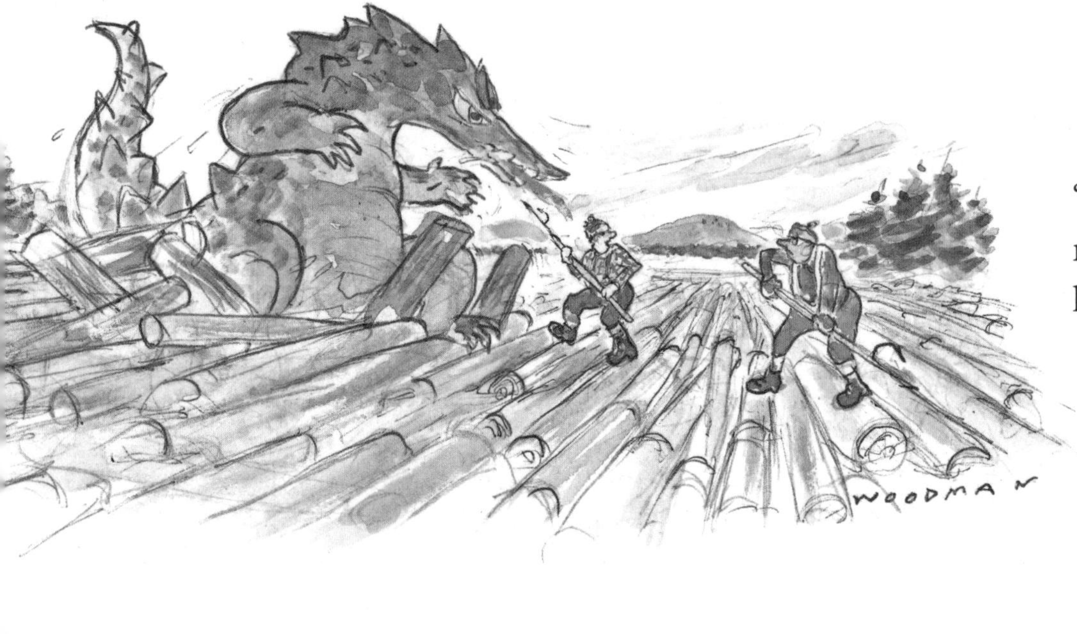
WOODMAN

"My mother told me there'd be days like this."

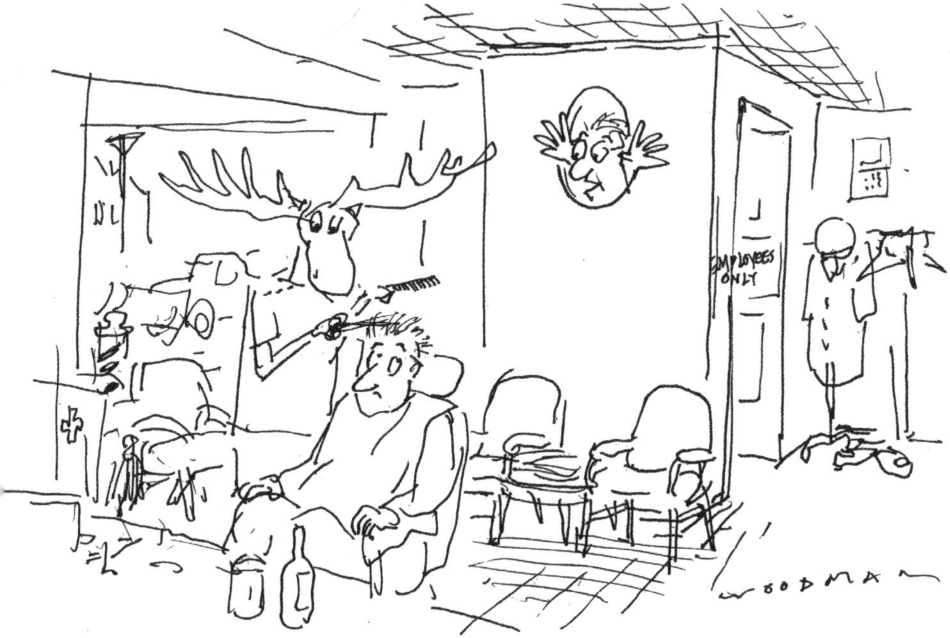
EMPLOYEES ONLY
WOODMAN

“We agreed to change places every now and then.”

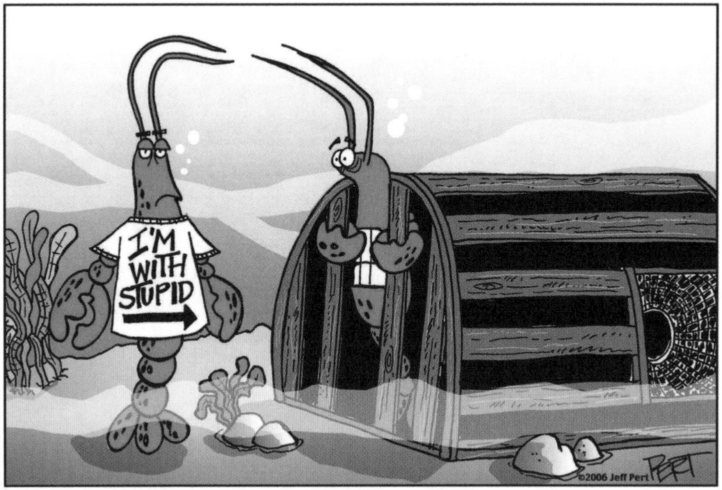
I'M WITH STUPID
©2006 Jeff Pert
PERT

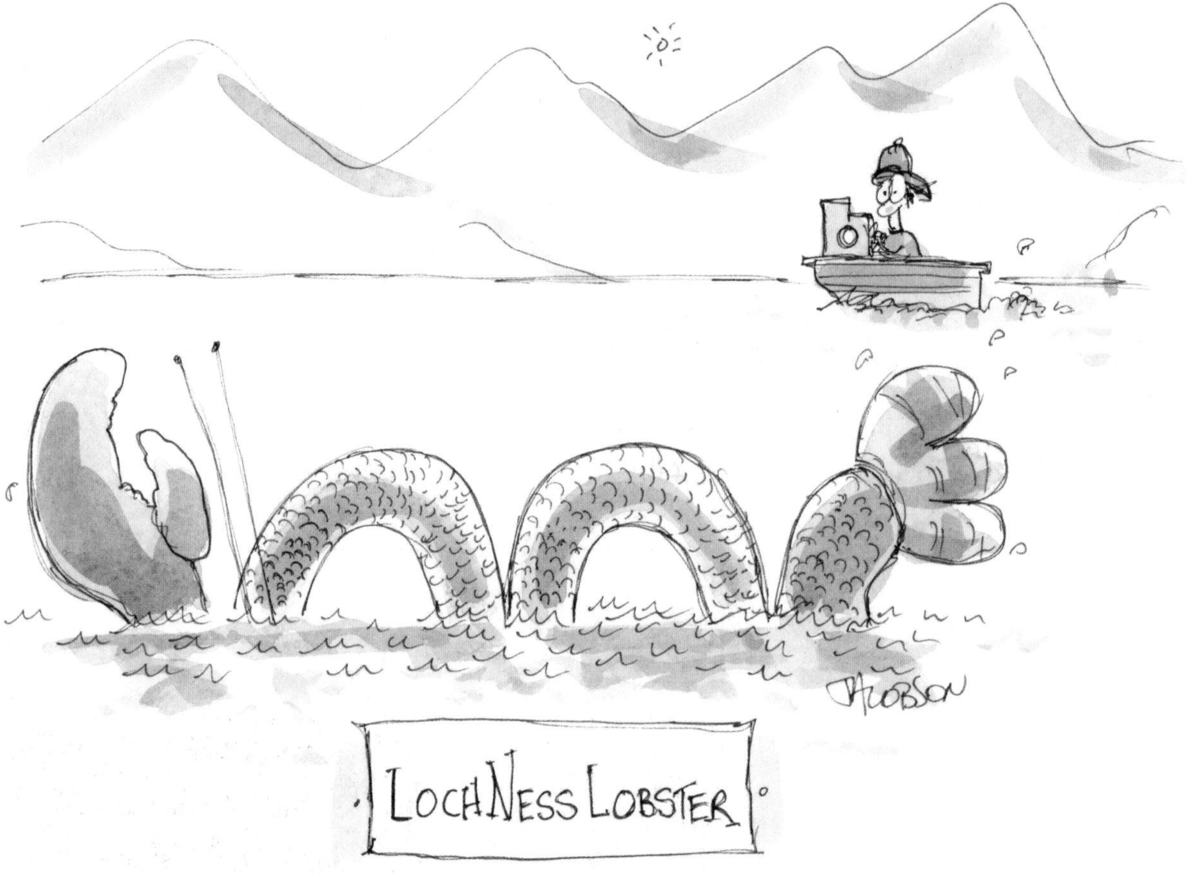
JACOBSON
LOCH NESS LOBSTER